2
&

Learning Through Living...

Some Assembly Required

By

Dr. Suzanne Metzger

"Each day grow older,
and learn something new."
   - Solon

Nicole, I hope you enjoy my stories
Suzanne

International Standard Book Number: 0-9741473-0-3

****

I would like to offer a very special "thank you" to my family and friends who have provided me with support, humor, affection, and an unlimited number of stories that helped me write this book.

Suzanne

****

For more information about Dr. Suzanne Metzger's keynotes, you may contact her at
Corporate Masters, Inc.
suzannecmi@earthlink.net
www.corporatemasters.com
317-718-1855

JANUARY 1
...KNOWING WE ARE NEVER ALONE

"Loneliness and the feeling of being unwanted is the most terrible poverty."
- Mother Teresa

⌘⌘⌘⌘⌘

I have been a lover of poetry since the days of Mother Goose and Grimms. I listened to poetry. I memorized, recited, wrote, and collected poetry. My fascination stemmed not only from the rhyme but also from the phrasing: that ability to say something in a new, more picturesque way that causes us to think about something or look at something in a different light.

One of my favorite collected poems came from a small, local newspaper. If my memory serves me correctly, for the poetry scrapbook has long since disappeared, the publication didn't even reveal the author and went like this:

> I think about God,
> But I talk of small matters.
> Now isn't it odd,
> How my idle tongue chatters.
> Of quarrelsome neighbors,
> Fine weather and rain,
> Indifferent labor,
> Indifferent pain,
> Some trivial style -
> Fashion shifts with the nod;
> And, yet, all the while,
> I am thinking of God.

I certainly wish I knew who this particular "Anonymous" was for I would like to thank him/her for making me see something in a new light: regardless of what we are going through — trivial or traumatic — we are never alone. The events we experience every day and think of as being so rigidly secular are part of a much greater whole that incorporates our life force, our soul, our spirit, and our faith. We are not alone.

⌘⌘⌘⌘⌘

"And, lo, I am with you always
even unto the end of the world."
Matthew 28:20

JANUARY 2
...STARTING EACH DAY IN A BETTER WAY

"Set out wisely at first; custom will make every virtue more easy
and pleasant to you than any vice can be."

- English Proverb

⌘⌘⌘⌘⌘

One of my favorite presentations is geared towards helping people be more positive in a "sometimes" very negative world. I start the session by asking the participants, "Do you have a conscious idea of how you start your day?" I typically get puzzled looks from my audience, so I explain. Most people start their day with an alarm — that which triggers a fire or police department response. Then we listen to the traffic report and realize that wherever it is we are going, we can't get there from where we are. Then comes the weather report; and, if you are a native Hoosier like I am, six months out of the year at 6:00 am it can be 90 degrees with a humidity index of 110, and the other six months out of the year at 6:00 am it can be 20 degrees with a wind chill of -30. The stock market report tells us we've lost money. The news tells us the terrible things that are happening in our own back yard. And, some of us even listen to country-western music. You know - those wonderful lyrics such as "You're the reason our kids are ugly," "Here's a quarter; call someone who cares," and "She got the diamonds; I got the shaft." [For all you country western fans, that was just a joke.] We begin our day in a negative frame of mind before our feet ever touch the floor.

There is a better way. Just set your clock radio five minutes earlier, and for that five minutes thank God for all the wonderful things in your life — both big and small. Then, when you do hear the weather report, the traffic report and the news, you can handle them better because you started your day off in a positive way.

There will always be negativity. How we handle what comes our way is the key to our success and living a more positive life.

⌘⌘⌘⌘⌘

"Your beginnings will seem humble
So prosperous will your future be."

Job 8:7

JANUARY 3
...SHARING SECRETS

"As awareness increases, the need for personal secrecy
almost proportionally decreases."
- Charlotte Pointer

⌘⌘⌘⌘⌘

I had the opportunity to meet and hear Jolene Godfrey when we both spoke at the same convention. She was once a very successful corporate woman and is now a very successful entrepreneur. Jolene has written a wonderful book about women entrepreneurs entitled *An Income Of Her Own* and has developed programs for schools to teach young women how to start their own businesses. Statistics indicate that women entrepreneurs are starting up their own companies at a rate four times greater than men entrepreneurs. Jolene's goal is to help entrepreneurial women get a head start on their business and have higher success rates.

During her luncheon presentation she talked about *An Income Of Her Own*. To write this book, she had asked several entrepreneurial women to lunch, asked them how they had started their businesses, and recorded the comments. She said that it was a little difficult to get them started talking about their businesses, but as they began to open up and share, she understood why: THEY WERE SHARING SECRETS. You see, many of them had no "formal" education in their area, had not written a business plan, and didn't have an entourage of staff or helpers. Their businesses had been started in basements, kitchens, and spare bedrooms without a "well defined" plan. All they had was a passion for success. And, they had succeeded! Their secrets were out!

Secrets can be an awesome thing at times. They are a part of us, and we have the desire to share them with others, to get them off our chest, and to accept responsibility or praise for what we have done. By sharing joyful secrets we can double our joy, and by sharing tragic secrets we can cut each tragedy in half. By letting people know some of the secrets we carry, we can trade life's experiences, let others know we understand what they are going through, and create camaraderie to support us in all those "less than perfect" days.

⌘⌘⌘⌘⌘

"And do not forget to do good and to share with others,
for with such sacrifices God is pleased."
Hebrews 13:16

...REALIZING THAT ALL THINGS HAPPEN FOR A REASON

"A little credulity helps one on through life very smoothly."
- Elizabeth Gaskell

⌘⌘⌘⌘⌘

I was very fortunate to meet a wonderful woman named Blaire. We participated in several organizations and attended classes together. Blaire and I wanted to get to know one another on a more personal level, so, we made plans for dinner. The first date we planned, I became ill; the second date, she had to go out of town; and the third date, she had car trouble. So we set the fourth date, and both of us were determined to keep it. On the evening we were to meet, I was going through one of the worst times in my life. My husband, then my fiancé, and I had broken up. My business wasn't doing well. These problems, coupled with several other "minor" things, were coloring my outlook on life a dismal shade of grey.

Since our dinner date had been cancelled so many times, I felt obligated to go. When we sat down at the table, Blaire looked at me and knew something was wrong. She asked if I wanted to talk, and all I was feeling and trying to deal with came pouring out of my heart, mouth, and soul in a stream of tears. She not only was kind and sympathetic, but she also gave me some of the best advice I have ever received. Blaire said that when life was too overwhelming for her, and she couldn't make wise decisions, she would ask God, "Please, if it is not in my best interest, take it away".

Thank you God for giving me the courage to make this statement, for giving me someone to talk to, and for Blaire. And, thank You for helping me go to dinner with Blaire even though I didn't want to go. You reaffirmed that all things happen for a reason.

⌘⌘⌘⌘⌘

"Trust in the Lord with all your heart
and lean not on your own understanding;"
Proverbs 3:5

JANUARY 5
...KNOWING SOME FRIENDS ARE LIKE STAPLES

"I felt it shelter to speak to you."
- Emily Dickinson

⌘⌘⌘⌘⌘

I have several friends who have been around forever. Well, it seems like forever! We have known each other for so long that I truly can't remember when we met. We all work in different fields and have very different lives, but it seemed as though we were "tied at the hip." Because our lives have changed so much over the years, we are fortunate to talk with one another occasionally and see each other two or three times a year.

The one thing that I have noticed about these friendships is that no matter how seldom we talk on the phone or meet for dinner, we still interact as if we had just parted yesterday. It is as if these friendships have been and will be around for all our lives.

It occurred to me one day while baking muffins, that some friends are like staples that you keep in the pantry. You know — the items you can't seem to function without when you cook: flour, sugar, salt. No matter how seldom you use or need these staples, when you do need them, they are there. They are your basics. They are the staff of your life. They are key ingredients you must have to complete not only your favorite recipe but to function in life.

Pantries are usually pretty crowded, and we don't have room for many staples, but the ones we choose to keep there seem to last forever. Our "staple" friends are no different. We don't have many in our lives, but they last almost forever in our hearts, minds and souls. I am so thankful that my "staple" friends are there for me when I need them, and I am there for them when they need me.

⌘⌘⌘⌘⌘

"If one falls down,
his friend can help him up.
But pity the man who falls
and has no one to help him up."
Ecclesiastes 4:10

JANUARY 6
...KNOWING THE VALUE OF SELF

"You can be pleased with nothing when you are not pleased with yourself."
                                        - Lady Mary Wortley Montagu

⌘⌘⌘⌘⌘

My mother had to work when I was growing up. We didn't always have dinners together, but when we did, she always served dinner in a special way. She never put a catsup bottle, a mustard jar or a bread sack on the table. Instead, she put the catsup and mustard in a little cup she had purchased at Woolworths for $.50 and the bread on a similar little plate. When you grow up having meals this way, you assume that everyone else has meals this way, also.

When I became old enough to go to other people's houses for dinner, many times the table would be set with a package of bologna, a jar of mayonnaise, a loaf of bread, and a knife. I was curious about this table setting to say the least.

I went home and asked my mother why we ate the way we did and why other people ate the way they did. Her response was, "Honey, most people save their very best for everyone else. You need to remember that there will never be anyone who walks through your front door that is any better than you are."

⌘⌘⌘⌘⌘

"For where your treasure is,
there your heart will be also."
                                        Matthew 6:21

JANUARY 7
...GIVING TO OTHERS AS THEY GAVE TO ME

"He who received a benefit should never forget it;
he who bestows should never remember it."
- Pierre Charron

⌘⌘⌘⌘⌘

The Lord has seen fit to bless me by putting some wonderful people in my path. These people were miles ahead of me in education, the corporate arena, life experience, worldliness, and sophistication, and they were also kind enough to open doors for me, enlighten me, encourage me, and show me the way in many different settings. They were the type of people who I could ask questions and not feel embarrassed at my lack of experience or knowledge because I knew they wanted to help me.

I wanted to somehow pay them back in kind for all they had done for me, but what could I possibly do for them? I mentioned this to one of my mentors, and he replied, "I was in the same situation. Others far ahead of me gave to me. I couldn't give to them, so I found some one who could use my help, and I just passed it on. That's what you can do; pass it on."

As others have done for me, I do for others and tell them to also pass it on. It is amazing to see the response from my mentees. They are relieved for they feel, just as I did, that there was no way to help their mentor, and they are gladdened at the prospect of helping others and being part of a ripple effect that has no end.

⌘⌘⌘⌘⌘

"It is more blessed to give than to receive."
Acts 20:35

JANUARY 8
...COMPLIMENTING OTHERS

"When someone does something good, applaud!
You will make two people happy."

- Samuel Goldwyn

⌘⌘⌘⌘⌘

Whenever I see that someone is having a "less than perfect" day, my goal is to say something to make them smile and forget their troubles for awhile. One day while going through a drive-through for an iced tea, I noticed that a teenage girl, working the window, looked as if she had the weight of the world on her shoulders. At her young age she already had deep furrows in her forehead and shadows around her eyes. I decided I would try to make her day go better by complimenting her on her earrings. I said, "Hey." She replied "What?" I continued, "Those are great looking earrings you have on!" She just stared at me for several seconds. A slow smile crept across her face; she leaned out the drive-through window, hung herself upside down so that her head was hanging in my car, and yelled, "See the barrette; it matches."

I began to laugh because her head was hanging in my car; she was laughing because she had done something impulsive; and, as I looked into the rear-view mirror, I noticed that everyone in line behind me was laughing at our interaction.

For a brief time, we connected. I made her smile and forget her troubles momentarily. She has no idea how often I tell that story in my seminars earning money and making others smile at the incident. Any small kindness nets incredible results.

⌘⌘⌘⌘⌘

"Let us not become weary of doing good,
for at the proper time we will reap a harvest if we do not give up."

Galatians 6:9

JANUARY 9
...BELIEVING WITHOUT SEEING

"In all affairs it's a healthy thing now and then to hang
a question mark on the things you have long taken for granted."
— Bertrand Russell

⌘⌘⌘⌘⌘

I was raised in a world that was very factual. It was an "I'll believe it when I see it" world. As I matured, I began to look at successful people — authors, leaders, athletes, speakers — and tried to figure out what made them more successful than other people in the same field. What they seemed to have in common was a belief system of success — an "I'll believe it and then I'll see it" world.

I began to read books by Norman Vincent Peal, Robert Schuller, Ruth Ross, Dennis Waitley, and Tony Robbins. They all talked about belief systems, positive affirmations, and expectancy. I wanted to find out who was the first proponent of positive thinking. In the New Testament Jesus stated "as a man thinketh in his mind, so is he." Then, one day, while browsing through Genesis, I realized this "I'll believe it and then I'll see it" philosophy goes back to our beginning. I don't know how many times I have read Genesis without really paying attention to a major point made in the chapter. Genesis states, "And the Lord said, Let there be light, and there was light." He thought it first and created it second. An "I'll believe it and then I'll see it" world was created for us, literally and figuratively, from Day One!

⌘⌘⌘⌘⌘

"And God said, 'Let there be light,'
and there was light."
Genesis 1:3

JANUARY 10
...INCORPORATING THE POWER OF PERSUASION

"If you would persuade, you must appeal to interest rather than intellect."

-Benjamin Franklin

⌘⌘⌘⌘⌘

From the first episode of Star Trek, I have been a "trekee." I was absolutely in love with the character of Mr. Spock. I was sure it would be wonderful to be in such control of your emotions and to be that intelligent. One day my college friends and I were discussing Star Trek. We all agreed that of the two characters – Spock and Kirk – Spock was definitely the more intelligent. If Spock were the more intelligent, why was he not the captain? A humorous reply was that he was an alien, but in all sincerity, it was because he lacked emotion. Spock played three dimensional chess, a game based on logic, with the computer and tied every time, but he could not play poker, a game that incorporates emotion, because he couldn't bluff.

Persuasion is the ultimate form of communication because it blends both logic and emotion. We have to have both to make any kind of change in this world! Pure statistics are factual but often boring, and pure emotion does not give you a firm foundation. The world's greatest speeches blend both together superbly. We hear speakers' logic, and we know that they speak the truth. Yet, it is not the logic we quote from their speeches. We quote the emotional phrases. The phrases that have made an impact on our lives. Phrases such as "I have a dream," "All we have to fear is fear itself," "Ask not what your country can do for you, but what you can do for your country," and "Blessed are those that mourn, for they will be comforted."

Persuasion, the blending of logic and emotion, is the ultimate attribute in our approach to life. It blends the mind and heart, the hard skills and soft skills, and the rational and emotional. By putting it all together and blending the incredible power of the brain and the soul, we can make people see things in a new light, make new information an active part of their life, and become change agents.

⌘⌘⌘⌘⌘

"Do not conform any longer to the pattern of the world,
but be transformed by the renewing of your mind."

Romans 12:2

JANUARY 11
...PUSHING THE DELETE BUTTON

"The most important thing in life is to see to it that you are never beaten."
- Andre Malraux

⌘⌘⌘⌘⌘

When I begin any new class that I am teaching for the university, I have all the students introduce themselves to the other class members. Because this can become pretty routine, I ask each student to tell something about themselves that is true but would be hard for people to believe.

I begin to get the students to relax and give them time to think. My "what you could hardly believe" is that I don't read a newspaper, watch the news on TV, or listen to the news on the radio. [My mother is very good about calling me with critical information on major events such as a war being declared or a tornado touching down so that I don't go into the world looking totally stupid.]

My students are usually stunned. Someone in the class always asks why. My response is that I am overburdened by the media trying to predispose me to how horrible this world is. I know there are troubles, but I don't constantly want them thrown in my face. I want to choose my environment and how I react to it. I want to start each day in a better frame of mind. I want to hold the vision of the church parking lot being filled each Sunday morning, and I want to remember hearing how much money we raised at Christmas to buy presents for children less fortunate than our own. I want to remember the feeling of packing up our previous choir robes and sending them to a village in Africa. When I have the opportunity to interact in a Christian environment with Christian friends, I still feel that the Millennium is a long way off.

Laurie Beth Jones put it best, "In this country, negative information is free. Positive information you have to search for, or, better yet – create." I think it is important for each of us to know we do have a delete button, and with that button we can choose what we consider "unnecessary" in our lives and eliminate it.

⌘⌘⌘⌘⌘

"Be very careful, then, how you live —
not as unwise but as wise,
making the most of every opportunity,
Ephesians 5:15,16

JANUARY 12
...SEEING OURSELVES AS OTHERS SEE US

"Nothing that God ever made is the same thing to more than one person."
- Zora Neale Hurston

⌘⌘⌘⌘⌘

I have two step-children, and I have learned a great deal about them, with them and from them. One afternoon, Stan, my husband, had gone to pick up Sarah, his daughter. (She was 14 years old at the time.) I was in the kitchen. When they arrived at the house, Sarah ran in, threw her books on the table and proudly announced that one day she knew she would grow up to be just like me. I was so pleased and honored – especially as a step-mother. I was envisioning Sarah as an entrepreneur, a Ph.D., an educator. I lovingly smiled at her and asked her what she meant. She said, "Today I had to go and buy a new bra, and it was a "C" cup. And, I said, yes, one day I'll be just like Suzanne".

I managed to keep the smile frozen on my face until she left the room. My smile faded, and, as I looked at my husband, who had just burst into hysterical laughter, I said, "This is what I have worked for all my life -- to be appreciated for my bra size!"

It is always good for us to see ourselves as others see us. It can be quite humbling — or invigorating — or confusing — or, as in this case, amusing, but it always makes us see ourselves in a new light. And, truly, only the Lord knows what the beams of this new light will highlight or shadow.

⌘⌘⌘⌘⌘

"No eye has seen
No ear has heard,
No mind has conceived
What God has prepared for those who love him."
I Corinthians 2:9

JANUARY 13
...NOT RESPONDING IMMEDIATELY

⌘⌘⌘⌘⌘

"Patience is bitter, but its fruit is sweet."
- Lida Clarkson

We learn many things as children, and we carry them into adulthood unaware of their origin. As adults, when we are asked a question, we think we have to respond immediately. I think it goes back to childhood experiences when we were caught doing something we shouldn't have been doing. We had an adult standing over us, yelling "Why did you do that?" In that moment, we knew we have to come up with an answer to save our lives.

We, as adults, do not always have to answer questions. Just because someone asks us something does not mean that we have to respond now. Adult lives are a little more complicated than the life of a child. In many situations we require more data, we need to get the correct information, or we are under a great deal of stress and cannot use our minds to their full potential at that moment.

I have learned there are times when I would be unwise to communicate. If I'm in a hurry, tired, ill, hassled, or I do not know the facts, I simply tell people I must think about that and get back with them. I try to be true to my word and get back with them after I have had a little more time to think things through or gather more data.

I have learned it is not always a good time to communicate or respond immediately in every situation. I have also learned it is much wiser for me to accept a person's sigh or huff because I won't give him/her an immediate response. Even though I don't like hearing those reactions, it's better not to give an immediate response and risk hurting someone's feelings, eating shoe leather every time I see them, or having to retract my response at a later date. This ounce of prevention is certainly worth the pound of cure.

⌘⌘⌘⌘⌘

"Perseverance must finish its work so that you may be
mature and complete, not lacking anything."
James 1:4

JANUARY 14
...KNOWING I CANNOT BE ALL THINGS TO ALL PEOPLE

"Consider well what your strength is equal to, and what exceeds your ability."
- Horace

⌘⌘⌘⌘⌘

We live in a world of mass communication. When we can meet people from all around the world from all walks of life, we can do a lot of comparing. It used to be if we were the fastest runner in our little town, we were the star. Now, with mass communication, we have to be the fastest runner in the world to be a star. Our field of comparison has changed.

We see magazine articles and TV shows and hear bits and pieces from others telling us of the great accomplishments people are making. They are just human, like us; we ought to be able to do the same. Women think they must be able to look like Loni Anderson, have a body like Cher, be as wise as Margaret Thatcher, as relationship-oriented as Dr. Joyce Brothers, as entertaining as Martha Stewart, and as good a cook as Betty Crocker. Men must be able to have a body like Arnold Schwarzenegger, the political insight of Henry Kissenger, the looks of Mel Gibson, the cooking skills of the Galloping Gourmet, the building skills of Bob Villa, the humor of Tim "The Tool Man" Tailor, and the athletic ability of Michael Jordan.

All the people I mentioned are "specialists" in their area. They each have spent a lifetime honing and developing, basically, one major skill: their area of expertise. We have to look at what our specialty is and capitalize on that. We must remember that we can't be all things to all people. We must know our mission. We must know what we can accomplish. We must know what we can spend our lifetime honing and developing to make us the best we can be in our world at our specialty.

⌘⌘⌘⌘⌘

"There is a time for everything,
and a season for every activity under heaven:"
Ecclesiastes 3:1

JANUARY 15
...MAKING PEOPLE FEEL IMPORTANT

"Language exerts hidden power, like the moon on the tides."
- Rita Mae Brown

⌘⌘⌘⌘⌘

If you have ever attended any type of empowerment seminar, many times people will be wearing buttons printed with MMFI = Make Me Feel Important. We all want to feel important about ourselves and what we cherish.

My husband and I have gotten so busy that we decided to hire a maid service to come in twice a month to do some deep cleaning. I called three services and interviewed each. The services were very similar, and the prices were very similar.

[It is important for you to know, at this point, that my husband and I have two four-legged children. We fit into the new marketing category of DINKODS - Dual Income No Kids Only Dogs. They are velocaraptors disguised as dogs. They are terrorists who would hold people hostage for a Milkbone. We are both aware of this.]

Even though the prices, services, and interviews were very similar, the third interview was a little different than the other two. The third woman, Kenwyn from Molly Maids, who came to the house for the interview had dog biscuits in her pocket. She gave the dogs their goodies, told me how beautiful Murphy and Coco were, what a joy they must be, and how well behaved they were. I know it is not polite to point it out when someone is lying, but, at the very least, this woman was stretching the truth. I know what our dogs are like. Even knowing our two four-legged terrorist/children well, I beamed when she praised, petted, and extolled them. They are our babies; they are important and special in our lives.

It is not difficult to guess which service got our business and why? Simply because Kenwyn made me feel important and special. She had taken time to notice what was important to me.

Because of this unsolicited kindness, I have passed on her name and the name of her company to many people, hopefully generating business for her. People who take time to make you feel special are quite special themselves.

⌘⌘⌘⌘⌘

"For we cannot help speaking about what we have seen and heard."
Acts 4:20

JANUARY 16
...KNOWING IT TAKES BOTH RAIN AND SUNSHINE TO MAKE A RAINBOW

"My heart leaps up when I behold
A rainbow in the sky:
So was it when my life began;
So is it now I am a man;
So be it when I shall grow old,
Or let me die!"

- William Wordsworth

⌘⌘⌘⌘⌘

One day I was driving home from South Bend, Indiana, through an incredible rainstorm. Several times I had to pull off the road because the downpour made it too difficult to drive. When I was about 10 miles from home, the storm stopped, and I was privileged to see one of the most gorgeous sights I had ever seen: three abundantly intense rainbows.

I was driving through a canopy of colors that touched the ground on both sides of the road. Trees, bushes, and houses were colored red, orange, yellow, green, and blue. My whole world had gone from gray to an illumination that was impossible to record with words. It was magical, mystical, and wonderful. The image itself was worth a pot of gold. I was so caught up in the colors and the glory of what was happening that, again, it was difficult to drive, but this time it was difficult because of the beauty of the rainbow not the severity of the rainstorm. It was then I realized that the hideous, nerve racking storm I had driven through was responsible for the delightful rainbows and the wonderment of God and nature.

Life is the co-existence of opposites – back and forth, up and down, hot and cold, good and bad, agony and ecstasy, the best of times and the worst of times – and we can't appreciate one unless we have experienced the other. As my mother has told me many time, "You can't appreciate the mountain top until you have been in the valley." To have one, you must have the other. The contrasts create spectaculars.

⌘⌘⌘⌘⌘

"It is beautiful in its loftiness
the joy of the whole earth."

Psalm 48:2

JANUARY 17
...BEING COMMITTED - NOT INVOLVED - TO KEY ISSUES TO OUR LIVES

"Do not put your spoon into a pot which does not boil for you."
- Romanian Proverb

⌘⌘⌘⌘⌘

When you order "Ham and Eggs," please remember that the hen was involved, but the hog was committed. There is a big difference here. When we become involved with something, we can choose to walk away. We may choose to walk away because the project is finished, there is someone else to do the job, or we have something else we would rather do. But when we are committed to a relationship, a new business venture, a child, running an organization, or even a pet, we have taken custody of it. It isn't that we cannot release the custody or commitment; it's just a lot more difficult. Commitment embodies our mind, energy, drive, values, and passion: difficult traits to abandon.

I had the opportunity to listen to a very wise/savvy business woman at a luncheon conference. She stated that she never committed to more than three projects a year. It was all she had time for. By committing to more than three, she either burned herself out or failed miserably at each one. Both of these scenarios are disappointing and rather long lasting.

We want commitment from others. Why would we expect that others want any less from us? Decide purposefully what your commitments will be and take custody of only those projects.

⌘⌘⌘⌘⌘

"Surely you will reward each person
according to what he has done."
Psalm 62:12

JANUARY 18
...TAKING PRIDE IN BEING A 30 MINUTE EXPERT

"Nobody knows enough, but many too much."
- Marie Von Ebner-Eschenbach

⌘⌘⌘⌘⌘

Years ago, I heard an interesting definition of an "expert": someone who has studied something for more than 2 years or less than 30 minutes. At first glance, this definition certainly does make fun of all those who profess to be omniscient on all topics. But, at second glance, it proves to have a little more value.

As I have aged, I have taken a great deal of pride in being a 30 minute expert on thousands of topics. Why? Just knowing a small amount on many different subjects allows me to engage in a conversation with almost anyone. Whether it is a topic as trivial or as mundane as the weather or seeing someone reading a book by a favorite author, it opens doors, interesting conversations, and, sometimes, long lasting friendships.

Whatever our gift or specialty is, we should be the seasoned two-year (plus) expert. But knowing a little about a lot allows us to cross paths and relate to many people. It allows us — for one brief moment in time — to be a part of someone else's life. We may never know what impact we may have on that person, or what a ripple effect we may be creating, with just 30 minutes of expertise.

⌘⌘⌘⌘⌘

"A wise man has great power,
and a man of knowledge increases strength;"
Proverbs 24:5

JANUARY 19
...KEEPING CONFIDENCES

"A thing we give to others to keep for us."
- Elbert Hubbard

⌘⌘⌘⌘⌘

Benjamin Franklin said, "Three may keep a secret if two of them are dead." I wish this quote had come to my attention years ago.

When I first started my speaking/presenting business, I, like so many other entrepreneurs, went through hard times and decided, more than once, to hang it all up. One time I even went so far as to send out resumes and interview with placement people. I did not realize that one of the women at a placement firm where I had sent my resume was the president of a very large woman's organization. Unbeknownst to me at the time, this woman's organization had decided to ask me to speak to their group. (This would have been wonderful for my career.) When my name came up at the board meeting for consideration as one of their speakers, this woman from the placement firm was in attendance. I found out later that I was rejected as a potential speaker because she told the other board members that I was shutting down my business. I have wondered many times how far that rumor went and how long it affected the success of my business.

Certainly this was an unusual situation. After all, I had made the first move and had sent out the resume. I had to take responsibility for what had happened. But this did cause me to stop and think about Franklin's quote.

All of us need to cultivate a select group of people to whom we can pour out our hearts. And, maybe, we should only share our innermost thoughts with those people who are going through similar experiences. Such people will likely know what is chaff and what is grain. If you're not willing to broadcast your innermost thoughts on e-mail, think before sharing those thoughts with just anyone.

⌘⌘⌘⌘⌘

"He who guards his mouth and his tongue
keeps himself from calamity."
Proverbs 21:23

JANUARY 20
...REMEMBERING EVERYONE DOES NOT LOVE US

"Always behave as if nothing had happened no matter what has happened."
- Arnold Bennett

⌘⌘⌘⌘⌘

As a speaker/trainer/presenter, it is easy to spot the people in the audience who do not agree with what I am saying or who are taking exception to me personally. Typically, they sit in the back of the room, write notes to a friend, fold their arms, glare at me, whisper to someone nearby, and never open their training manual. They are rather easy to spot.

When I first began speaking/presenting, I would tend to focus all of my attention on such people and try to win them over. It took me quite a while to realize that if someone didn't like me when they entered the room, they probably wouldn't like me any better when they exited the room. I don't know why. I could look like someone in their past that made their life miserable; they could be ill or out of sorts. For whatever reason, they don't like me or agree with me. I had to come to terms with that. I had to change my attitude for I certainly couldn't change theirs.

I'm reminded of what my psychology professor told me in college when I was earning my undergraduate degree: even Jesus wasn't popular in his home town. He had been a carpenter there for 30 years. Why should anyone listen to a carpenter preach the gospel?

We need to stop focusing our attention on the people we cannot reach and focus our attention on the ones we can.

⌘⌘⌘⌘⌘

"A man finds joy in giving an apt reply —
and how good is is a timely word!"
Proverbs 15:23

JANUARY 21
...DEVELOPING OUR OWN YARDSTICK

"Every new adjustment is a crisis in self-esteem."
- Eric Hoffer

⌘⌘⌘⌘⌘

I tend to be a practical joker – at times. When I was going through college, there were several girls who just loved to go on and on about having a 24 inch waist to those of us who did not. And, frankly, I got sick of hearing about it. So, I decided to put an end to their comments. I went home, took a piece of elastic and a black marker, and made my own "elastic" tape measure. With an "elastic" tape measure, you can have any size of waist you want. It was great for a laugh.

As an adult, the memory of this practical joke reinforced the very human need we all have to "measure up." We are constantly trying to measure up to everyone else's standards - weight charts, income levels, number of children, fat grams, number of hours in the gym, etc. Where do **our** standards come into play? I don't think we can ever measure up to someone else's standards. They are their standards, not ours.

For us to be successful we need to develop our own yardstick, set our own standards, and determine what our level and measurement of success is. The experts tell us that people respond well to their own data. By developing our own standards with our own data, we will know what we want to achieve and when we have reached that level. We will be responding and measuring to our yardstick; not someone else's.

⌘⌘⌘⌘⌘

""Finally, brothers, whatever is true, whatever is noble,
whatever is right, whatever is pure, whatever is lovely,
whatever is admirable — if anything is excellent or praiseworthy —
think about such things."
Philippians 4:8

JANUARY 22
...QUESTIONING BEFORE I CONDEMN

"If we must have new knowledge, we must get a whole world of new questions."
- Susanne K. Langer

⌘⌘⌘⌘⌘

Condemning others has become an Olympic event for some of us, and many of us have become gold medallists in the "sport of condemnation." We need to learn to question before we condemn. It will save us many agonizing arguments and get us to think about what we are saying.

A young college friend of mine lived with several other students on the top floor of a condo. A little old lady lived on the bottom floor. She had a small dog that she let out early every morning. As with many small dogs, the little dog loved to bark. For a college student who doesn't go to bed until 2:00 or 3:00 am, a dog barking early in the morning is not what anyone wants to hear. One day my young friend made the statement that some morning he was just going to throw water on the dog. I was outraged. I love dogs. My initial reaction was to scream, "Don't you dare. I will never do anything for you again. I'll never forgive you. I'll hate you until the day I die." Realizing this response would not be well accepted and could put a wedge in our relationship, I listened internally to what I preach. I thought about how best to rephrase my response. Finally, I asked, without screaming, "What makes you think it is right to persecute an animal for something that is human's fault?"

Nothing was said. No argument ensued. No hard feelings developed. No dog was persecuted. And, a thought process took place. Instead of condemning my friend and his actions, I questioned his thought process, and so did he.

⌘⌘⌘⌘⌘

"Blessed are the peacemakers,
for they will be called sons of God."
Matthew 5:9

JANUARY 23
...SEEING OUR OWN POSSIBILITIES

"The important thing is this: to be able at any moment
to sacrifice what we are for what we could become."

- Charles Du Bos

⌘⌘⌘⌘⌘

Women have unbelievable inner strength. It's that inner strength that
either consciously or subconsciously is recognized by others in times of stress or
elation. It's a strength that is in our beauty, our voice, our touch, our laugh, and
our humanity.

We use these strengths to be the comforters, the encouragers, the
caregivers, and the motivators, and we use these strengths for the important
people in our lives. Well, almost all the important people in our lives. There is
often one forgotten person in a woman's life that could use care, encouragement
and motivation. We forget to do these things, most often, for ourselves.

We try so hard to be all things to all people. If we do not comfort,
encourage, care for, and motivate ourselves, there will be little, if any, of these
attributes to share with others.

We look at others and see endless possibilities. Why do we not look at
ourselves and see the same? We must learn not only to see the possibilities in
others but also the possibilities in ourselves. Our lives are as important as the lives
of any of our other heroes.

⌘⌘⌘⌘⌘

"Everything is possible for him who believes."

Mark 9:25

JANUARY 24
...KNOWING CHANGE IS A CONSTANT

"There is a time for departure even when there's no certain place to go."
- Tennessee Williams

⌘⌘⌘⌘⌘

How often we look at our situation — either good or bad – and think that it will last forever. And, how untrue that is. Situations in our lives resemble clouds in a summer sky. They move along with an invisible push. We don't know where the clouds come from or where they are going. Depending on their place in time and their relationship to the sun, they will create a brightness, a beauty, and an atmosphere that makes us feel incredible, or they will cast shadows and make everything on earth seem gray and forlorn. The shadows cause us to stop and think, remembering the sunshine and hoping to see it again soon.

Our good times are like those moments of sunshine. They create those feelings of happiness, success, and excitement — that "nothing can stop me" attitude. And, even though we are feeling on top of everything, we know it will not last forever. That may make us sad. Yet, there is a happy side to this. Likewise, when we are down in the dumps, and things aren't going well, we know that this will not last forever either.

Sharon Donlon, a dear, sweet friend, made the comment to me one day that "it has come to pass — not to stay."

⌘⌘⌘⌘⌘

"So there is hope for your future," declares the Lord."
Jeremiah 31:17

JANUARY 25
...SWEATING THE SMALL STUFF

"The displacement of a little sand can occasionally change the course of rivers."
> - Manuel Gonzalez Prada

⌘⌘⌘⌘⌘

I often hear people say "don't sweat the small stuff." I find that expression odd and a personal source of irritation. The small stuff is what the big stuff is built upon. You don't have big stuff without small stuff.

I was reminded of this when my husband and I became acquainted with the two new families across the street. We live in a nice neighborhood, and the builder had done some extras — small things -- to make each home buyer feel special. When we moved in, the builder had provided a large plastic trash can with the company name on the side. Inside the trash can were convenience items of importance for any new home owner: paper towels, snack goods, light bulbs, drinks, gift certificates to a local pizza shop, etc. It was a nice "gift" even if it was in a plastic trash can.

Our neighbors were told, when they moved in, they would receive their "gift" soon. It has now been two years, and they still have not received their "gift." They know it is a plastic trash can, but that makes no difference. They want the gift that was promised!

They live in beautiful, expensive homes with all kind of "expensive" extras, and each time we get together, instead of talking about the expensive extras, they still talk about not receiving their "gift" – a plastic trash can.

A small thing – yes. But, over the course of two years, it has become a big thing that they discuss with many people. Neglect breeds mischief. We must all pay attention to detail.

⌘⌘⌘⌘⌘

"It is like the mustard seed,
which is the smallest seed you plant in the ground.
Yet when planted, it grows and becomes the largest of all garden plants,
with such big branches that the birds of the air can perch in its shade."
> Mark 4: 31-32

JANUARY 26
...BECOMING

"Growth itself contains the germ of happiness."
- Pearl S. Buck

⌘⌘⌘⌘⌘

Ruth Hamner, a fellow entrepreneur, once remarked that "winning was only the beginning." We set our goals and work so hard to reach them. Things are finally falling into place! We are getting the recognition that we want. People are calling us – for a change. Business is coming through the door. We can pay ourselves a salary. What could go wrong? We could. If we sit back and rest on our laurels, we could lose it all.

Our pursuit of goals and destinations is usually more exciting than reaching them. Think of Christmas as an example. We invite, shop, plan, trim, wrap, bake, serve, decorate, and clean. We spend 24+ days for one 24-hour period. Christmas morning guests arrive. We unwrap presents that we have been shopping for since the After-Christmas Sales last year. Wrapping paper that we have spent much money buying and much time wrapping is ripped off the boxes in milliseconds. Thanks are exchanged, clothes are tried on, compliments are given, the "loot" is taken to the car, the discarded wrapping paper and bows are put into green trash bags, and everyone comes in and sits down to wait for lunch.

We eat a meal, that we have been up preparing since 6:00 am, in less than an hour. We clean up the dining room and kitchen. Then, many of the guest leave to go to other houses only to go through the same routine during the evening hours.

About 2:00 PM an exhausted and forlorn atmosphere seems to invade the house. There is a quiet lull broken only by the ticking of the Grandfather Clock. We finally realize it was more fun planning for the Christmas holiday than experiencing the day itself.

As thinking beings, we need the goals, destinations, and plans as a marker of what we are accomplishing with our lives. That wonderful successful feeling based only on our past accomplishments is short lived. We must keep the feeling alive and current and on a progressive path. We must become. After all, the word "retirement" does not appear in the Bible.

⌘⌘⌘⌘⌘

"...they are like the new grass of the morning —
though in the morning it springs up new,
by evening it is dry and withered."
Psalm 90: 5-6

JANUARY 27
...APPRECIATING REAL LIFE EXPERIENCES

"Experience is a dear teacher, but she sends in terrific bills."
- Minna Thomas Antrim

⌘⌘⌘⌘⌘

My undergraduate degree is in education. Basically, I spent three years studying the subject matter, six months on the theory of teaching, and six months as a student teacher. The first day I walked into my own classroom, I realized it was going to take a lot more than those last four years of study to make me a good teacher. The text books and theory did not prepare me for 120 seventh-graders with different needs, education levels — and puberty. I needed experience!

As I have aged, I have gained experience and compassion for those going through menopause, breast cancer, and arthritis because they have become part of my own life. I have become insightful and intuitive about business success and failures because they, too, have become part of my life. I now understand why my mother, in her 40's, came home at night tired from too much mental stress and why she couldn't spend eight hours on yard work each Saturday because I am now past 40 years old. I know how people feel when they lose a loved one, watch someone with a debilitating illness struggle to recover, and try to rally their strength when they are overcome by stress. These have, also, become part of my life.

I have developed a greater appreciation for the fine arts as I write and read more. I have a new appreciation for music and the composer's ability to intertwine notes as I have gone from being a soprano to an alto. I have smiled often watching the exuberance of youth as I remember some of the crazy things I did as a child because I was a child. I have come to love to talk about the old days with people in their 20's and speak of wringer washing machines, summer canning kitchens, iceboxes, push mowers, and walking a mile to school. I have learned to love the lines in my face because they are smile lines not frown lines. And, I love to look at my husband who complains about balding, having a Budda belly, and having a sagging chin. I still see the twinkle in his eyes and the smile of a child.

There is a miracle that comes from these real life experiences. The more we know what others go through, the more consideration and respect we have for where they are now. We develop compassion and wisdom that comes only with age. "The years have learned things that the days will never know."

⌘⌘⌘⌘⌘

"...let the wise listen and add to their learning,
and let the discerning get guidance — "
Proverbs 1:5

JANUARY 28
...APPRECIATING TECHNOLOGICAL GIFTS

"An invention or new combination can be successful only if all of
the elements necessary for the recombination are present in the culture."
- Peter Farb

⌘⌘⌘⌘⌘

We are always talking about our gifts. They are wonderful. This morning
I realized what wonderful technological gifts I have chosen to have in my home.
While relaxing with my morning coffee and doing spiritual meditation, I am also
doing dishes, washing clothes, and baking bread. Now, while writing, dinner is
cooking in the crock pot, and the dogs, because we have installed an electric
fence, are outside getting exercise and enjoying their life, too. My computer, fax,
postage machine, and telephone permit me to have an office in my home cutting
down on overhead and allowing me to do things around the house at the same
time. My car makes it possible to get to clients in 30 minutes, and I can fly to an
appointment on either coast in 3 hours.

We love the simple pleasures in life, and we love doing many different
things. By selecting what technologies will work for us – from the bread machine
to the computer — we can make time available to us for many of the wonderful,
natural, technical, and simple things in life that make life so much more enjoyable.
While spending time at the keyboard, I am listening to classical music, rocking in
my platform rocker, looking out the window at the dogs playing, seeing the buds
on the trees and the tulips coming up, fixing a great supper for my husband, and
getting the clothes clean.

In reality, we know we can't get it all done all the time, but it certainly is nice
to do it all some of the time. It gives us that momentary feeling of being a
Wonder Woman or a Superman. It gives us a glad heart, a gleeful smile, and a
momentary rush. Thank goodness for technology and our ability to use it wisely.

⌘⌘⌘⌘⌘

"Perseverance must finish its work so that you may be mature and complete,
not lacking anything."
James 1:4

JANUARY 29
...KNOWING THE DIFFERENCE BETWEEN VALUE AND SUCCESS

> "I must admit that I personally measure success in terms of the
> contributions an individual makes to her or his fellow human beings."
> - Margaret Mead

⌘⌘⌘⌘⌘

Albert Einstein said, "Try not to become a person of success but rather a person of value". Value is not only a fair price, but it is also the worth of something in usefulness and importance. We have and are working hard for our success however we have defined that to be. Along our road for success, we also need to stop periodically and decide if we are a person of value.

When is the last time you have asked yourself these questions: Do my friends only judge me for what I have accomplished in business? Is all my conversation related to business topics? Have I created a balance in my life so that if one spoke of my wheel is broken, I shall still role? Have I gotten where I am by working hard at business and at business ethics? Have I and am I helping others along the way? When I have time for myself, do I always reach for my lap top computer?

In determining our value and our success, we must not only consider what is a fair price but also realize that sometimes a price for success can be too high to pay. Our success is important during our lifetime. It shows we "have arrived." Our value is important for eternity. It shows our life was worth living — for ourselves and for others.

⌘⌘⌘⌘⌘

> "How much better to choose wisdom than gold,
> to choose understanding rather than silver!"
> Proverbs 16:16

...ENJOYING EACH STEP ALONG THE WAY

"People need joy quite as much as they do clothing.
Some of them need it far more."
- Margaret Collier Graham

⌘⌘⌘⌘⌘

So many of us are like Marie Curie. She said, "I never notice what has been done. I only see what remains to be done." I'm not exactly sure if I have ever read a statement that rings any more true for women than this. How many hundreds — no thousands — of times have we tackled projects, struggled to complete them, only to shrug off our achievement and go on to something else? What seems to be even more tragic is the fact that no matter how hard we have worked to finish the project, when someone recognized that this was a difficult task and that we did a very good job, we usually brush it off by saying we were just lucky. Lucky! From the time we were little we were taught not to take credit for our accomplishments, to compete with ourselves, and to complete one project and go on to another. We were taught to deny and refuse to receive that ego gratification that promotes our self-esteem.

To help boost our self-esteem we need to celebrate not only the completion of each new project and the skill we have in getting the projects done, but we also need to celebrate each advance and each step along the way. We should not only take time to "smell the roses," but we should also take time to revel in the fact that we dug up the earth, planted the roses, fertilized and watered the roses, and tended the roses. Each accomplishment we have achieved and the skill we have displayed and developed in its completion should be admired.

⌘⌘⌘⌘⌘

"Let me hear joy and gladness;"
Psalm 51:8

JANUARY 31
...LIFE'S SUCCESS IS NOT A STRAIGHT LINE

> "I am one who never knows the direction of my journey
> until I have arrived."
>
> - Anna Louise Strong

⌘⌘⌘⌘⌘

I have several friends who are pilots, and I have flown with them. The first time I got a good look at the cockpit of a plane, I was amazed at the gauges that recorded almost everything. While we were flying, the person piloting the plane was constantly adjusting the plane's course and speed to compensate for wind, air pockets, bad weather, etc. Watching the constant readjustment caused me to realize that we had spent most of the air time getting to our destination being off course.

In math, I learned that the shortest distance between two points is a straight line. In life, when we are at one point, we may be sure of the location that we are travelling towards but not exactly sure of the actual point of the destination. Or, we may know where we want to go but not know the best way to get there. These situations make a straight line hard to follow.

We cannot always achieve our success by going the shortest distance. In any new endeavor, trial and error is a key factor. We must develop our "sea legs'"and learn to adjust to the rolls, the winds, and the curves. Our ability to readjust and set a new course helps us be successful in our journey.

If pilots, with years of training, get to their destinations by being off course about 90% of the time, we need to realize there will be times when we must stop, evaluate our progress, retrace steps, readjust, and start off on a new course to get to the same destination.

⌘⌘⌘⌘⌘

> "Thus you will walk in the ways of good men
> and keep to the paths of the righteous."
>
> Proverbs 2:20

FEBRUARY 1
...SEIZING OPPORTUNITIES

"The start of great enterprises."

- Demosthenes

⌘⌘⌘⌘⌘

I have always thought that the proverbial "window of opportunity" was a great deal like the Cheshire Cat in *Alice In Wonderland*. The window, just like the cat, presents itself for a very short period of time. For a few select moments the window allows you to see, to communicate, and to react, and then it vanishes until the timing is right for it to appear again.

I know there are times when we can help create our own opportunities. We create that space in time that allows the window to appear for us to take advantage of. Once it appears, it is again ours to react to. Too often, as the window appears, we are so awe struck with actually seeing the window that it disappears before we can react. Our reaction time is what we must change.

Opportunity does knock more than once; but if we are not prepared to answer, it will not make any difference how many times it knocks.

When you finally see the window of opportunity, don't just stand there and gaze. Be prepared to jump through.

⌘⌘⌘⌘⌘

"No eye has seen,
no ear has heard,
no mind has conceived
what God has prepared for those who love him"

1 Corinthians 2:21

FEBRUARY 2
...WAITING FOR OUR OWN SPRING

"The spring's behavior here is spent to make the world magnificent."
- Adapted from John Drinkwater

⌘⌘⌘⌘⌘

Spring is such an incredible time. It almost overwhelms our senses. We see the beautiful yellow-greens of new growth against the dark-greens of age. We watch anxiously for the daffodils, crocus, and tulips to venture forth after spending the winter underground. The pale pink and white flowers on cherry and crab apple trees are breathtaking. Robins and song birds return to sing melodies for us all summer long, and the ducks and geese honk their way through the long hot days.

It's a wonderful time of newness and change. Sometimes, when we are surrounded with all this beauty and change, we look at ourselves and think "how can all these changes occur when I am still stuck in the same old place."

We all wait for our own timing — our own spring. We are like the trees which stood up against the harshest winter in a dormant stage before starting life again, the bulbs which have spent a long winter in cold, frozen ground, or the birds which have stayed the winter and spent time being hungry and cold or those which returned after flying thousands of miles to come home.

The timing of spring is special and individualistic. We must wait for our own time to blossom and start our season anew.

⌘⌘⌘⌘⌘

"See! The winter is past;
the rains are over and gone.
Flowers appear on the earth;
the season of singing has come,
the cooing of doves
is heard in our land.
The fig tree forms its early fruit;
the blossoming vines spread their fragrance.
Arise, come, my darling;
my beautiful one, come with me."
Song of Solomon 2:11-13

FEBRUARY 3
...NOT BLAMING

"Blame is especially useful in situations in which there is no apparent villain —
those moments that prove, despite our advancement of learning,
how susceptible we are to high winds and wet roads."

- Roger Rosenblatt

⌘⌘⌘⌘⌘

Blame is a very interesting concept. It means to place a responsibility for
something on a person or happening. Which person or happening is the key. It
certainly can't be **our** fault.

When I began writing, my goal was to write seven entries a day. I finally
realized I didn't have it in me to do seven "good, creative" entries a day, so I fell
way behind. Then, I extended my time period and assigned myself four entries a
day. Initially, I blamed myself for setting the first goal too high to reach; but when
I had made the goal more attainable and still had trouble getting all the entries
written, I had to blame the holidays, the phone, the clients wanting proposals, and
the meetings I had to attend. (When you don't have people to blame, you have to
use happenings.) It wasn't that I stayed up too late, didn't get going early enough
in the morning, or spent too much time watching TV. So, if I wasn't at fault,
something else had to be!

I have opened my eyes to a really incredible phenomenon. Even when we
have something or someone to blame, it doesn't change anything. I was spending
way too much time agonizing over finding an outlet for not meeting my goals, and
all I accomplished was taking up more time which, in turn, made me feel even
more incompetent.

Why is it necessary to blame? It doesn't change a thing.

⌘⌘⌘⌘⌘

"He whose walk is blameless is kept safe,"

Proverbs 28:18

FEBRUARY 4
...STRETCHING OURSELVES

"Out of the stain of Doing,
Into the peace of Done."
- Julia Louise Woodruff

⌘⌘⌘⌘⌘

What is truly beyond our reach? When we reach or stretch out for what we are after, we usually get it. We may not use conventional methods, but we can be pretty creative with our unconventional methods.

The sock that falls between the washer and dryer is out of our reach; but, if we use a yardstick, we can get it. The apple that is high up and out on a limb is too far overhead to reach; but, if we shake the tree or throw a rock at the apple, we can get it. The boxes we filled when we moved were too heavy for us to lift; but, by opening them up and taking out the contents an item at a time, we could get the contents into their new place. We stand on chairs to get things off shelves; we walk heavy furniture into place; and we take one object apart to see how to put another together.

Louisa May Alcott said, "Far away there in the sunshine are my highest aspirations. I may not reach them, but I can look up and see their beauty, believe in them and try to follow where they lead." By looking into the sunshine which gives us warmth and encouragement and seeing where we might reach, somehow, we can figure a way to stretch ourselves and obtain that which we want so dearly.

⌘⌘⌘⌘⌘

"Everything is possible for him who believes."
Mark 9:23

FEBRUARY 5
...HAVING AND BEING A FRIEND

"The only way to have a friend is to be one."
- Ralph Waldo Emerson

⌘⌘⌘⌘⌘

When I first started my own business, I made a list of all my friends on a calendar and planned to see them every month or, at least, every other month. How sad I felt when I looked at that calendar and saw no check marks by their names in that monthly column. Then I thought I'd get them together all at one time for a party, but where would I find the time to clean and cook and arrange. So, I let my friendships slide. It is easy to make other friends, right?

Then, when I hit my first business "black hole," who did I have to turn to for comfort, advice, or support. There was no one to share disappointments with, no one to share the accomplishments with, no one to tell I had a cold or a sore throat. I knew things had to change.

It may be a phone call, a message left on an answering machine, a note through the mail, a thirty minute cup of coffee before a meeting, or even a copy of my newsletter, but I try to keep in touch with my friends. I'm not always as successful as I want to be in this endeavor, but I will continue to strive to maintain friendships.

Having and being a friend. What warmth there is in that statement.

⌘⌘⌘⌘⌘

"Dear friends, let us love one another,
for love comes from God."
1 John 4:7

FEBRUARY 6
...KNOWING "IF IT IS TO BE, IT IS UP TO ME"

"(That which) must be shown, by each of us in his appointed place,
not merely in the patience, but in the activity of our hope...our labor."
                                                        - John Ruskin

⌘⌘⌘⌘⌘

When I first became an entrepreneur, one thing I vowed was that I would
not get out of bed again at 5:30 AM unless it was for the Second Coming. Today, I
had another very clear example that even when we are setting our own schedule,
sometimes, we do need to set the alarm for 5:30 AM for special events.

There was a breakfast meeting scheduled for 7:30 AM, and the speaker was
an authority on the value of advertising your business. This was of interest to me,
so, I set the alarm for 5:30 AM and went. As I drove downtown, I was
remembering my vow of not getting up this early — because it was cold and rainy
and dark. I was wondering what had happened to this self-commitment.

The presentation was nothing like I thought it would be. The speaker talked
mostly about himself, and I was very disappointed in his presentation. However, I
did meet a woman who handed me five new business leads.

This was truly an incredible morning even if it was cold and rainy and dark.
The contact and this wonderful networking occurred because I got out of bed at
5:30 AM.

So many times we can get too comfortable, too relaxed, and even too set in
our ways.
If it is to be, it will take our energy and our life force, our exposure and our
experience, and our willingness and our strength to succeed. By utilizing all of
these, we can gain riches of many kinds.

⌘⌘⌘⌘⌘

"Oh, the depth of the riches of the wisdom and knowledge of God!"
                                                        Romans 11:33

FEBRUARY 7
...PROTECTING MY NATURAL RESOURCES

"Rest is the sauce of labor."
- Plutarch

⌘⌘⌘⌘⌘

Many people are heavily involved in activists groups trying to save our earth's natural resources. I, for one, am very glad. We tend to think of natural resources as being outside us. However, there are natural resources that are much closer to me and to you. These natural resources are our mind, our talent, our drive, our patience, our energy, our humor, and our self-esteem. As with all natural resources, each has its limits, and it is just as important that we guard these "personal" natural resources as we do those occurring outside ourselves.

Please don't misunderstand. I'm not telling you to be completely selfish and not share any of yourself. You will end up very lonely. What I am trying to tell you is to be selective and discerning with your natural resources and how they are spent. I think, in most situations, everyone gives in order to get back. It's an old belief system. What we need to make sure of is giving and spending our natural resources where they will do the most good in the long run.

If we constantly give out our natural resources without ever taking time to replenish and rejuvenate, we will surely burn out just as the sun does at the end of each day. And we cannot be 100% for others without being 100% for ourselves first. I know we must give in order to receive. I also know we must rest in order to give.

⌘⌘⌘⌘⌘

"Six days do your work, but on the seventh day do not work,
so that your ox and your donkey may rest and the slave born of your household,
and the alien as well, may be refreshed."
Exodus 23:12

FEBRUARY 8
...MOTIVATING FROM WITHIN

"True revelation comes through the clear intellect."
- Solomon B. Freehof

⌘⌘⌘⌘⌘

I have found that most people have some sort of motivational or inspirational guru. They buy the books or tape set, listen to them once, and then set the books or tapes on the shelf.

Motivational speakers are wonderful. I love to listen to them myself. Their message is truly inspiring. After studying the results of motivational speakers on the individual, we have learned that we forget nearly 50% of what they have said by the end of the first day and another 25% by the end of the second day. Just one session will not give us what we want: helpful motivation to carry us through.

Tony Robbins — a wonderful motivational speaker — bills himself as a "success coach." That is what we need. I purchased Tony Robbins' set of tapes. There are 30 of them. I listened to them once and did the exercises, but I didn't stop there. I listen to one almost every morning. We don't just listen to a coach one day and expect to play all the games remembering what he said during the first practice. We need the reinforcement. I also have a drawer in the nightstand by my bed that contains many "yellow highlighted" books. I pick one up periodically and reread what I've highlighted.

Because success coaches aren't in abundance, we have to become our own success coach. On a regular basis, listen to your tapes, reread your favorite passages, and review your goals to know where you stand and where you still want to go.

⌘⌘⌘⌘⌘

"Since you are my rock and my fortress,
for the sake of your name lead and guide me."
Psalm 31:3

FEBRUARY 9
...BEING WHOLE

"Resolve to be thyself; and know,
that he who finds himself, loses his misery."
- Matthew Arnold

⌘⌘⌘⌘⌘

I believe that many people go into business and marriage for the same reason – to find some part of someone or something to make them whole.

In math, we learned that "two halves make a whole." In math this is true, but in math we are talking about an equal mix. People and businesses are not an equal mix. This is another lesson I had to learn the hard way. Because I had such an uneventful time in my own high school years and was never part of the "in" group, I think one of the reasons I stayed in teaching as long as I did was to take my turn at popularity. Not a good reason for working with young people. Until I was in my 40's, I was certain every man I met would rescue me, and I, in turn, would become a better person. It wasn't until I rescued myself and became a whole person — personally and professionally — that I saw success in relationships and business. My whole person had presence! That presence was recognized and responded to.

Goethe said, "Before you can do something, you must be something." Before we go into a business or a marriage in which we want to be successful, we need to consider if we are a whole being from the start. Can we go into this endeavor whole knowing who we are, where we are going, what we want and what we have to contribute? Being aware of our strengths will help us to implement them, and being aware of our weakness will help us know how to compensate for them.

Only by knowing our true self will we be able to know what we are capable of. Through better knowledge of ourselves, we will be able to create more successful professional and personal relationships.

⌘⌘⌘⌘⌘

"If anyone thinks he is something when he is nothing,
he deceives himself."
Galatians 6:3

FEBRUARY 10
...KNOWING WHEN NOT TO COMMUNICATE

"Nothing is often a good thing to say,
and always a clever thing to say."
- Will Durant

⌘⌘⌘⌘⌘

Having studied communication for over 25 years, I have learned – the hard way – that there are times when I should not communicate.

I had once volunteered to do a presentation for a singles club. When I had first agreed to do this, I did not have any other presentations scheduled that day. But, as fate would have it, a client called and needed me as a substitute for their very ill trainer. So, after working an 8-hour training session, I arrived at the singles club to do another 90 minute presentation. I was tired, but I made it through.

Now, you can always spot the "one in every crowd" kind of person. He was sitting in the back of the room on my left. After the applause died down, he jumped out of his seat, semi-trampling some of the other attendees and made a beeline for me. He waited his turn in line; and when we were finally face to face, he said, "Can you take some constructive criticism?" I thought serious about it and replied, "I've had a very long day, and I'm very tired. No, I cannot ,but thank you for offering."

The look on his face definitely reflected disbelief, and I'm sure he didn't think this was the most Christian response he had ever heard. Knowing what "constructive criticism" usually means and knowing that I was not in any mood to receive it, I opted not to communicate on this issue. We must all realize that it is not always a good time to communicate.

⌘⌘⌘⌘⌘

"Make it your ambition to lead a quiet life,"
1 Thessalonians 4:11

FEBRUARY 11
...REFRAMING

"Our life is what our thoughts make it."
- Marcus Aurelius

⌘⌘⌘⌘⌘

I attend the largest Methodist Church north of the Mason Dixon Line. We have over four thousand members and another two thousand people that simply attend. And, it is growing steadily each month.

The church was not designed to hold this many people. It has been expanded once and is now being expanded again. Because of the size of the congregation, on some Sundays parking can be a problem! There is a spot in front of the church that holds about 40 cars; and, if you time it just right, you can get a parking spot for the second service by being there when people from the first service are leaving.

One Sunday I was running late – really late. I pulled up in front, and there were no parking places. I drove in back; no parking places. I drove to the side lot; no parking places.

I was so angry because I couldn't find a place to park. All of a sudden, I was sad and embarrassed at what I had been thinking. I realized, especially in this day and age, I should have been overjoyed that the parking lots were that full and so many people wanted to hear the Lord's word and commune with other Christians. I reframed and apologized to the Lord. And, lo and behold, after I reframed and apologized, someone who was also running late — really late — came out of the church, got into their car and pulled away, and I had a parking spot.

⌘⌘⌘⌘⌘

"For my thoughts are not your thoughts,
neither are your ways my ways, declares the Lord."
Isaiah 55:8

FEBRUARY 12
...BY LETTING OTHERS BE THE CENTER OF ATTENTION

"Half of the harm that is done in this world
is due to people who want to feel important."
- T. S. Eliot

⌘⌘⌘⌘⌘

We all have something that makes us special. It may be a special dish we prepare, an outfit, a car, a dog, or the color of our eyes. We work hard to make whatever we have that is special stand out, and we love it when people notice whatever it is. It adds so much to our self-esteem.

A friend had a beautiful Husky named Tasha. This dog was not only beautiful, but she was also sweet, well trained, and entertaining. She'd play with her squeaky hamburger and howl when you tried to tickle her feet. Everyone enjoyed Tasha. At a party, Tasha was the center of attention. There was a man there listening to the accolades Tasha was receiving. Every time someone would say something nice about Tasha, he would make some type of comment about his dog. If someone admired Tasha's coat, his dog's coat was prettier. If Tasha was beautiful, his dog was more beautiful. If Tasha did a cute trick, his dog did something spectacular.

This created an awkward situation. At the beginning of the party, you could see the woman beam when someone noticed and praised her dog. As the party wore on and the man continued with his "one-upmanship," praise to the dog waned because people were tired of listening to him, and you could tell the woman was saddened by this. This man had robbed her of one of her joys in life.

We all have something special. We should be allowed to revel in this joy. No one should rob us of it. If someone flies a plane, don't monopolize the conversation with your flight along the Alaskan Highway. If someone belly dances, don't talk about all the times you have been center stage. We must allow everyone to have a chance to be the center of attention. We must allow everyone a sense of joy.

⌘⌘⌘⌘⌘

"But each man has his own gift from God;
one has this gift, another has that."
1 Corinthians 7:7

FEBRUARY 13
...DEVELOPING MASTERY IN ONE AREA

"Anyone who has achieved excellence in any form
knows that it comes as a result of ceaseless concentration."
- Louise Brooks

⌘⌘⌘⌘⌘

At a lecture on communication the instructor was talking about the glut of information people today are faced with. The perfect example he gave was that if a person wanted to read one copy of the New York Sunday Times word for word, cover to cover, it would take 18 hours for 18 days. We have more information in this one issue of this paper than people 150 years ago had in a lifetime. To be successful in this world of technology, we must be both a specialist and a generalist. We must know a little about many things and a great deal about one thing. That will be our claim to fame.

One definition of an expert is someone who has studied something for more than two years or less than thirty minutes. Now, I take a great deal of pride in being a thirty minute expert on thousands of topics. Why? This allows me to talk with almost everyone about something. I take an even greater pride is being a two (+) year expert in the area of communication and motivation. This is truly my claim to fame and how I will help others in this very complex technical world. Our technology is wonderful and puts the world at our finger tips, but it is still the "old fashioned" art of one-on-one, face-to-face communication that helps us relate, interact, and proceed through life bonding with other human beings.

⌘⌘⌘⌘⌘

"The spirit of the Lord will rest on him —
the Spirit of wisdom and of understanding,"
Isaiah 11:2

FEBRUARY 14
...WORKING BACKWARDS

"The secret of success is constancy to purpose."

- Benjamin Disraeli

⌘⌘⌘⌘⌘

Trying to make it through college when you are just entering early adulthood and independence can be difficult at times. My undergraduate degree was in English Literature. (I know some of you are wondering why anyone would major in English Literature. I did. Somebody had to.) Majoring in English Literature, you read novel after novel after novel. At first glance it was overwhelming. I couldn't possibly read all those pages by the due date. After once getting behind and paying the consequences in my grade, I realized I needed to develop a system that would work for me. When I had a novel completion due, I would look at the number of pages, divide it by the days available, and figure out how many pages I had to read a day to get the novel read. It worked great!

As a matter of fact, this plan worked so well for me, I use it in almost all areas of my life. Whether it is reading a new text, creating a new presentation, or planning a meal for a dinner party, I figure out what has to be done, how long it is going to take, and when I need to start.

I did not realize I was goal setting even before it was popular. To me, goal setting is working backwards. It is seeing where you want to go and planning the way of getting there. Oliver Wendell Holmes said, "I find the great thing in this world is not so much where we stand, as in what direction we are moving."

⌘⌘⌘⌘⌘

"And we know that in all things God works for the good of those who love him, who have been called according to his purpose."

Romans 8:28

FEBRUARY 15
...CELEBRATING OUR DIFFERENCES

"Differences challenge assumptions."
- Anne Wilson Schaef

⌘⌘⌘⌘⌘

I know we've all had the "light bulb" experience, and, one day, walking through the mall, a light bulb went off – for me – that could have lit up the entire north-east side.

I probably had walked by 20 store fronts; when all of a sudden, I actually realized what I had been seeing. As I walked by a man's clothing store (MCS), in the window would be slacks, coats, ties, shirts and suits. As I walked by a women's clothing store (WCS), in the window would be tailored business suits. Another MCS – slacks, coats, ties, shirts, and suits. Another WCS – beautiful dresses with lace and flower trim. Another MCS – slacks, coats, ties, shirts, and suits. Another WCS – jog suits, stretch pants and oversized sweaters. MCS – the same. WCS – long wrap shirts or skirts with the slit up the side and silk blouses. MCS - the same. WCS – vests, big shirts, short skirts, and legging.

There was our different life styles and personalities right in front of my eyes. The man's wardrobe was a corporate uniform – a uniform as any team member would wear for his position, and the women's wardrobe offered a different outfit to meet the need for our diverse, multi-task lifestyle.

For women, simply knowing what to wear at what time is a visual sign of our self-trust. It is not the only secret of our success, but it is one that does help us establish balance to meet all our needs as women. Our lives are as diverse and excitingly different as our clothing.

⌘⌘⌘⌘⌘

"For who makes you different from anyone else?"
1 Corinthians 4:7

FEBRUARY 16
...FEELING PASSIONATE ABOUT WHAT WE DO

Only passions, great passions, can elevate the soul to great things."
- Denis Diderot

⌘⌘⌘⌘⌘

My seminars and training focus on helping people be more effective communicators. Many times, after one of my communication seminars, I have clients call and ask me if I will do a presentation on team building, and I say, "No." They say, "Pardon me." And, I say, "No" and then proceed to explain. "I've been an entrepreneur for over 15 years. I like working by myself. If I am on a team and people don't do things my way, I have to kill them. This works very well for me, but it may not be successful in your organization." Then, they usually ask me if I can recommend someone, and I do so gladly. I want to recommend someone who has as much passion for team building or time management as I do for communications. That's what makes each of us successful -- passion. [I don't really kill people; I just have no passion for team building and would not do a good job presenting this type of workshop.]

How many times have you gone to a session of - let's say - time management. The person doing the presentation doesn't want to be there, has no interest in the subject matter, or is tired from over-presenting. The audience knows this in less than 60 seconds, and every minute they spend there is an eternity. Knowing a subject and speaking from the mind may get the information across, but if you want the information to have a lasting effect and make changes in a person's life, you must add passion for the subject and speak from the heart as well as the mind.

⌘⌘⌘⌘⌘

"You will go out in joy
and be led forth in peace;"
Isaiah 55:12

FEBRUARY 17
...KEEPING DELIGHT IN MY LIFE

"Happiness does not lie in happiness, but in the achievement of it."
- Dostoyevsky

⌘⌘⌘⌘⌘

My husband and I sing in the church choir. I'm an alto, and he's a tenor; so, we even get to sit reasonably close to one another. Something else we share together is a love for donuts; however, being a little more health conscious as we age, we basically had given them up — that is until we started singing in the choir. Our church has three services. The choir sings at the 9:30 and 11:00 service. We have a half hour break in between the two services. To facilitate interaction of the church members between services, in the Great Hall the church serves coffee, juice, bagels, and donuts. Our one truly decadent treat during the week is our Sunday morning donut.

One Sunday, while imbibing, I watched a four year old boy walk through the Great Hall with a chocolate covered donut. Instead of eating the entire donut, he was licking the chocolate off the top of the donut, and the ear-to-ear smile told of his delight.

So often in life, especially as adults, we do what we have to do, and in doing what we have to do, we eliminate what can be the delightful things in our life. We take a shower instead of a long hot bath; we microwave canned soup instead of making something from scratch; or we eat the entire donut instead of licking off the icing, the part most of us like the best.

Long hot baths, home made meals, icing. Whatever is a delight to you, whatever brings you joy, try to incorporate into your life occasionally. It's a wonderful way to keep the inner child tickled and looking forward to the next delightful moment.

⌘⌘⌘⌘⌘

"Be joyful always;"
1 Thessalonians 5:16

FEBRUARY 18
...MAKING A DIFFERENCE WITH THE SMALL THINGS

"We find great things are made of little things,
And little things go lessening till at last
Comes God behind them."
- Robert Browning

⌘⌘⌘⌘⌘

We "had" one dog: an 80 pound black and gold Lab mix named Murphy. She has grass allergies and takes antihistamines. One afternoon, I went to the vet to get a refill on a prescription. When I walked in, there was an elderly man at the counter paying a bill. He had picked up his Wired-haired Dachshund named CoCo that had been boarded at the vet's for the last month. She was so happy to be out of that cage. She ran up to everyone, sat up, and pawed the air for attention. She had just been groomed and was wearing an orange and white Halloween bandana. She was precious. I thought how great it would be to have a small lap dog.

I was eavesdropping on his conversation to the receptionist. He said he had been at the hospital for the last month with his mother who had heart surgery. He had sold his home and was going to move in with and take care of his mother. He couldn't keep his dog. He didn't know what to do with her, so he was going to take her to the pound. My heart stopped. I looked at CoCo and then the man and told him he couldn't take her to the pound. She was too precious. I brought her home praying that my husband would love her, and she would get along with our retriever.

It was as if it were meant to be. She looked just like a dog my husband used to have, and Murphy and she became fast friends almost overnight.

Bringing her home was such a small thing. She doesn't eat a lot or take up a great deal of space. Walking two dogs is not much different than walking one. And, she is a wonderful companion for Murphy.

I'm reminded of the story of the man on the beach throwing each starfish he found back into the ocean. He couldn't make a difference to all the starfish, but he did to each one he found and saved by throwing back.

I love dogs and wish I could save all of them. I know I can't, but I can care for these two. I have made a positive difference in the life of these God-made creatures, and they in turn have made a wonderful positive difference in my life.

⌘⌘⌘⌘⌘

"A little yeast works through the whole batch of dough."
Galatians 5:9

FEBRUARY 19
...DISPLAYING COMMON COURTESY

"Manners must adorn knowledge and smooth its way through the world."

- Lord Chesterfield

⌘⌘⌘⌘⌘

Phrases and cliques are (excuse me) "a dime a dozen." We have heard them so often that, most of the time, we don't question their origin or meaning or even realize if we agree with them.

One phrase I have a definite problem with is "common courtesy." To me, common denotes ordinary, mundane, or taken for granted. I think common courtesy is a misnomer. I don't think there is anything common about courtesy!

The way we treat others — family or strangers — should never be taken for granted. Our family is supposed to be made up of the most important people in our life. Should our interaction with them be ordinary or mundane? No, I don't think so.

Courtesy, the little extra kindness, praise, and notice, is something we should be certain that we give to others. For isn't it in giving that we receive? How thrilled we are when someone opens a door, tells us we did a good job, or notices a new outfit we are wearing. Comments such as these never go unnoticed. Each time someone is courteous to us, our self-esteem and pride goes up a couple of notches. Our day goes better, and we look forward to interacting with this person again.

Isn't this how you would like to be remembered and viewed by the people you interact with each day? Be courteous to people in an "uncommon" way, and they will be "uncommonly" courteous back to you.

⌘⌘⌘⌘⌘

"Be kind and compassionate to one another,
forgiving each other, just as in Christ God forgave you."

Ephesians 4:32

FEBRUARY 20
...NOT UNDERSTANDING EVERYTHING

"To be conscious that you are ignorant is a great step to knowledge."
- Benjamin Disraeli

⌘⌘⌘⌘⌘

Do you remember a TV character by the name of Arthur Fonzerelli? Most people believe he is a rather humorous enigma. I don't think so. I think the Fonz is a dominant gene on our DNA. None of us like to admit we are wrong or we don't understand for the fear of looking foolish. So investors talk to us for hours telling us about the future of our money, and we nod and say "uh huh" not really understanding what is happening to our money. Someone mentions a name and/ or story, and we chime in in agreement not really knowing much, if anything, about the matter. We agree to things that "everyone" understands, know people that "everyone" knows, and buy things that "everyone" must have. Why? Because we believe we have to understand everything.

Our world is too complicated to understand everything, and "I don't understand" does not make anyone less of a person. In many ways "I don't understand" can help build relationships. When we are not the world's expert on every topic, other people get an opportunity to tell what they know. It is great for their self image and value, and, who knows, we just may learn something in the process.

⌘⌘⌘⌘⌘

"Trust in the Lord with all your heart
and lean not on your own understanding;"
Proverbs 3:5

FEBRUARY 21
...KNOWING MOST OF OUR CREDENTIALS ARE INVISIBLE

"Maybe being oneself is always an acquired taste."
- Patricia Hampl

⌘⌘⌘⌘⌘

Credentials, that which entitles one to confidence, credit, or authority, is generally understood to be in the form of sheepskins, awards, or titles. It is important for us to realize that many of our most powerful, inspiring, and impressive credentials are invisible as far as sheepskins, awards, or titles.

What displays our confidence, credit and authority? Our walk, the tilt of our head, the gleam in our eye, our smile, our soft touch, our kindness. Too often, because these are intangibles, we tend to think they have little value or worth. Without these intangibles, the tangibles such as the sheepskins, awards, and titles won't get displayed to the world. It takes us imboding what we have earned, mixing what we are with what we have learned, and presenting this to the rest of the world. This establishes our credibility. These are our credentials.

⌘⌘⌘⌘⌘

"Understanding is a fountain of life to those who have it,"
Proverbs 16:22

FEBRUARY 22
...GIVING FIRST

"Let him that desires to see others happy,
make haste to give while his gift can be enjoyed,
and remember that every moment of delay takes away
something from the value of his benefaction."
- Samuel Johnson

⌘⌘⌘⌘⌘

A good friend of my mother's would be considered, by most, a recluse. She lived in a very rural farm house out in the middle of a field. She did have electricity but no indoor running water. All water for human consumption came from a pump. On a visit to her home (to go mushroom hunting), I was asked to bring water in from the pump. Sure. They then gave me a bucket already filled with water. I couldn't understand why I needed to bring in water when we already had some water. That was when I learned you had to prime the pump. You had to pour water down into the pump before you got the water you wanted up from the pump.

We want respect before we give it. We want help before we give it. We want friendship before we give it. We must give to receive. It is not a difficult lesson to learn, but once learned, we tend to forget it from time to time.

It is especially important to let the younger generations see us in the act of giving. Giving is something we learn in our early years. It is important for young people to see us give requiring nothing in return. They will learn to give to us, to others, and to pass the act of giving along to generations to come.

⌘⌘⌘⌘⌘

"It is more blessed to give than to receive."
Acts 20:35

FEBRUARY 23
...WAITING FOR PERSPECTIVE

"'Tis distance lends enchantment to the view."
- Thomas Campbell

⌘⌘⌘⌘⌘

For about seven years I attended church in a very passive capacity. I was just going to church and not being involved in church. I would sit in a part of the church with the stained glass windows on my left and enjoy the colors as the sunlight streamed through.

About three years ago, I decided to become an active part of this church. My husband and I serve on several committees and sing in the choir.

When sitting in the choir loft, you face the stained glass windows. One Sunday, while listening to the minister and staring at the windows, I realized I was not just seeing panes of color. I was seeing a fish, a scythe, a book — religious symbols. I was seeing the glass from a new perspective. It had taken me eight years of Sundays to finally see the windows as they were meant to be seen.

I thought about some of the issues I was dealing with in my personal life. Things were just not moving fast enough for me. [Patience is not quite as strong as my other skills.] Suddenly, it dawned on me that if it took me eight years just to see the patterns in the panes of glass at church, it could possibly take a little longer on some of the major issues in my life.

Perspective comes with distance and time. These two entities are not always immediate or obvious.

⌘⌘⌘⌘⌘

"Therefore, judge nothing before the appointed time;"
1 Corinthians 4:5

FEBRUARY 24
...SPEAKING SO ALL PEOPLE UNDERSTAND

"Fine sense and exalted sense are not half so useful as common sense."
- Alexander Pope

⌘⌘⌘⌘⌘

Keeping updated on the latest in any profession is wise. Especially if you are an entrepreneur and want repeat business from clients. Knowing that people respond well to their own data and that they like immediate results, I was intrigued with a new "thinking model" called Whole Brain Thinking. Whole Brain Thinking divides the brain into four quadrants, and the self-test determines what our thinking preference is.,

I trained and studied and read. I also sent off to the originator and ordered the game and overheads. One of the overheads was a chart of some of the world's great thinkers. Scanning the people listed, I was amazed to see that Matthew, Mark, Luke and John were on the chart – each in a different quadrant of the brain.

The Four Gospels are, basically, the same story, each with a different interpretation or a different highlight. In talking to people about the Four Gospels, it is very common for a person to pick one of the gospels as a favorite over the other three. I would assume that each one of us picks the gospel that is written most closely to the way we prefer to think.

The understanding of words is in the interpretation. We all interpret differently. If the Gospel can be written four different ways to have meaning for all, maybe it would be advantageous for us to think of different ways to present ourselves so that all people can relate, identify, and understand the meaning behind our words.

⌘⌘⌘⌘⌘

"Wisdom is supreme; therefore get wisdom.
Though it cost all you have, get understanding."
Proverbs 4:7

FEBRUARY 25
...CREATING CEREMONIES

"The wine of human experience."
- Morris R. Cohen

⌘⌘⌘⌘⌘

Because I am out so many evenings speaking at dinner meetings, my early morning is like everyone else's late evening. It is my time to relax, regroup and plan.

This is my morning ceremony. I put on grubbie clothes, and the dogs and I go for our mile walk. I then feed the dogs and put them out on the deck to bark at the birds and the neighbors. I make a cup of espresso and fix my plate with fresh fruit and a "giant" muffin (one of the four basic food groups). I read my Daily Word and a chapter in the book d'jour. I meditate, thank the Lord for all my blessings, and ask for the day to go smoothly. I let the dogs in, retreat to the bathroom, and get into the Jacuzzi tub for about 30 minutes. With this completed, I get dressed, put on make-up and curl my hair. After this two hour refresher, it is 9:00 am, and I am ready to start the day.

There is a comfort in ceremonies. The timing of them, all they accomplish, and the joy of the renewal. It's the guidance and the structure that we create that allows us to handle all the unstructuredness that we face everyday. Our ceremonies can be the backbone of our life. They provide us with the strength and the support upon which the daily unpredictable events temporarily lodge.

⌘⌘⌘⌘⌘

"...ask where the good way is, and walk in it,
and you will find rest for your souls."
Jeremiah 6:16

FEBRUARY 26
...FEEDING THE SOUL AND NOT JUST THE BODY

"When we are not physically starving,
we have the luxury to realize psychic and emotional starvation."
- Cherrie Moraga

⌘⌘⌘⌘⌘

Studies change the way we live our life. Look at how our diets have changed over time. When we were younger and worked harder, we could eat almost anything. Then, we began to age and put on a few pounds. So, we started to think about our eating habits to see what needed changing.

First we counted calories — not fat. Now we count fat grams. Then we had to exercise. Then we had to work out until we "felt the burn." Recently we have been told that just 30 minutes of walking is considered beneficial. Then we had to avoid red meat. One day we were supposed to eliminate high carbohydrates and now high carbohydrates are supposed to be the base of our pyramid diet (which, incidentally, is different than the four basic food groups that I grew up with).Whole or 2%? Fat free or sugar free or both? Lactose free? Salt free? Do we buy in bulk or individual servings? Yogurt or fat free ice cream? Prepackaged food or home made? Frozen vs. canned? Grocery or specialty store? Eat in or out? And, is exercise just for weigh loss, or will it stop the aging process?

We spend countless hours studying our diets – what we intake for our body. What do you think our lives would be like if we spent as much time feeding our soul? A smile or a frown? A positive or a negative outlook on life? Infinite vs. finite possibilities? Timebound or timeless? Endless or ending?

If we spent just half as much time thinking about what we feed our soul as what we feed our body, how much more filled and fulfilled we would be today!

⌘⌘⌘⌘⌘

"Do not work for food that spoils,
but for food that endures to eternal life,"
John 6:27

FEBRUARY 27
...SMILING WITH THE MORNING

"I really do believe I can accomplish a great deal with a big grin.
I know some people find that disconcerting, but that doesn't matter."
- Beverly Sills

⌘⌘⌘⌘⌘

Have you every had one of those mornings when you wake up greeting the day with "Good God, it's morning" instead of "Good morning, God"? I was having one of those days. I walked into doors, stubbed my toes, dropped almost everything I picked up, tripped over the dogs, and spilled most of my breakfast on my freshly laundered robe. I was feeling very "put upon" and out of sorts. I just wanted to go back to bed and forget about the day's commitments. I was positive I couldn't function in this world with all the "terrible" things that were happening to me!

Trivial, petty incidents cloud our view and steal our smile. Sometimes, when we allow this to happen, and then, during the day, we hear of an accident victim who will never walk again, suddenly, all those petty incidents seem **really** petty and certainly not worth all the effort and time we have spent thinking about them. It is rather sad to have to hear of someone else's tragedy to make our own life seem better.

I personally have learned that any day above ground is a good one, and cuddling with my husband, seeing the sun, listening to the rain, watching it snow, hearing the birds, or having two dogs jump up and kiss me good morning brings a smile to my face. During the day, when I stop and remember my morning should have started with a "Good morning, God," I can smile despite all those truly petty, insignificant things that just simply happen.

⌘⌘⌘⌘⌘

"...but the cheerful heart has a continual feast."
Proverbs 15:15

FEBRUARY 28
...REMEMBERING CHILDHOOD JOYS

"The older I grow the more earnestly I feel that the few
intense joys of childhood are the best that life has to give."
- Ellen Glasgow

⌘⌘⌘⌘⌘

My mother always told me I was a rather inquisitive child. She created
many games to keep me occupied. When we traveled in the car on vacation, to
keep me from asking "are we there yet," she would give me a nickel for each
horse I counted as we drove to our destination. Being very goal oriented and
wanting the spending money, I sat silently with my eyes glued to the window hour
after hour counting horses.
My favorite childhood joy was catching lightning bugs. Again, to keep me
busy in the evenings while she sat on the porch resting from a day at work, Mother
told me that on the backs of some lightning bugs rode fairies. If you caught a
lightning bug with a fairy on its back, you could get the fairy to grant you any wish.
So, night after night, I ran from one end of the yard to the other catching lightning
bugs. I never did find the one with the fairy on its back, but I sure did have a
great time.
To this day, every time I see a lightning bug, I giggle inside remembering
the fun I had as a child.

⌘⌘⌘⌘⌘

"And the child grew and became strong in spirit;"
Luke 1:80

MARCH 1
...WATCHING OUT FOR THE RUSH

"Our patience will achieve more than our force."
- Edmund Burke

⌘⌘⌘⌘⌘

As I've stated before, patience is not as strong as my other virtues. I guess because I've become used to remote controls, faxes, microwaves, 24-hour shopping, the Internet, etc., I seem to want everything now. It is no different with my driving. Wherever it is I have to go or be, I want to be there now! I want no traffic jams, red lights, Sunday morning drivers, or construction. I don't want delays! When I have long stretches of uninterrupted highway, I tend to push just a little harder on the accelerator to get where I'm going a few minutes ahead of schedule.

One Saturday, several friends and I drove to the southern part of the state for some outlet shopping. Timewise, we thought everything was under control, and we would be back home for evening engagements with an hour to spare. We did not take into consideration that the southern part of the state is in a different time zone; consequently, we were running late. I tried to make haste at every opportunity and said everything but blessings for people who got in my way and slowed down my progress. Just as I came to a stretch of road where I could make up some time, a man pulled in front of me doing a great deal less than the speed limit. I hit the brakes. My reaction and attitude toward this gentleman were not favorable.

Just a second or two after I had hit the brakes, a car going in the opposite direction lost a tire. It came flying across the road barely missing us. Then, a rod flew across the windshield at eye level. If I had not slammed on the brakes when I did, my friends and I would probably not be alive today.

This taught me a great lesson in patience. Now, when delayed on the road, I pause and reflect on this incident and realize that maybe the Lord just doesn't want me in a particular spot at a particular moment. Some days it is not good to be caught up in the rush.

⌘⌘⌘⌘⌘

"Yet the Lord longs to be gracious to you;
he rises to show you compassion.
For the Lord is a God of justice
Blessed are all who wait for him!"
Isaiah 30:18

MARCH 2
...REVELING IN MY RESOURCEFULNESS

"A single idea, if it is right, saves us the labor of an infinity of experiences."
- Jacques Maritain

⌘⌘⌘⌘⌘

Marcia, my neighbor, and I are quite different in many ways — age, children, and careers. Even with these differences we do have three things in common: we both have two black dogs — one large and one small; we both have the same type of flooring; and we both have a hideous time keeping scratches, dirt and dog hair off the floor.

She recently had her third child. All her family and in-laws were flying in for the baptism. She wanted the house immaculate (tough with two dogs). She put the dogs outside and spent several hours scrubbing and waxing these "hard to clean" floors. Just as she finished, it started to rain. Naturally, the dogs wanted in. What to do?

From the laundry Marcia retrieved 4 pairs of her older boy's socks and put the socks on the dogs' feet. Picture two black dogs wearing 4 white socks! It was quite an amusing sight.

Her resourcefulness accomplished many things: it kept the floor clean from scratches and mud; it saved her hours of rewaxing and rescrubbing; and it provided all of us with a wonderful laugh.

[My resourcefulness with cherry floors and two dogs is to allow people to come over only when it is dark or overcast. I'm not as creative as Marcia.]

⌘⌘⌘⌘⌘

"He has filled them with skill to do all kinds of work
as craftsmen, designers, embroiderers in blue, purple and scarlet
yarn and fine linen, and weavers —
all of them master craftsmen and designers."
Exodus 35:35

MARCH 3
...BY KEEPING IN TOUCH WITH MY SPOUSE

"Husbands are like fires. They go out when unattended."
- Zsa Zsa Gabor

⌘⌘⌘⌘⌘

Both my husband and I have been previously married. Before we were married, we dated for about five years. We spent time discussing what type of future we wanted. We both knew we weren't 16 any more; we each had a past, responsibilities, careers, and investments. We wanted a marriage that would last for the rest of our lives. It was difficult for us to exactly define what we wanted, but we certainly knew what we didn't want. One of the major things we didn't want was to lose touch with one another. In a marriage of today it is so easy to get caught up in paying the bills and cutting the grass that you lose touch with one another.

We created a plan to keep in touch with one another. In all of our discussions of what we enjoyed, we came up with three things we enjoyed doing as a couple. First, we have dates – still. We go to movies, have nice dinners, walk our dogs, and hold hands. Second, we take gourmet cooking classes, cook together, and have friends over for our cooking parties. Third, we sing in the church choir together. We have choir practice every Thursday night and sing in two services every Sunday morning. After church, we go to Sunday brunch.

These things aren't extraordinary. Actually, they are pretty ordinary. But they keep us together — in love, in sight, and in touch.

⌘⌘⌘⌘⌘

"Do two walk together unless they have agreed to do so?"
Amos 3:3

MARCH 4
...SETTING PRIORITIES

"That which determines the material."
- Thomas Carlyle

⌘⌘⌘⌘⌘

In a one block radius of my childhood neighborhood were 10 kids all the same age, same class, and same church. And summers were for play. We played dolls, red rover, jacks, board games, and tag. Tag seemed to be our favorite. We would play tag until dark, and we had to come in.

A new kid moved into the neighborhood, and his parents had a cookout for all of us so we could get acquainted. As usual, after we ate, we decided to play tag. The mail box on the front porch was base. I was hiding on one side of the house. When who was "it" ran around to the other side of the house, I ran behind the bushes toward the base. The problem I ran into reaching base in this unfamiliar yard in the dark was a well in front of a basement window. Just as I neared the front porch I fell into the window well filled with gravel. I laid there scratched, bruised, and bleeding. My best friend walked up to me touched my hand with her right hand, the base with her left hand, and said "free." She had her priorities clearly set. First, she made sure I has "home safe," and second, she would see if I were still alive.

We all set our priorities – in our own mind, and they are right for us. They may not be what others think should be first on our list, but they are not living our life. Others are not aware of our hierarchy, needs, interests, or desires.

It is important for us to remember that when people are not doing things as we think they should, it is because we each set our own priorities; we do not allow others to set them for us.

⌘⌘⌘⌘⌘

"See to it that no one takes you captive through hollow and deceptive philosophy, which depends on human tradition and the basic principles of this world rather than on Christ."
Colossians 2:8

MARCH 5
...PUTTING ON AND TAKING OFF LAYERS

"Self-preservation is the first principle of our nature."
- Alexander Hamilton

⌘⌘⌘⌘⌘

Bob Gregory is one of our local weathermen. Several years ago he did a commercial where a young boy, who wanted to go out and play in the snow, had on so many layers of clothing that he could only move stiff legged and stiff armed. You can't play very well or have very much fun when you can't move, run, build snowmen, make snow angels, throw snowballs, or sled.

I have been this layered kid. We had a huge blizzard in '78. With the wind chill factor, the temperature was -60 degrees, and the snow had drifted in places up to 10 feet high. We had four horses that had to be fed and watered. I bundled up in insulated underwear, jeans, jackets, hats, scarves, boots, and insulated coveralls. With the layers of clothes restricting my movement and the wind and snow slowing my progress, it was everything I could do to get to the barn and back. To be honest, once I had made it to the barn I was scared I couldn't get back to the house.

When we put on layer after layer of our attitudes, interactions, and soul searching, we are just like the little boy who had so many layers on that he couldn't really do what he wanted to.

There are times when we need the extra layers as protection not only from frost bite but from people bite, so we pile the layers on. But when protection becomes less of an issue and when we want to accomplish things, let's start peeling the layers off — one at a time — and relax, get more things done, and see what and who is actually underneath.

⌘⌘⌘⌘⌘

"You are my hiding place;
you will protect me from trouble
and surround me with songs of deliverance.
Psalm 32:7

MARCH 6
...KNOWING THE GREATEST AMONG US WAS ALSO THE MOST HUMBLE

"The first test of a truly great man is his humility."
- John Ruskin

⌘⌘⌘⌘⌘

Spending a great deal of time at organizational and corporate meetings, I have many opportunities to observe people. In observing people, the phrase "all walks of life" comes to mind. When I watch people enter a room, they usually come in one of two ways. One way is barking orders, telling everyone of the latest success, pointing out who did what wrong, and being loud just to be the center of attention. The second way is different. This person enters with a smile, greets people, asks how they are doing, and subtly becomes the center of attention because other people respect, what I like to call, their "gentle authority."

When you have gentle authority, you don't have to tell people you are in charge; they somehow know you are in charge. You don't put people down to make yourself look better or superior; you build people up, and they, in turn, give you respect and look up to you. You don't constantly shout to get yourself noticed; you are noticed the minute you enter a room because you are who you are.

This gentle authority is humility. It is taking the lead for others to follow. It is having others follow you not out of fear but out of respect. Others look to you for guidance instead of orders. It is setting the example of how to deal with others effectively, of how to live a life, and of how to have peace in your life and help bring peace to others.

⌘⌘⌘⌘⌘

"If anyone wants to be first, he must be the very last, and the servant of all."
Mark 9:35

MARCH 7
...PRESENTING MY BEST

"Every man is entitled to be valued by his best moment."
- Emerson

⌘⌘⌘⌘⌘

My grandmother used to read an old English nursery rhyme to me that went, "I bargained with life for a penny, and life would pay me no more." At a very early age she was trying to tell me that life gives to you what you expect – in most cases – and people respond to the type of person you present to them. Somewhere along the line, I forgot this lesson.

I had been travelling all over the globe for about three weeks. I was suffering horribly from jet lag. A friend called and wanted me to go out to lunch. I said NO. She asked why. I said because I didn't feel like getting cleaned up, and I was afraid I would see someone I know – especially a client. She told me it was 1:00 in the afternoon, and everyone I knew would be back in their offices. So, I said I would go if she would come and get me.

The following was my appearance – how I greeted the world: I had barely combed my hair, had on little or no makeup (which at my age is a very scary proposition), had on a print blouse, harem pants with the crotch that hung to the knees, and flats with no hose. Just as I walked into a local restaurant, I ran into the Director of Human Resources for one of the big accounting firms who was also a client. Without smiling, she scanned my presence from head to toe. In true Irish fashion of using humor when all else fails, I said, "Jane, I've just had open heart surgery and been released from intensive care." She chuckled and asked what was really the matter. I told her of the jet lag and trying to regroup, and she said she understood. This happened in 1989, and in all the time since then, I have not gotten one other piece of business from them, nor do I expect to.

My visual impression said it all. "Corporate Masters must not be doing so well." It was a very hard lesson to learn. Without a doubt, I believe to get the best from others you must present your best to each and every one. Don't bargain with life for "only" a penny.

⌘⌘⌘⌘⌘

"For God did not give us a spirit of timidity,
but a spirit of power, of love and of self-discipline."
2 Timothy 1:7

MARCH 8
...TAKING SMALL BITES

"In an ant's house the dew is a flood."
- Persian Proverb

⌘⌘⌘⌘⌘

Unfortunately, like so many others, I, too, occasionally eat at my desk. I get in a hurry to complete a project, plan a presentation, or send a proposal out while needing some nourishment. I am trying to do several things at one time.

Now, if you are like me, when no one is around to watch you eat, you drink the last of the soup from the bowl, cram the last handful of broken potato chips in you mouth at one time, and take very large bits of whatever the main course is. And, it never fails; just as I have crammed about 1/6 of my sandwich in my mouth, the office phone rings.

My answering service automatically picks up on the fourth ring, so I have very little time to react. I can either choke down what's in my mouth or spit it out on the plate to answer the phone. Neither choice is very appealing, and it certainly isn't gracious!

What I have learned to do is take very small bites. This way, when the phone rings, I can finish chewing what's in my mouth and pick up the phone before the call goes into the answering service.

I have adopted this technique in most aspects of my life. Events and projects are so much easier to handle when we do one small piece at a time.

⌘⌘⌘⌘⌘

"Whoever can be trusted with very little
can also be trusted with much, and whoever is dishonest
with very little will also be dishonest with very much."
Luke 16:10

MARCH 9
...KNOWING THE VALUE OF MY "SOFT" SKILLS

"Fair and softly goes far."
- Cervantes

⌘⌘⌘⌘⌘

When I was in high school the "race for space" was on. Almost overnight, we went from a liberal, fine arts educated society to a math and science educated society. Math and science majors were singled out, given special opportunities, courted by corporations, always asked their opinion, and were considered the hope for tomorrow. Even without any management or people skills, math and science majors were asked to run companies.

Hard skills were valued; soft skills were fluffy, feminine, and frivolous. Romance languages were abandoned. Art and music classes were slighted. And literature and poetry? Get real!

After 15 years of math and science leading the way, some curious things happened to some companies. Companies where people skills were not valued began to faulter. Futuristic insight and projections based solely on hard skills overlooked people's reactions and "feelings" about products. Interacting on social levels proved difficult and uncomfortable for many people because they did not understand a literary, artistic, or musical reference mentioned in passing. Corporate loyalty was a thing of the past; people were not valued – only a positive bottom line had worth.

Many companies learned the hard way that hard skills were not the be all and end all of everything. It takes soft skill interaction with people to produce hard skill results.

Here's to both the math and science and the liberal, fine arts education, and here's to knowing the value of both soft skills and hard skills.

⌘⌘⌘⌘⌘

"A gentle answer turns away wrath,
but a harsh word stirs up anger."
Proverbs 15:1

MARCH 10
...VALUING MY SENSES

"There is no way in which to understand the world
without first detecting it through the radar-net of our senses."

- Diane Ackerman

⌘⌘⌘⌘⌘

One of the composition classes I teach has a very interesting exercise for the adult learner. The exercise was designed to get each student comfortable with expressing their thoughts and speaking in front of the group. On the board I write the following:

Favorite Childhood Memory

They have about five minutes to think about this. Then, each person in the class responds. We hear about picnics, fishing, riding bikes, pets, gardens, special outfits for holidays, something a grandmother cooked, or walking hand in hand with a dad. Actually, everything from soup to nuts.

We discover several things from this exercise. One, we all have something of value to share. Two, we learn what the term "looping" means: one story or idea makes you think of another. And, three, our senses have memory. You do not have to have a sheet that has been dried on the line or an American Beauty Rose under your nose to know what they smell like. The feel of velvet and puppy fur will always be remembered. The taste of homemade meals lasts forever. The sight of gorgeous gardens is embedded in our memory for instant recall. The giggle of a child rings in our ears until eternity.

How wonderful it is to know that our senses have memory and that we can call upon these memories anytime for a break from the day to day, the drudgery, and the negative. We have something inside that can make us pause, smile, and relax.

We know the value of our senses.

⌘⌘⌘⌘⌘

"He makes me lie down in green pastures,
he leads me beside quiet waters,
he restores my soul.
                    Psalm 23:2-3

...APPRECIATING THE HAPPY LINES IN MY FACE

"When grace is joined with wrinkles, it is adorable.
There is an unspeakable dawn in happy old age."
- Victor Hugo

⌘⌘⌘⌘⌘

This year I will be 50 years old – one half a century. Many of you may wonder why I don't mind telling people I'm going to be 50. The reason is that, to date, I know of only one way to permanently stop aging. Thank you, I'll age.

When I look in the mirror, I don't see a person who looks like she is 50 years old. I'm fortunate to come from Anglo-Saxon "stock" that holds their age very well. I've tried to hold the worry lines — furrowed brow, frown lines, etc. – down to a minimum by not scowling or frowning.

I do have lines in my face, but they are happy lines. It's those little lines that show up under my eyes when I smile. It's the indentations around my mouth that go up, not down, when I smile.

It shows, to me, that I have spent a great deal more time smiling than frowning in the last 50 years. That, in itself, says a great deal about my life. I'm looking forward to the next 50 years.

⌘⌘⌘⌘⌘

"Instead, it (your beauty) should be that of your inner self,
the unfading beauty of a gentle and quiet spirit,
which is of great worth in God's sight
1 Peter 3:4

MARCH 12
...THINKING BEFORE I SPEAK

"In His will is our peace."
- Dante

⌘⌘⌘⌘⌘

Teaching communication skills for over 25 years has made me more aware of what I say and how I say it. I try to keep my speaking pattern similar to the military pattern of READY - AIM - FIRE or thinking before you speak. Unfortunately, when many people speak, their communication pattern is READY - FIRE - AIM or speaking before you think.

I have had to learn this lesson over and over and over to stop making a fool of myself. The first time I remember making a fool out of myself in front of a large group of people was during my sophomore year in high school. We had a foreign exchange student from the Middle East. She was in many of my classes, and we had lunch together. We talked about many things in America and in Indiana. She spoke little of her home land or home life. During our annual School Open House, I saw her with a much older man and assumed he was her father. At lunch, the next day, I asked her why she hadn't introduced me to her father. She replied, "That was my husband." I then understood why she hadn't introduced me: I would have made a fool out of myself in front of him, also.

As I have aged [and made more than one error similar to the story previously recounted], I have grown tired of looking foolish, of stirring up trouble, and of having to back peddle to cover up for my thoughtlessness. Over the years I have learned to think before I speak. And, in doing so, I have saved face, temper, and relationships.

⌘⌘⌘⌘⌘

"Blessed are the peacemakers,
for they shall be called the sons of God."
Matthew 5:9

MARCH 13
...INTERACTING JOYFULLY WITH OTHERS

"People need joy quite as much as clothing.
Some of them need it far more."
- Margaret Collier Graham

⌘⌘⌘⌘⌘

Twice a year I go to the dentist to get my teeth cleaned. Not one of my favorite things to do, but necessary. During the cleaning, when the hygienist didn't have her hands and tools in my mouth, we struck up a conversation. We talked of kids, parts of the country, husbands and daily activities. We ended up talking about church and found out we both attend the same church. I told her that my husband and I sing in the choir. She told me I must talk with their accountant for she also attended the same church.

As I was checking out with the accountant, the hygienist came up beside me and told her that my husband and I sang in the church choir. Immediately her face lit up, and she began asking all sorts of questions. How often do you practice? Do you have to audition? Do you have to read music? What are the other choir members like? I answered each question while smiling at her interest. Then she began a series of statements telling me the joy she felt when listening to the choir. "The choir is so dynamic. The music that is selected really touches the soul. Adding the bells, tympani, and brass make it so special. I can't keep from crying at the beauty of the songs the choir sing." You could tell she was genuine in each of her statements.

I was joyful knowing what we did was so appreciated, and she was joyful to be able, at last, to tell one of the choir members how she felt about their performances.

Without this interaction, this joy could not have been appreciated, shared, or passed on.

⌘⌘⌘⌘⌘

"I have great confidence in you;
I take great pride in you.
I am greatly encouraged:
in all our troubles my joy knows no bounds."
2 Corinthians 7:4

MARCH 14
...LIVING IN THE PRESENT

"Know the true value of time;
snatch, seize, and enjoy every moment of it.
No idleness; no laziness; no procrastination;
never put off till tomorrow what you can do today."
- Lord Chesterfield

⌘⌘⌘⌘⌘

Positive thinking has become a way of life for me. In combination with other things, it has helped me get over the loss of family and friends, low ebbs in personal growth and finances, and breast cancer. Positive thinking has helped me learn to live in the present because that is all I really have. I always plan for tomorrow, next month, and next year. I also realize those times are tentative and may not occur. I have now, this moment, today.

The past is over. Nothing we do will change that unless we have the ability that Superman had when he flew around the world and spun it backwards, reversing time, to save Lois Lane from the cave in. I do not have that ability. As much as I would like, I can't change anything that has happened. I can't count on tomorrow for sure because it may not happen. All I have is now!

I once heard a friend sum it up very well. He said, "I'm not here for a long time just a good time." When the present is truly all we have to rely on, we need to live in the present, appreciate the present, and praise the present.

⌘⌘⌘⌘⌘

"What I mean, brothers, is that the time is short."
1 Corinthians 7:29

MARCH 15
...CHANGING THE CONVERSATION

"Like a salad (conversation), should have various ingredients and
should be well stirred with salt, oil and vinegar."
-Joaquin Setanti

⌘⌘⌘⌘⌘

At times we can get trapped into conversations with people that we would prefer not to get trapped in. It is usually a story that we have heard 100 times before and seemingly has no solution; consequently, we know it will never come to an end. As we listen to the other person go on for what seems an eternity, we become angry. We aren't really angry with the other person for we can't change them; we are angry with ourselves because we are listening to the same thing again without calling a halt to this repeated scenario.

Being angry with ourselves is not something we can afford. If I become angry with you, I can walk away; but when I am angry with me, I'm stuck. There is no getting away.

To end this self directed anger, to put an end to the same conversation, and to move on to a more positive, productive conversation, I simply ask the person, "What can you do about it?" If they continue in the same vein, I again ask, "What can you do about it?"

After a few times of asking the same question, the other person finally catches on. This situation reminds me of a quote from Edith Wharton. In *The House of Mirth* she states, "She wanted to get away from herself, and conversation was the only means of escape that she knew."

By changing the conversation and asking the person what they can do about it may just help the person get in touch with themselves and understand what they are really doing to themselves and others.

⌘⌘⌘⌘⌘

"Let your conversation be always full of grace,
seasoned with salt,
so that you may know how to answer everyone."
Colossians 4:6

MARCH 16
...SMILING WHEN IT DOESN'T FEEL GOOD

"The most wasted day is that in which we have not laughed."
- Chamfort

⌘⌘⌘⌘⌘

We have all experienced days when things don't go as planned, when a weight is crushing our chest and we can't breath, and when we are so angry we could literally chew nails.

I was having one such day with all the aforementioned things happening, and it was only 7:00 am. I was standing in front of the mirror putting on make up and wondering how I could get out of this day's commitments. I opened up my compact of blush, picked up the brush, and smiled to apply the color in the right places. While looking in the mirror to eliminate the possibility of looking like Ronald McDonald, I suddenly realized that, when smiling, the weight on my chest had disappeared, I could breath easier, and the feeling of anger had gone. All this happened because I was smiling.

Having come from a military family and attending a military high school, I know that erect posture helps elevate our mood. Until that moment I never realized a smile could do it, too.

Smiles are a universal sign of friendship. They are offered to cheer someone who is down. They help share joy and laughter. And when we smile, even though it may not feel good at the moment, it gains us friends, cheers our own mood, and makes us laugh all at the same time.

⌘⌘⌘⌘⌘

"You have made known to me the path of life;
you will fill me with joy in your presence,
with eternal pleasures at your right hand."
Psalm 16:11

MARCH 17
...AVOIDING SOME HUMOR

"A difference of taste in jokes is a great strain on the affections."
                                                                    - George Eliot

⌘⌘⌘⌘⌘

Not only is beauty in the eye of the beholder but so is humor. Humor is very personal. It is so different that I think it must be difficult for a comedian or comedienne to appeal to both men and women. Humor makes fun of things. It makes fun of age, looks, size, intelligence, religion, sex, race, culture, and heritage. Things we hold near and dear when they refer to us. Humor depends on our frame of mind and who is telling the joke. Blondes can tell blonde jokes to other blondes. Irish can tell Irish jokes to other Irish. Crossing lines can be a little treacherous! It boils down to the fact that humor is very personal.

Depending on the situation, people involved, and subject matter, some things do not strike us as funny. People may accuse us of having no sense of humor when, in fact, it may be that they don't know what is funny to us. Because we use humor as a way to bond with other people, we try things occasionally that do not prove to be successful.

If our humor is not successful, as the joke teller, we can cease to tell more jokes along this line, or as the listener, it becomes our responsibility to tell people we do not appreciate this type of humor or simply walk away.

We all desperately need humor in our lives, and it must be acceptable to all parties involved.

⌘⌘⌘⌘⌘

"The teacher searched to find just the right words,
and what he wrote was upright and true."
                                                                    Esslesiastes 12:10

...KEEPING PRODUCTIVE COMPANY

"No man is much pleased with a companion who does not increase,
in some respect, his fondness of himself."
- Samuel Johnson

⌘⌘⌘⌘⌘

Don't you love this quote about people? "Some people make things happen; some people watch what happens; and some people stand back and wonder what happened." If given a choice, I think most people prefer to be around the people who make things happen, but that isn't always possible.

A friend and I decided to do the Master Mind Program together. Because we were both in a place and time that we preferred not to be, we met every week and shared goals and plans for a better future. Each of us had been dating men for some time with whom we were having trouble predicting a future. We would spend a long portion of our time together complaining about our predicament. Some days we would spend so much time complaining that we overlooked our goals, plans, and thoughts for our futures.

We finally realized we were feeding on each other's unhappiness; so, we called a halt to the Master Mind Program until we could get our personal lives together. We are now both happily married. When we have an opportunity to spend time together, it is productive time of sharing joy and happiness, and, because we have little to complain about, we can truly focus on our successes. We walk away from our meetings feeling happy and uplifted not drained and despondent - what keeping productive company is all about.

⌘⌘⌘⌘⌘

"He who walks with the wise grows wise,
but a companion of fools suffers harm."
Proverbs 13:20

MARCH 19
...NOT BEING THE LOW PRICED SPREAD

> "Surely there comes a time when counting the cost and paying the price
> aren't things to think about any more. All that matters is value —
> the ultimate value of what one does."
>
> - James Hilton

⌘⌘⌘⌘⌘

One of the most difficult things for an entrepreneur to do is set prices.
When you first begin your business, there is always a feeling of financial
desperation. Can you pay the bills? Can you meet payroll? Can you get a line of
credit at the bank? Consequently, when clients call, to help lessen your financial
worries, you quote prices that are far below what you know, with your talent and
skills, you should be making.

Some times you will get the work, and this may not be good. You may
have promised too much for too little. You may have committed to things that
are not really your strength. You may have agreed to do something that takes
much more research time than you have to spend so that you are strapped to get
it done. It is not done well, and your client is not pleased. The words of unhappy
clients do get around.

Or you may not get the job because you are the low priced spread. Many
potential clients — especially those who are used to dealing with more high
powered entrepreneurs — want people who have skills of "value." If you don't
think that what you do has value, why would someone else?

⌘⌘⌘⌘⌘

> "Do you not know that in a race all the runners run,
> but only one gets the prize?
> Run in such a way as to get the prize."
>
> 1 Corinthians 9:24

MARCH 20
...LEARNING MY GIFT

"Everyone must row with the oars he has."
- English Proverb

⌘⌘⌘⌘⌘

We all have something about us that makes us special. Whatever this special gift is, it makes us superior to everyone else in the world, and everyone else in the world has some gift that makes them superior to us. This gives us our ego. It helps us survive the day to day.

My special gift is words. I can put them together in lectures or writings to help make others see things in a different light. I have noticed that beside our one special gift we also have small gifts over others that vary from person to person.

A major film star was in town for the 500 Festival Fashion Show. I think this particular actress is one of the most gorgeous women I have ever seen, so I spent a great deal of time looking at her. All of a sudden, it occurred to me that she was wearing a dress, and I had never seen her in a dress before. I wondered why? As I was looking at her, I realized why I think she doesn't wear a lot of dresses: she has thick ankles. All of sudden, I realized that my gift over her was that my ankles were thinner than hers. Now, that is the **only** part of me that is thinner than she; but, at my age, I'll take joy where I can find it.

On a serious side, please remember what Desire Joseph Cardinal Mercier said, "We must not only give what we have; we must also give what we are." Learn what your gift is, and share it with the world.

⌘⌘⌘⌘⌘

"Great and marvelous are your deeds,
Lord God Almighty."
Revelation 15:3

MARCH 21
...KNOWING TO WHOM MUCH IS GIVEN MUCH IS EXPECTED

"The only gift is a portion of thyself...the poet
brings his poes; the shepherd his lamb...the
girl, a handkerchief of her own sewing."
- Ralph Waldo Emerson

⌘⌘⌘⌘⌘

I have a lovely friend, Sharon Donlon, who is gracious, wise and genteel. I enjoy talking and spending time with her. It is refreshing. You walk away with a feeling of warmth and a joy of being treated to a dose of old world civility.

For many years she and I had an office in the same building. We had the opportunity to chat several times a day. We also had the opportunity to complain several times a day.

As we are all aware, some days are easier than others. On one such day when I had had no sleep the night before, had many things on my mind, and had to return what seemed like a million phone calls, I went down to Sharon's office for a break. I sat down in one of her chairs while giving a heavy sigh, and she said it looked as if I had something on my mind. I said I did and proceeded to unload on her. After my five minute "poor me" tirade, I summed it up by saying I was tired of being the "Shell Answer Man" for everyone.

Sharon smiled and responded, "Suzanne, you have been given many gifts and talents to share with the rest of the world. You must remember to whom much is given much is expected."

Sometimes the simplest statements can make you pause and reflect and do an immediate paradigm shift.

⌘⌘⌘⌘⌘

"From everyone who has been given much,
much will be demanded;"
Luke 12:48

MARCH 22
...BEING COMFORTABLE

"One cannot rest except after steady practice."
- George Ade

⌘⌘⌘⌘⌘

My husband and I have had Murphy, our 80 pound retriever, since she was 6 weeks old. She is one of our current 4-legged children, and we have spoiled her rotten. We are not the type who want to keep a dog in a portable kennel; dogs are our companions, and we like to have them with us. They have full run of the house. We have been fortunate in the fact that, as a puppy, Murphy didn't take much notice of things in the house. (That could be because she has so many puppy toys that our family room resembles "Puppy Toys R Us.")

Having the run of the house, she has become a creature of comfort. The leather coach in the family room, the polished cotton flowered sofa in the living room, and our queen size bed are all more comfortable than the floor, but even Murphy can make her resting places even a little more comfortable.

On our bed we have four decorative pillows. One day, while my husband and I were in the bathroom getting ready for church, we heard Murphy making some kind of strange noise. We looked into the bedroom, and there she was on the bed pulling the decorative pillows around with her paws making a new arrangement: one that was more suitable to Her Majesty. She got the pillows in a pile in the middle of the bed, snuggled down amongst them, and let out a big sigh of relief.

That sigh said it all. She had worked and worked to get the pillows just right – to be comfortable. Once done, in her dog language she was making the point of being relieved and delighted.

We all have to work to be comfortable whether it's arranging our own pillows or putting the house back together after entertaining or after completing a big project or proposal at work. In our language, we need to let the rest of the world know that we are also relieved and delighted. We are comfortable.

⌘⌘⌘⌘⌘

"Whatever you have learned or received or heard from me,
or seen in me – put it into practice.
And the God of peace will be with you."
Philippians 4:9

MARCH 23
...LAUGHING AT SANDBOX BUDDIES

"A single soul dwelling in two bodies."
- Aristotle

⌘⌘⌘⌘⌘

It all started with a phone call from our choir director Dr. Chuck Goehring. Stan had been out shoveling snow; and when he came in to take the call, he was out of breath. Chuck, the director, mentioned that Stan should have a snow blower to use instead of working so hard at shoveling. Stan agreed, and Chuck asked if he needed any support confirming this suggestion to me. Stan laughed and said, "Sure." I asked Stan what he was laughing at, and he told me of the conversation. I said mockingly, "Do you need any help? Spare me this sandbox philosophy!" And, we laughed.

Naturally, he went to work and told all of his buddies about the sandbox philosophy. (They, as a group, all talk about the most recent things their wives have said and done or what they would like their wives to say or do!) His buddies all thought this was hysterical, too. They now have an official group called "The Sandbox Buddies."

I am happy this turned out this way. Most of the time I don't understand men's humor, mid-life crisis, finite details of medicine or sports, or why you can spend as much time in a hardware store as you can the Smithsonian. I am a woman and can't share in these manly interactions.

Men need the company of other men just as women need the company of other women. When Stan comes home and tells me about what the Sandbox Buddies talked about today, even when I don't understand the humor, I laugh, and I'm happy because he is happy.

⌘⌘⌘⌘⌘

"God is able to provide you with every blessing in abundance,
so that by always having enough of everything,
you may share abundantly in every good work."
2 Corinthians 9:8

...APPRECIATING WHAT OUR MOTHERS HAVE DONE

"My mother is a woman who speaks with her life
as much as with her tongue."
- Kesaya E. Noda

⌘⌘⌘⌘⌘

Today is my mother's and my aunt's birthday (they were born on the same day nine years apart). As I have matured, I have developed a profound admiration and respect for what my mother has gone through.

She was a first generation career woman. It was she who fought the battle of home vs. career. She, as a first generation career woman, didn't want a career. She wanted a house, picket fence, braided kitchen rug, and children. She got me and a career in statistics. WOW! A single mother with a daughter to raise and a career in math. Very juxtaposed.

As a child I never understood what she was going through. As an adult, I now understand why she came home tired, cried at "family" movies, and taught me to be strong and independent. Her life was much different than what she had wanted and expected, and she didn't know what the following decades would hold for me.

Thanks to my mother, I now have a career, three college degrees, and a wonderful family life with a husband and two step children. I am also strong, self-confident, and happy with my life.

What I am I owe to my mother. I appreciate all she has done. She not only paved the way for me, but she also made the path easier to travel.

⌘⌘⌘⌘⌘

"As a mother comforts her child,
so I will comfort you."
Isaiah 66:13

MARCH 25
...BEING A ROLE MODEL

"Outside show is a poor substitute for inner worth."
- Aesop

⌘⌘⌘⌘⌘

I have been teaching the adult education classes at one of our local universities for about eight years. In that time, I have met some very interesting people. They have impacted my life in many ways, but I never knew how much I had impacted theirs until last month.

About five years ago, I had the opportunity to meet a woman, Melanie, dedicated to her education and development. She not only was in the core classes I taught, but she also signed up to take many of the electives I taught. I sincerely thought she was just interested in communication. Little did I know her interest was in me. And, last month, I found out what this was all about.

I met her in the hall one evening. She asked me if I knew the instructor that she now had for class. Yes, I replied. Melanie said he had given her the compliment of a lifetime. He had asked Melanie if she knew me. She said yes and asked why. He said, "I don't know what it is, but somehow you remind me of Suzanne." She said this made her heart glad. She then told me that when she first met me, she was amazed at what I did. She realized we were about the same height, the same weight, and the same age. Where she did not look forward to getting up in front of people, I had no problem getting up in front of people. She said I was confident, poised, and sophisticated. What she had wanted to be. So, she decided to emulate me. Without knowing, I became her role model. A most glorious day for her was when someone else recognized the connection she had been making between us.

It may take years for us to know that we are role models for people, and many of us will never know. What we do need to know is that we don't have to stand on pedestals and shout to the rest of the world "Look at me, I'm doing a great job." We simply have to lead the type of life that shows the rest of the world that the life we are leading is working -- and working well.

⌘⌘⌘⌘⌘

"By the tender mercy of our God,
the dawn from on high will break upon us,
to give light to those who sit in darkness...
to guide our feet into the way of peace."
Luke 1:78-79

MARCH 26
...ENJOYING COMFORT FOOD

"Talk of joy: there may be things better than beef stew
and baked potatoes and home-made bread — there may be."
- David Grayson

⌘⌘⌘⌘⌘

My grandmother cooked everything from scratch. She never used a recipe or anything new-fangled. Even her measurements were old: "butter the size of an egg." Her food stuck to your ribs (and hips), and she always tried to make your particular favorite.

Some of the most wonderful aromas were potato soup with dumplings, peanut butter and jelly coffee cake, and corned beef. Sunday night supper was traditionally salmon patties, potato cakes and peas. The warmth from her kitchen wasn't just from the oven. Warmth radiated from her heart and soul as she prepared and served your favorite food. We always blessed the hands and heart that prepared the meal.

When I get over-stressed, over-loaded, and over-stretched, I want, at least temporarily, to go back to simpler times. I want to go back to my grandmother's warm kitchen where someone took my interests to heart. I want to sit at the table, once more as a child, with little worries, with much anticipation of good things to come, and with that comfortable feeling that people cared for me and what I was doing and going through.

My grandmother has been gone for many years. I miss her deeply. When I want to think of her and the warmth and goodness she gave to me, I go somewhere where I can order comfort food: thick soups, salmon patties, pudding, coffee cake, and mashed potatoes.

It's not a substitute for my grandmother. It is a reminder, a memory jogger, that causes me to think of passed laughter, tears, and dreams shared at the dinner table.

⌘⌘⌘⌘⌘

"My soul will be satisfied as with the richest of foods;"
Psalm 63:5

MARCH 27
...DE-JUNKING MY LIFE

"The strongest principle of growth lies in human choice."
                                                    - George Eliot

⌘⌘⌘⌘⌘

Gina attended a seminar on a new way of structuring the way you live your life. One of the last exercises she did was on learning new ways to de-junk your life: getting rid of things that have no value or worth, that are distracting, and that are detrimental to your growth.

Many of the things you could do were very simple. Don't go to a wholesale store when you only need a gallon of milk; you waste too much time looking at everything else. Don't turn on the TV unless you intend to watch it; the noise can be distracting and irritating. Don't make one huge stack of things to do (read magazine, cut recipes, file) and keep it in a very visual spot; it is a constant reminder to you that you can't relax and hear God in your life; you always have too much to do – always.

There are hundreds of ways to de-junk your life and open up time for thought, creativity, reading, communing with nature, spending special time with your spouse, etc. It's those little minutes we gather that add up to hour upon hour every week and year, helping us keep our life and house in order and peace.

⌘⌘⌘⌘⌘

"For where your treasure is, there your heart will be also."
                                                    Matthew 6:21

MARCH 28
...SETTING STANDARDS

"Conduct is three-fourths of our life and its largest concern."
- Matthew Arnold

⌘⌘⌘⌘⌘

I taught junior and senior high school English for 14 years. As with all situations, we learn much of what we impart -- sometimes we learn even **more** than we impart.

As a result of scheduling, in sixth period College Prep English, I had most of the senior boys going on to college. It was a fun class. One student, Bobby Smith, sat right in front of my desk. He was quiet, reserved, and mannerly: a pleasure to have in class. One day I overheard the other senior boys kidding him about his behavior in Physics. I was stunned to hear what he had said and done. I asked Bobby if his behavior were different in classes other than English, and the other boys laughed heartily.

Almost bashfully, he replied, "Yes." I asked why. He replied, "You set the tone. No one would dare act up in your class because they know it would not be tolerated."

I wasn't sure how to respond. I did manage to thank him. I thought of what my grandmother said about wisdom coming out of the mouth of babes.

It is never to early to set standards for ourselves and others. We all rise to the occasion.

⌘⌘⌘⌘⌘

"Whatever happens, conduct yourselves in a manner
worthy of the gospel of Christ."
Philippians 1:27

MARCH 29
...BEING A SEEKER UNAWARE

"Understanding human needs is half the job of meeting them."
- Adlai Stevenson

⌘⌘⌘⌘⌘

I have been singing in the church choir for about a year. I have enjoyed it tremendously. In a church as large as St. Luke's United Methodist, it is nice to have a place where you feel you belong and are cared for.

Since I'm an alto, I know the altos better than the people in the other sections. I especially know the ones in my row – the back row – and the ones that sit on each side of me.

Dr. Kent Milliard, our minister, has the ability to touch your heart with his sermons. At times, it is difficult for us to sing the last hymn being so moved by one of his sermons. One Sunday, his sermon was particularly moving, and I was trying to hold back tears so that no one would notice my emotional state. As Dr. Millard said his last prayer and all our heads were bowed, I was blotting up tears. Debbie, my fellow alto friend, seeing me in need put her arm around my shoulders as an act of comfort and friendship.

I was comforted, and I thanked God for letting people be seekers unaware: those wonderful people that see a fellow human being in need and come to their aid.

I am thankful for finding a place in St. Luke's choir and for learning the value of meeting the needs of others unexpectedly.

⌘⌘⌘⌘⌘

"If you have any encouragement from being united with Christ,
if any comfort from his love,
if any fellowship with the Spirit,
if any tenderness and compassion,
then make my joy complete by being like-minded,
having the same love, being one in spirit, and purpose."
Philippians 2:1-2

MARCH 30
...QUESTIONING INSTEAD OF CONDEMNING

"Man's finest quality."
- Solomon Ibn Gabirol

⌘⌘⌘⌘⌘

For some of us, condemning is an Olympic Event, and we are "going for the gold." In teaching communication, I try to get others to realize how destructive condemning is. I use the following scenario to show what an impact condemning has.

It is one of the rare occasion when both husband and wife are home for dinner. (I heard one speaker refer to it as the Annual Hot Meal.) One of you has been home preparing a gourmet meal, and the plan is to have dinner at 6:30 – together. It is now 6:45, and the other person is not home. You call the office, the pager, and the car phone. Finally, you get a reply, and you say, "Well, I might have known I couldn't count on you to be home on time. I have spent two hours cooking. This meal is ruined. I have wasted my time and energy for nothing. I will never do this again for someone who is so insensitive." If you are the person in the car, doesn't that just make you want to push the gas pedal a little harder to get home a little sooner and interact with this person? Not!

Instead of the previous tirade, what about saying, "Hon, I know we planned on having dinner at 6:30, and it is going on 7:00. Is there a problem?"

The response to either scenario is the same: "I'm sorry. Just as I was leaving the hospital, E.R. called and needed a scan on a young man who had been badly injured in an accident. Everyone else in the department was gone, and I stayed to do the scan. It didn't do much good though. He died during the procedure."

By using the question instead of the condemnation, you have saved yourself feeling foolish, unreasonable, and out of control. By just asking a question and listening, you have allowed this person – the one who is suppose to be the most important one in your life -- to express his/her reasons or concerns, share a hurt, and bond with you in a way that does strengthen marriages and relationships.

⌘⌘⌘⌘⌘

"I will question you,
and you shall answer me."
Job 38:3

MARCH 31
...NOT WHINING

"There is not any advantage to be won from grim lamentation."

- Homer

⌘⌘⌘⌘⌘

My husband and I have not been married very long – just going on three years. Two months after we were married, I discovered I had breast cancer. I was fortunate in the fact that I did not have to have a mastectomy, just a lumpectomy; but because two of the lymph nodes came back positive, I had to go through chemotherapy, radiation therapy, and hormone therapy.

I started the chemotherapy the first week of December. (What a birthday celebration that was.) The week before Christmas, my hair was coming out in handfuls, and by Christmas, I was completely bald.

My hair has always been an agony and ecstasy to me. It is fine and silky, falls at the first hint of humidity, and is hard to do and keep up. I also receive tons of compliments on its cut and color. Every morning I would stand in front of the mirror saying out loud that I hated having to do my hair everyday. In December, I remember the maxim "Be careful what you wish for. You just might get it."

I don't whine about doing my hair any more! As a matter of fact, I'm tickled to death to have hair to do. I love washing it, drying it, curling it, buying hair care products for it, and receiving compliments about it.

It is amazing how quickly we can change our perspective about something in our life. Losing something we value – even when it is sometimes difficult to deal with – will stop us from whining and increase our appreciation at least 100 fold.

⌘⌘⌘⌘⌘

"I pour out my complaint before him;
before him I tell my trouble."
Psalm 142:2

APRIL 1
...NOT BEING A "WALKING, BREATHING TO DO LIST"

> "The one with the primary responsibility to the
> individual's future is that individual."
> - Dorcas Hardy

⌘⌘⌘⌘⌘

I think many of us measure our life by our accomplishments. I know there are times I do. But there is more to our life than what we have done. Part of our life is simply who and what we are or want to be. Unfortunately, making a list of what needs to be done and checking off each item as we complete it gives us instant gratification and a visible sign of our worth. Maybe this is why the concreteness and finality of this action often outweighs our planning.

What we are or what we want to be is more important — especially in the long run — than lists of errands, jobs, and meetings. Because it takes longer to become something than it does to do something, we need to be prepared for the long run. We need to prepare ourselves for revelry for each small step in this longer journey. This will help us get the gratification and visible signs of our worth that are so important for us and our survival.

While being a "walking, breathing to do list" gives us worth, it does not give us our values. Our values – what we are — will long be remembered after us. Our values will be here long after we have folded each load of laundry, long after we have adjourned each meeting, and long after we punched out on each time clock.

⌘⌘⌘⌘⌘

> "And we pray this in order that you may live a life worthy
> of the Lord and may please him in every way:"
> Colossians 1:10

APRIL 2
...NEEDING LITTLE

"Seek not proud riches, but such as thou mayest get justly,
use soberly, distribute cheerfully, and leave contentedly."
- Francis Bacon

⌘⌘⌘⌘⌘

I was, at one time, a buyaholic. I really didn't enjoy shopping; I enjoyed buying. It didn't make any difference if it were jewelry, shoes, or clothing. With each new purchase, I was sure I would achieve perfection one more time.

New shoes made my legs look sexier. New perfume attracted new beaus. New jewelry drew more attention to my face. New clothing made me look like I had lost another 10 pounds. A new shade or color of shadow brought out my hazel eyes. Or, at least, this is what I believed for awhile.

Once the novelty of the new item had worn off, I was back at the stores trying to recreate those feelings...again and again. I had over 100 pairs of shoes with matching bags, 30 pair of jeans and 70 suits. I now realize I was waiting for something on the outside to transform me on the inside, and it wasn't happening.

One afternoon, I was watching Lauren Hutton on TV. She was being interviewed, and the interviewer was remarking how together she was and how she lived and dressed so simply. She replied, "How many sets of sheets can you have?"

All the suits, shoes, and jewelry would not make the difference in my life. I would. I needed little in the way of material possessions and much in the way of spiritual possessions to make changes in my life.

⌘⌘⌘⌘⌘

"The Lord abhors dishonest scales,
but accurate weights are his delight."
Proverbs 11:1

APRIL 3
...STOP WAITING FOR THE LAST STRAW

"The crosses we make for ourselves by overanixety."
- Francois de Fenelon

⌘⌘⌘⌘⌘

I was getting ready for a presentation for the Noblesville Chamber of Commerce. I had prepared the material, run off the handouts, gathered my brochures and cards, packed my briefcase, put on my suit and was headed for the door.

Now, with the briefcase on my shoulder on the way down the stairs, I decided I could pick up the laundry and carry it to the laundry room. As I started down the stairs, I saw a haze of dust on the railing, so with one of the wet washrags in my hand, I was cleaning down the railing. Here I am in my suit, briefcase on my shoulder, handouts in one arm, laundry in the other, whipping down the stairs.

At the bottom of the stairs I just stopped, wondering what I was doing with my life. I was working crazy hours, had two dogs that added incredible dirt to the house, and was trying to write a book, keep up with a husband, keep the business running, do things with family and friends, spend time at choir practice and church activities, and clean the house.

I made up my mind to call a maid service and have them come in a couple times a month to help with the deep cleaning. What a relief!

Why do we have to wait for the last straw? Why do we let ourselves go to the brink, finally breaking, and then do something? When will we realize it is better to take care than repair. We must learn not to wait for the last straw, become angry, let all the balls drop, and then start anew. Starting anew, each time, keeps putting us back at ground zero and lengthens our time to completion on all our endeavors.

⌘⌘⌘⌘⌘

"By the seventh day God had finished the work he had been doing;
so on the seventh day he rested from all his work."
Genesis 2:2

APRIL 4
...REMEMBERING THE "MM" PHILOSOPHY

"Grieve not that men do not know you;
grieve that you do not know men."
- Confucius

⌘⌘⌘⌘⌘

We learn many things as a child that could be very useful to us as an adult, but we often discount what we have learned as a child because we were only children. If the names Bobby, Sharon, Darlene, Tommy, Karen, Cubby, and Annette ring a bell, you were probably like me and raced home every day at 3:30 to watch the Mickey Mouse Club.

At the end of each program, the Mousketters were grouped together on the stage and sang "M-I-C." Jimmy would say, "See you real soon." Then, they would sing "K-E-Y," and Jimmy would say, "Why, because we like you." We should remember this profound wisdom.

There are thousands of people out there who do what you do for a living. People don't do business with buildings or corporations, they do business with people — with you, and why? Because they like you. People choose to be your friend because they like you. People do things for you because they like you. People introduce you to others because they like you.

This very simple Micky Mouse (MM) Philosophy is the basis of our daily interaction with the world. We do for others because we like them, and they, in turn, do for us because they like us. Many times our success is based on a "mutual admiration society."

⌘⌘⌘⌘⌘

"So in everything, do to others what you would have them do to you,
for this sums up the Law and the Prophets."
Matthew 7:12

APRIL 5
...ACCEPTING INSIGHT

"There is none so blind as they that won't see."
- English Proverb

⌘⌘⌘⌘⌘

So often we say, "Lord, if you would just show me what I'm supposed to do, I'd do it." We ask for insight or divine guidance, but when it comes, we don't believe it.

I had been beating down doors with Corporate Masters for about four years, and it had been moving along but at a snail's pace. I had gotten tired: more than tired -- completely drained of energy, enthusiasm, and drive. I had been working part time for one of the academies, doing a marketing study for a company, and teaching part time for the university. Corporate Masters, my true love, was in addition to all this but still on the back burner because it wasn't paying the bills. Being so divided with no central focus, it was no wonder I was advancing at a snail's pace.

I was sitting at my desk at the height of my frustration and said, "Lord, I have been working at Corporate Masters for four years, and I'm tired. I think Corporate Masters is what I'm supposed to do, but I need to know for sure. I need some kind of sign. Won't You please give me some kind of sign?" I just sat there staring at my computer. About forty minutes after I asked for my sign, the phone rang. It was from a national headquarters asking me to speak at my first national convention.

I knew then that Corporate Masters was what I was supposed to be doing. I finished the marketing project and took no more. I resigned as director of the academy. I focused on my teaching and building my business. And, the results? Well, with the help of God, it has become more successful every year.

Sometimes when we ask for guidance, we do receive it. Once received, we must make a decision to act on it.

⌘⌘⌘⌘⌘

"I will lift up mine eyes unto the hills,
from whence cometh my help."
Psalm 121:1

APRIL 6
...BEING SELECTIVE WHEN OFFERING AN OPINION

"Truth filtered through the moods, the blood,
the disposition of the spectator."
- Wendell Philllips

⌘⌘⌘⌘⌘

My grandmother had an expression about opinions: "every one has one." [I'll spare you the rest of the quotation.] She was right; all of us have opinions, but that doesn't mean we should express them readily. There are times when it is best to keep our opinions to ourselves.

My step daughter might be labeled a free spirit, and she is certainly not of my generation. Last year, on spring break, she got her belly button pierced; something that most of us adults find a little unusual. This year, before she went on spring break, she was warned not to come back with a tattoo. She didn't; she got her nose pierced. It was the following year she came back with a tattoo.

I didn't get my ears pierced until I was 24 years old, and even though I was 24, my mother still was upset. You see, as a latent silent generation, only "those kind" of girls got their ears pierced. She wondered what everyone else would think!

Now I'm the older generation looking at my step daughter with her nose pierced wondering what everyone else will think about her. I know that they won't think what a beautiful face she has, what an outstanding student she is, how good she did running track, what a great job she did being on the National Honor Society, or what a super job she did as the lead in the last two plays. No, the older generation will think "why did she get her nose pierced."

It was done. I couldn't change or influence it. When she asked her dad and me what we thought, I just let her dad reply. While I don't have any trouble expressing an opinion, I realize there are times when expressing it will fail to have a positive impact.

⌘⌘⌘⌘⌘

"Do not judge, or you too will be judged."
Matthew 7:1

APRIL 7
...UNDERSTANDING THE SMILE OF A FRIEND

"Friendship needs a certain parallelism of life,
a community of thought, a rivalry of aim."
- Henry Adams

⌘⌘⌘⌘⌘

Gina and I have been friends for about 14 years. We bonded so closely so quickly, I can't help but think our relationship is ancient.

We meet with each other in many settings: trade shows, meetings, restaurants, parking lots. Sometimes, when we first see one another, one of us will be speaking with someone else. Most often we look up, recognize each other, and smile.

That smile means at least 100 different things to each of us. It can show genuine warmth and pleasure at seeing each other again. It can contain hidden private jokes, hidden meaning, and, at times, hidden stress. It can be a smile that comprehends sorrow. It can be a smile that shares deep understanding of what someone is going through. It can be a smile that offers encouragement. But, most of the time, it is a smile that brings joy, happiness, and contentment at seeing my friend one more time.

Mother Teresa said, "Let us always meet each other with a smile, for the smile is the beginning of love."

What a wonderful thing it is to see her smile and know that I have a friend.

⌘⌘⌘⌘⌘

"A man that hath many friends must show himself friendly."
Proverbs 18:24

APRIL 8
...ACCEPTING OTHER PEOPLE'S PLACE IN LIFE

"Those that know the least of others think the highest of themselves."
- Charles Caleb Colton

⌘⌘⌘⌘⌘

The women I have as friends have very exciting diverse lives and hobbies. Not only are most of them caretakers of their family, but, in addition to this, they either have their own company or have reached the upper rungs of corporations. Their hobbies amaze me! They train horses, fly planes, sing in trios, cook gourmet meals, decorate homes, show dogs, etc. Community involvement is a given for these women. Singing in the church choir, serving on charity boards, and attending organizational meetings are only a few of the things they are involved in. And, many of them are going back to school for advanced degrees.

Despite the diversity, there seems to be one thing they have in common: they don't get along well with their mothers. My mother and I were talking about this one afternoon, and we think we came up with the reason: the daughter's life is invalidating the mother's life.

Most women my age (50) were first generation career women. Most of their mothers were home makers. They took care of a husband, a home, and the children and probably thought they had done well with their lives until they compared themselves to their daughters. Without verbally saying a word, the daughter's life of being a home maker, career women, and involved in many outside activities has made the mother's life seem less by comparison.

Neither mother nor daughter can really change the world or the time that each has lived in. It is also difficult for me or others to understand what we are not accustomed to. What we can do to validate each other is appreciate and accept what each has done in their own life without making any comparison.

⌘⌘⌘⌘⌘

"You are worthy, our Lord and God,
to receive glory and honor and power,
for you created all things,
and by your will they were created
and have their being."
Revelation 4:11

APRIL 9
...WALKING THE DOGS

"People seem to think there is something inherently
noble and virtuous in the desire to go for a walk."
- Max Beerbohm

⌘⌘⌘⌘⌘

I know I have mentioned my dogs – Murphy and Coco – before. They are
a major love of my life. Being adventuresome, young dogs, life inside a house can
be pretty boring when there is a world of things to smell and investigate outside.
They love to go for a walk!!!

They see robins to chase, kids to bark at, cars to lope along side, strangers to
stare at, paper goods to investigate, and other dogs to sniff. A walk is very
stimulating in a dog's world. It gets all those puppy endorphins going, reduces
anxiety of being cooped up too long, and keeps their weight down. Unless the
weather is really inclement, I try to take them walking at least once a day.

I've noticed some interesting things about my walk with the dogs. After
being cooped up in my office, the fresh air rejuvenates my mind. I relax as I hear
the birds sing, and I smile as I pass each flower garden. I get a chance to meet and
chat with my neighbors which also stimulates my mind. I come back to the house
refreshed and ready to go back to work.

The walk that I take with the dogs gets my human endorphins going,
reduces my anxiety of being cooped up too long, and helps keep my weight down -
- in the last year I have lost seven pounds, without changing my diet, just by walking
the dogs.

In many ways we have a lot in common with God's creatures. This walk –
getting back to nature and relaxing – is good for all creatures, both the two-legged
and four-legged kind.

⌘⌘⌘⌘⌘

"A cheerful heart is a good medicine,"
Proverbs 17:22

APRIL 10
...RECOGNIZING VS. REALIZING

"Reality is that which, when you stop believing in it, doesn't go away."
- Philip K. Dick

⌘⌘⌘⌘⌘

The more I taught my English Classes and studied words, the more aware I became of the nuances in definitions. One of my greatest discoveries was in understanding the difference between recognize and realize. Recognize means " to know or be aware of." Realize means "to comprehend completely." I realized that there are things in this world that I recognize, but I choose not to realize. There are some things in this world that I don't want to comprehend completely or take internally to carry with me.

I recognize there are cruel people in this world. I recognize that every day when I pass people on the street, that some of these people are cheats, liars, and frauds. I recognize there are crimes, cruelty, and abuses in this world. But I don't want to realize these things. I want to realize the good that is in this world.

The people and situations I have in my life are the ones I have chosen to have there. These are the people and situations I want to realize, to take internally, and to be a part of my life.

We are inundated with bad news, daily. I don't want to carry this around with me. I think the more we realize the good, the more we will be surrounded with it. Let's all focus and realize the good, the positive, and the virtue of this world.

⌘⌘⌘⌘⌘

"Stop judging by mere appearance,
and make a right judgment."
John 7:24

APRIL 11
...MAKE BELIEVE

"There are no days in life so memorable
as those which vibrated to some stroke of the imagination."
- Emerson

⌘⌘⌘⌘⌘

We have no reservations as children. We live each day in our "play time" world of our choosing — for the most part. Wise adults even help and encourage us in our creation of our make believe world.

I remember a large woods by our house with oak trees. Mother and I would gather acorns and break them apart to make cups and saucers for my doll house. If you put blankets on each side of the bunk beds, you could pretend you were a big bear in your cave. Cardboard boxes were everything from trains to sleds to rooms of a make believe house. Dolls were real babies, and a plastic horse head on a stick was just as wonderful as Trigger, Flicka, or Champion.

My husband had a make believe friend named Robert. Any time something was wrong, it was Robert's fault, or when he was at the store with his mother and threw a candy bar into the grocery cart, it wasn't for him; it was for Robert.

The world of make believe was one without trials, tribulations, worries, responsibilities, and drudgery. There were no bills to pay, no one ever died, no one shed real tears, no one was cruel, and no one was unhappy. It was a world of intense joy without boundaries or limitations.

As adults, for our peace of mind and sanity, it is important for us to visit our make believe world some times. When we hear a Straus Waltz, we can make believe we are in a beautiful ball gown dancing with a handsome prince. When we hear our favorite song, we can pretend we are the recording artist. When we see a beautiful suit two sizes small for us, we can image how we would look if we were in it.

Because our adult world is full of so many trials, tribulations, worries, responsibilities, and drudgery, it is important for us to get away from it temporarily even if it is only in our mind.

In *The Heart of a Woman*, Maya Angelou said, "If one is lucky, a solitary fantasy can totally transform one million realities."

⌘⌘⌘⌘⌘

"Because you have seen me, you have believed;
blessed are those who have not seen and yet have believed."
John 20:29

APRIL 12
...WAITING FOR THE DESCANT

"Music is edifying, for from time to time it sets the soul in operation."
                                                                    - John Cage

⌘⌘⌘⌘⌘

We have some wonderful sopranos in our choir. [You know who they are; they have those lovely long thin necks.] It is such a pleasure to hear them sing. Many of them have majored in music and sing in more than just our choir. Some are multi-talented and write music and play several instruments as well. Music is a large part of their life, and they love to share this with others.

The Introit, the first song we sing with the congregation, seems to set the tone for the service. We usually sing the first three or four stanzas in unison, and then comes the big finale. Just before the last stanza, the organist plays several inspirational measures to set the tone. As the organ is playing, we have the opportunity to look up at the congregation. All of the congregation's eyes are focused on the sopranos as they wait for the descant: those wonderful high notes that so few can reach.

When the descant starts, I watch the congregation. Many of them are so in awe of the music that they stop singing and just listen. Many eyes fill with tears as the people hear the descant blend beautifully with the melody of the hymn. Many bow their heads in silence and are alone with their most private thoughts.

It is refreshing to know that the human voice, whether in word or song, can still impact people in many different ways: to stop and pause in time and space, to be moved in emotion, or to cause to reflect on life's moments. The human voice: an instrument created by God.

⌘⌘⌘⌘⌘

"Clap our hands, all you peoples;
shout to God with loud songs of joy."
                                                                    Psalm 47:1

APRIL 13
...APPRECIATING SOPHISTICATION

"It seems to me that invisibility is the required provision of elegance.
Elegance ceases to exist when it is noticed."

- Jean Cocteau

⌘⌘⌘⌘⌘

My husband and I are DINKODS: Dual Income No Kids Only Dogs.
Most of our friends are DINKODS, also. And, when we say dogs, we do mean
more than one.

One of our good "couple" friends, Robin and Curt, have two Yorkies
named Martha and Emily. Robin refers to them as the "Terrorists." Her dogs,
like ours, bark at almost everything. One day while on the phone solving the
world's problems, I could hear Martha and Emily continuously barking in the
background. Robin had not given them their morning treat, and not only were
they unhappy, they were not about to let the matter pass her attention. Robin
said, "They are very demanding in their petitions."

If Robin could have seen me, she would have seen a smile that went from
ear to ear. It was not so much what she had said but the way she had said it. It
was the old world charm of sophistication. It was thinking before speaking, and it
was thinking of the person you were speaking to before speaking. It was the
elevation of minds: a gentle thought provoking boost.

It is easy in the day to day to get caught up in the easy way, the short cuts,
the "killing two birds with one stone" way. "Thru" is easier to spell than
"through." The "&" is easier to write than "and." We don't have to think. We
just do it.

By thinking and speaking in the sophisticated way, we have the opportunity
to reflect on our own interaction with the world. We realize we have something
to learn from others and that we don't have all the answers.

Sophistication helps us set standards. It is like a tide that raises all boats. It
helps all of us be less naive and more worldly-wise.

⌘⌘⌘⌘⌘

"He has caused his wonders to be remembered;
the Lord is gracious and compassionate."
Psalm 111:4

APRIL 14
...STARTING OFF ON THE RIGHT FOOT

"A good beginning makes a good ending."
- English Proverb

⌘⌘⌘⌘⌘

On Christmas Even when I was a sophomore at college, I fell down two flights of stairs at my grandmother's house breaking both bones in my left ankle and pulling all the muscles apart in my left knee. I was in a plaster cast for three months. I believe this major event was responsible for many of my questionable personality traits. [You try not taking a bath or not being able to drive for three months and see how you feel!]

The timing was awful. It was the dead of winter, and I was walking all over campus amid the snow and ice with a full leg cast. My French Class was in one of the older buildings, and I had to climb about 30 stone steps to get inside. Not an easy task in a full leg cast. And, if you think going up was bad, you should try going down. As long as I started with the left foot, I could manage fairly well. However, one day, my mind had left me. I started down the steps on the right foot, the left leg wouldn't bend; and if I hadn't dropped my books and grabbed the railing, I would have fallen down those 30 stone steps. I know this wouldn't have been good for my body to say nothing of a leg that was already broken. I had not thought this situation through. I had not started out on the right foot (in my case, the left foot), and things could have turned out badly.

Every time I climbed these stone steps to French Class, I thought about this "almost" disaster. It was a constant reminder to me during major events in my life. When I had to start a project, interact with someone on a personal level, or deliver unpleasant news for some reason, and things didn't go well, I knew I should have thought it through before I spoke. Figuratively, I didn't get started on the right foot.

If we plan our course of action so that we do have enough time to think things through and get started on the right foot, we can avoid repeating ourselves, hurt feelings, misunderstandings, and "almost" disasters. Our will to plan is just as important as our will to succeed.

⌘⌘⌘⌘⌘

"For we walk by faith, not by sight:"
2 Corinthians 6:7

APRIL 15
...LEARNING WHAT I NEED TO LEARN AND MOVE ON

"I know the most important faculty to develop is one for hard, continuous
and varied work and living; but the difference between knowing this and
doing anything consistent about it is often abysmal."

-James Agee

⌘⌘⌘⌘⌘

It seems to me that every time I'm doing something that I should not be
doing, the Lord allows something to happen to make my life so miserable that I
have to change. In situations like this, I suppose we could curse the person and the
situation, but cursing doesn't seem to change things. I suppose we could scream to
everyone how unhappy we are, but screaming doesn't seem to change things. I
suppose we could stew in the misery of our fate, but stewing doesn't seem to
change things.

When I'm miserable, wanting to change things and cursing, screaming, and
stewing aren't working, I need to figure out what will work. Everything that
happens to us is an opportunity to learn, and sometimes the most painful learning
steps will lead us in a new direction we wouldn't have taken unless we were forced.

I was trying to phase out of a particular job — a particularly well paying job.
Our season ended in August, and I would resign. The owner of the company
decided to do three more shows which gave me the opportunity to earn a
minimum of $15,000. A tough sum to turn down! So, I was trying to be patient
and bide my time until November. It was August, the day I had decided to resign,
and I had just landed in Detroit on my way to meet the owner of the company. As
I pulled my 60 pound sample case from the overhead compartment, the wheels
fell off. I knew I was going to have to carry 60 pounds from one end of the Detroit
Airport to the other. I was so angry. I stood at the front of the plane beating my
head on the bulkhead, saying, "Lord, I told You I was going to quit this job.
Won't You, please, just give me a break?" I made it through the airport,
worked with the owner of the company, and resigned before the day was over.

When I have to learn through uncomfortable situations, my prayer is,
"Lord, just let me learn what I need to learn and move on, please." Learning and
moving on are more preferable and productive than cursing, screaming, and
stewing.

⌘⌘⌘⌘⌘

"In the same way, the Spirit helps us in our weakness.
We do not know what we ought to pray for, but the Spirit himself
intercedes for us with groans that words cannot express."

Romans 8:26

APRIL 16
...REALIZING WE ALL HAVE SOMETHING TO OFFER

"The child is not a prisoner of its inheritance;
it holds its inheritance as a new creation which its future actions will unfold."
- Jacob Bronowski

⌘⌘⌘⌘⌘

Several years ago, Indianapolis began to renovate the downtown area. After much work and fanfare, they opened a refurbished Union Station. Adjoining Union Station is an old bridge that is 13' 2" tall. A truck driver driving a semi through downtown thought he could make it under this bridge. He couldn't. He got the semi tightly wedged under the bridge.

He tried backing it out, but that didn't work. He tried revving up the engines and driving out, but that didn't work. He called in a wrecker, but the truck wouldn't budge. Finally, he called in some great minds of transportation, and their solution was to unload the truck and collapse the frame.

Just as they were getting ready to unload the trailer, a little six year old boy, who had been sitting on the curb, walked up to one of the men, tugged on his coat, and uttered these words of wisdom and insight: "Let the air out of the tires."

Whatever our age, education, sex, race, religion, or culture, we all have something to offer.

⌘⌘⌘⌘⌘

"Every valley shall be raised up,
every mountain and hill made low;
the rough ground shall become level,
the rugged places a plain."
Isaiah 40:4

APRIL 17
...REPETITIOUS WAY

"There is a repetition everywhere, and nothing is found only once in the world."
                                                                    - Goethe

⌘⌘⌘⌘⌘

My husband and I eat at Cracker Barrel about once a week. We enjoy the type of food they serve; we call it "grandma food" because it reminds us of the food our grandmothers used to cook.

For those of you who eat at Cracker Barrel, you know each table has a triangular game with golf tees called "All But One." The goal of the game is to jump all the golf tees but one — hence the name "All But One."

I have never won this game, much to my dismay! I have worked from the center out and lost. I have worked from the outside in and lost. I have worked each corner in and lost. I have even taken out all the pegs but one and tried working it backwards — and lost!@!@!

Each time we are seated at the table, I am determined not to play this game again. I can't win; so, why bother? And, yet, after the server has taken our order and left the table, my eyes stray to the triangle, and I find myself jumping golf tees - just one more time.

I think our tenacity of trying just one more time helps us accomplish most things in life. Our ability to "take a licking and keep on ticking" helps us deal with tragic losses, near fatal illness, the death of loved ones, unemployment, and "almost adult" children testing the waters. Setbacks: those things that slow us down but don't stop us.

Every time you go into Cracker Barrel, drag that triangle in front of you and jump those golf tees one more time. This silly game is a reminder to us that we may have setbacks, but we do not give up.

Hope springs eternal in all arenas.

⌘⌘⌘⌘⌘

"Always be prepared to give an answer to everyone who
asks you to give the reason for the hope that you have."
                                                        1 Peter 3:15

APRIL 18
...MAKING TIME FOR SIX MINUTES OF HEAVEN

"Heaven is under our feet as well as over our heads."
- Thoreau

⌘⌘⌘⌘⌘

Stan and I share a love of classical music. The other day he presented me with a new CD of some of my favorite classical pieces. The sixth piece on the CD is Pachelbel's Canon. I'm always mesmerized when I hear that piece of music. [As a matter of fact, I liked it long before it became popular as television commercial music.] The strings and harpsichord blend so beautifully together. It's soft and melodious.

It touches my heart and soul. As it plays, I envision relaxing pastoral scenes, weddings, a string quartet immersed in the music, lovers' smiles, and clouds. It creates a wonderful euphoric state for my senses.

When it finished playing, I looked at the digital display; it read 6:00 minutes. That is the playing time of this version. I realized that this is truly six minutes of heaven for me.

I listen to Pachelbel's Canon when I'm in traffic, when I'm angry or stressed, or when I'm sitting in a parking lot waiting for someone. It calms me. It brings peace to my whole self.

We should all choose what is six minutes of heaven for us. It could be music, holding a sleeping baby, prayer, sitting outside communing with nature, or reading an inspirational piece. Six minutes is just one-tenth of one hour. This is not much to ask out of our day for all the joy six minutes of heaven brings to us and, in the long run, to others.

⌘⌘⌘⌘⌘

"Is not God in the heights of heaven?"
Job 22:12

APRIL 19
...PAMPERING OURSELVES

"Let us live while we live."
- Philip Doddridge

⌘⌘⌘⌘⌘

Once a month, I take one day and do nothing but pamper myself. I take a long Jacuzzi bath and then go to one of the coffee houses for breakfast and delicious coffee. I go to the mall and browse always finding at least one thing I can't live without. I share a light lunch at a restaurant with a new magazine. Then I head for the salon to have my hair highlighted (very polite term) and receive a facial while listening to relaxing music and breathing in aromatherapy. I finally arrive back home, get cleaned up, and take my husband out for a lovely dinner. It is a fabulous routine I look forward to each month because it helps me get through the other 29 or 30 days.

When we have to be so many things to so many people, it is important for us to take care of ourselves first. We will never be able to be 100% for someone else until we are 100% for ourselves. There is nothing selfish in this idea. It is not selfish; it is self-actualizing and self-preservation.

Most of the creatures in this world take care of themselves first so they are capable of taking care of their young. It is the older, mature plants that propagate the new, young starts. In both the plant and animal world, it is the healthy and strong who are capable of doing for others.

This one day of incredible comfort and relaxation helps get me ready for all the extra errands, meetings, and company that will come my way during the month. I can face helping each person and situation with a cheerful heart instead of clenched fists and teeth.

We all realize there is little we can control. One thing we can control is how we prepare ourselves to meet each situation. When we pamper ourselves, we are refreshed and more capable of meeting life's challenges head on.

⌘⌘⌘⌘⌘

"What is your life?
You are a mist that appears for a little while and then vanishes."
James 4:14

APRIL 20
...OVERLOOKING THE SMALL THINGS WHEN WE LOVE

"Men trip not on mountains, they stumble on stones."
- Hindustani Proverb

⌘⌘⌘⌘⌘

Ben, my step-son, had married his finance Jill. Because I'm twice her age and married to Ben's father, we occasionally discuss our husbands. "How do you say this? How do you get him to do that? Do they all do this?" And, so on. You see, Ben and his Dad are literally "two peas from the same pod." I told Jill if she wants to know what Ben will look like and act like in 30 years to take a look at his Dad.

Ben and Jill moved to Ohio. For a newly wedded couple to be away from "influential" people is a good thing. They will have time to work things out with one another instead of with well meaning family and friends.

Jill and I were talking one evening when she asked me what was the most difficult thing about being married. I laughed and replied, "The little things are the things that will drive you crazy."

Stan, my husband and Ben's father, doesn't drink, isn't physically or emotionally abusive, doesn't gamble, doesn't carouse, and doesn't hoard money. But he wads up the wet kitchen towels and leaves them on the counter where they mildew; and when he gets up from the kitchen table, he never pushes in his chair.

I'm sure I have habits and do things that "get under his skin," but he never mentions them because neither do I drink, am physically and emotionally abusive, gamble, carouse, or hoard money.

We usually know the big things before we get married; it's the little things, the "ants" of marriage, that we are unaware of until we live together. The little things that we overlook with either a sigh or a laugh because we love the person. The love we have for their goodness and character so far outweighs the "ants" in our marriage that we turn a blind eye in their direction.

⌘⌘⌘⌘⌘

"He will not grow tired or weary,
and his understanding no one can fathom."
Isaiah 40:28

APRIL 21
...PUTTING UP BIRD FEEDERS

"Not a gift of a cow, not a gift of land, not yet a gift of food,
is so important as the gift of safety,
which is declared to be the great gift among all gifts in this world."

- Panchatantra

⌘⌘⌘⌘⌘

Some things in our lives, that seem pretty simple or insignificant, bring us incredible pleasures. One morning while looking down on our new deck, we noticed three Bluebirds sitting on the railing of the deck. They were tiny and precious and gorgeous. We watched them through the binoculars and lamented over the fact that we did not have a bird feeder for them. If we had, we could have appreciated their beauty a little longer as they stayed to feed.

To semi-rectify this situation, we went out and bought a bird feeder and books on developing a sanctuary for the birds. We have added a finch feeder, hummingbird feeder, mister, bird bath, bird house, and mulched areas for the ground feeders. We also re-landscaped the back yard adding the necessary trees and bushes they prefer for their shelter and protection. We put out "Critter Mix" for the squirrels, raccoons, and chipmunks and corn for the ducks. We gathered rocks to surround the feeding area to help keep the creatures safe as they feed, and the bird bath that we purchased is only a foot tall so even the non-flying creatures could get a drink in really dry weather. We have also added a butterfly garden and butterfly house.

The Bluebirds have not yet returned, and we are saddened at that, but what we have reaped by putting up the bird feeders and accessories has added incredible pleasure to our lives. We now have three pet squirrels — Moe, Curly, and Larry — who feed every morning, a pair of chipmunks that hide in the woodpile and chatter at the dogs, a pair of ducks that parade their brood by us each spring and summer as we watch their down turn to feathers, a baby raccoon who hides in the trees at night (we see his eyes), rabbits who have eaten most of the flower bulbs, doves that nestle on the rocks and coo each morning, and an array of cardinals, red-winged black birds, blue jays, yellow and purple finch, starlings, crows, and butterflies.

This entourage passes by our deck and gardens every day. They put a smile on our faces, give us funny stories to tell, and add hours of pleasure to our lives.

⌘⌘⌘⌘⌘

"The eternal God is your refuge,
and underneath are the everlasting arms."
Deuteronomy 33:27

APRIL 22
...SUSPENDING JUDGMENT WHEN YOU DON'T KNOW THE FACTS

⌘⌘⌘⌘⌘

For many reasons, I choose not to have children. As with all decisions we make, there are always moments when we either regret or wonder if we did the right thing. I honestly was never prepared to have children, and then I married Stan. Stan has two children. When we met and started dating, Ben was 19 and Sarah was 14.

When Ben got married, one of Stan's and my conversations turned to grandchildren. Because I've always been a very private and quiet person about personal matters, Stan asked me how I would interact with grandchildren. I opened my mouth to respond but took my own advice of thinking before I speak and realized that not only did I not have all the facts, I didn't have any facts.

My response was, "You are asking me to make a judgement call about something on which I don't have the facts. I've never been around small children. How am I to know if I will be good at something that I have never done or been? I suppose children are just like adults: some you like and some you don't like. I will have to wait until the situation presents itself and see how I do."

I know this was not the answer he wanted, but it was the only answer I could give honestly. An answer that would not come back to haunt me. We all need to realize we should not judge until we have all the facts.

(I did tell Jill, Ben's wife, that I would be partial to girls because I love to cut out clothes for paper dolls and play dress up. I guess that's an answer in itself.)

⌘⌘⌘⌘⌘

APRIL 23
...OVERCOMING LAZINESS AND FINDING INSPIRATION

"Indolence is a delightful but distressing state:
we must be doing something to be happy."
- William Hazlitt

⌘⌘⌘⌘⌘

When I tell people that I am collaborating on different projects with
people, one of the first questions asked is why do I do projects with someone else.
I choose to work with people for several reasons:

1) We each have our areas in which we excel.
2) We compensate for each other's weaknesses.
3) At times, we may be two old souls who have known each other for
   many life times.
4) We have a great time together.
5) We accept where each other is in the current space and time and
   try not to judge or interfere — just help.

As you can see, I collaborate for many reasons, but a major, yet unlisted
reason I go for the dual endeavor is because I tend to get lazy, and I need
someone to hold me accountable. I've often wondered why I get lazy about things.
Maybe it is because I'm almost 50 years old, and I think I deserve to rest. Maybe
it's because I've been an entrepreneur so long that I'm used to doing things on
"my" time. Maybe it's because I have so many irons in the fire that it is hard to
prioritize and decide what to do first.
Or maybe I'm not lazy; maybe I need inspiration. Jesus had his disciples.
Arthur had his knights. A judge has his jurors. Companies have stock holders. It
seems to me that we all need people to inspire us and keep us on track.
There are times when our collaborators resemble a disciple with words from
the Lord, a knight who comes to our rescue, a juror asking questions about our
purpose, or a stock holder taking interest in our progression.
Not only does collaboration help me overcome my laziness; it also produces
a friend.

⌘⌘⌘⌘⌘

"And, lo, I am with you always,
even unto the end of the world."
Matthew 28:20

APRIL 24
...APPRECIATING ALL AGES

"It is not new for the older generation to bewail the indolence of the young, and there is a tendency for the latter to maintain much of the older ethic screened by a new semantics and an altered ideology."
- David Riesman

⌘⌘⌘⌘⌘

Some of my clients expressed a concern about effectively blending the different generations in the workforce. Consequently, my new seminar for 1997 was "Mixing Generations." I spent about six months doing research, interviewing and studying the Silent Generation, the Boomers, and the Generation X'ers. Not only did I make some new friends, I enjoyed the study and developed a new appreciation for each generation.

I realize we tend to misunderstand and have low levels of tolerance for people who are not like us. But, with a little education and insight, we can appreciate other peoples' points of view. Those of us who are not of the Silent Generation tend to think they are too conservative with their money and ideas. But, as one member of the Silent Generation pointed out, "If your entire 'depression era' winter wardrobe came from the Goodwill and cost 20¢ (5¢/@ for 2 sweaters and 2 skirts) and for dinner you were lucky to have potatoes or potato skins to eat, you would become a little more conservative, too." Or, if you accuse a Boomer of being omniscient, you might have a clearer understanding if you realize they were the first demographic group to be seriously studied (and pigeonholed) and told, because of their education, they should "always" have the right answer. Or, when you look at a member of Generation X and criticize their dress, lack of manners, corporate loyalty, and different interactive skills, it might be advantageous for you to realize they are the first generation of "latchkey" kids in the workforce. Who told them how to dress, what fork to pick up, or whom to be loyal to?

We know that each generation is different, and our differences give each of us something special to offer. The Silent Generation = foundation/tradition. The Boomers = amassed education. The X'ers = technoliteracy.

Age comes to us without effort. We have earned it by just being a member of the human race. It does not transform us, accommodate us, or adjust to us. It just allows each of us to see ourselves and others more clearly. And, in that clarity, maybe we realize that we all have something to give.

⌘⌘⌘⌘⌘

"Is not wisdom found among the aged?
Does not long life bring understanding?"
Job 12:12

APRIL 25

...ELIMINATING DISTRACTIONS

"We're all muddlers.
The thing is to see when one's got to stop muddling."
- Iris Murdoch

⌘⌘⌘⌘⌘

The fourth Sunday of each month is Baptism Sunday. It is wonderful to see the families and their unity, their faith in the future, and their legacy to the world. The babies are not only precious in the baptismal gowns, But they are also cute. One will grab the microphone, splash in the holy water, giggle or do something to bring a smile to the congregation.

Sometimes, after the ceremony, a baby will get cranky and start to cry. One Sunday, just as Dr. Millard was beginning the sermon with a prayer, one of the babies started to cry. He said, "Let us pray" and paused while the parents left the sanctuary with the fussy infant. It was handled so well and was certainly the best thing to do, for, when a baby cries, it is difficult to focus, listen, or concentrate on what else is being done or said.

I certainly think eliminating distractions is what we should do in many situations in our daily lives. So many times we are trying to concentrate, listen or focus amid distraction; and when the distractions overwhelm us, and we can't focus, listen or concentrate, we become angry and frustrated.

Daily distractions are like ants at a picnic. Both are inevitable. When we have just arrived at the picnic, and we are fresh and the ants are few, we are able to deal with them rather satisfactorily; however, as the day wears on, and we have become hot and tired and put up with one too many ants, it's time to pack it in and go home.

Knowing when it is time to pack it in or gracefully eliminate distractions is a compliment to our spirit. It is an act of revival.

⌘⌘⌘⌘⌘

"I am saying this for your own good,   not to restrict you,
but that you may live in a right way in undivided devotion to the Lord."
1 Corinthians 7:35

APRIL 26
...SHEDDING TEARS OVER AMAZING GRACE

"There is something pleasurable in calm remembrance of a past sorrow."
- Cicero

⌘⌘⌘⌘⌘

We have several students majoring in music from a nearby university who sing with our choir on occasion. One young gentlemen sang "Amazing Grace" at a very special performance. His mother had come down from Chicago to be in his audience. This was her father's and his grandfather's favorite song. Unfortunately, his grandfather couldn't be there that day. His grandfather was in the hospital, gravely ill.

As he began the last verse while looking at his mother, tears streamed down his face; and when he finished the song, he went to his mother, also crying at the beauty of her son's voice and the concern for her father, and they hugged one another tenderly. Trust me when I tell you they were not the only ones shedding tears.

I don't know what there is about "Amazing Grace." Maybe because it is sung at so many funerals, or because of the words, or because of its history and being written by a slave trader saved by God. Whatever it is, it always reduces me, and most other people, to tears.

A friend of mine made the comment one day that "the Lord gave me tears to use, and I'm not ashamed to use them." As sad as I feel after hearing "Amazing Grace," I'm still relieved that I can shed tears, feel emotions and have compassion for others. I am also relieved that others can do the same for me.

It is our life experiences that give us compassion. It is the blending of the words, the music, the passion, and the life experiences that cause those tears to fall. We should welcome our tears because they too are a gift from God and contain the power of the soul.

⌘⌘⌘⌘⌘

"Sorrow is better than laughter,
because a sad face is good for the heart."
Ecclesiastes 7:3

APRIL 27
...RELEASING OUR ANGER WITH OURSELVES

"It is easy to fly into a passion — anybody can do that —
but to be angry with the right person to the right extent
and at the right time and with the right object and in the right way —
that is not easy, and it is not everyone who can do it.

- Aristotle

⌘⌘⌘⌘⌘

In some psychological studies I have read, much evidence leads to the fact that heart disease is aggravated by anger and rage. I have felt these two emotions occasionally, and when at their peak, they seem to toxify my system for days. No wonder they affect the heart – or at least mine.

In my seminars on "Living Positive in a Negative World" I speak to the attendees about anger and how detrimental it is to each of us. I point out a particular situation to them. If I get angry at every one of them in the seminar, I can gather my material, walk out the door, and I never have to deal with them again. However, if I get angry at myself, I'm stuck! I can't get away under any circumstance. It's my blood pressure, my heart rate, my pulse, my anxiety level, my rage, my anger, and my stress on my own heart.

There are times when we do get angry with ourselves. We need to try and eliminate the anger as soon as possible. We can do that by living in the present moment - not the past or the future. An ill deed done to us in the past is over. We need to find a way to express our unhappiness and go on. A perceived ill deed that could possibly be done to us in the future is not a given, only a possibility, and we should not get angry about something that may not happen.

Living in the present helps eliminate self-anger. In Matthew we are told to stick with today's troubles for today's troubles are enough for today. Anger can make us look stupid; anger can make us look out of control; and anger can shorten our lives.

Our lives should be filled with passion for the life we are living, not anger at self for what has been or might be. He's right. Today's troubles are enough for today.

⌘⌘⌘⌘⌘

"Let not the sun go down upon your wrath."
Ephesians 4:26

APRIL 28
...BEING FRIENDS ON OUR TERMS

"Though all men be made of one metal,
yet they be not cast all in one mold."
- John Lyly

⌘⌘⌘⌘⌘

Another "Lesson From Murphy" – our two year old, 80 pound retriever. My husband and I wanted a mixed breed so we might possibly avoid some of the health problems that so many of the pure breeds have; consequently, Murphy is a mix: her mother was a Black Lab, and her father was a Golden Lab. We were sure we would have few problems with her. Much to our dismay, Murphy has grass allergies, narrow back hips, and a bad case of nerves.

Now, we have always tried to treat her with kid gloves. She is truly our four-legged child. With a bad case of nerves and a fear of people, she can come on very aggressive. Screaming at her didn't help. Jerking on her choker chain didn't help. Putting her outside or in the garage didn't help. What did help was a wise friend who had dogs as pets all his life. He came over, and, naturally, Murphy began barking, displaying an aggressive posture, and snorting. He just sat down on the landing and let Murphy walk around him and sniff and bark; and, before you knew it, she was waging her tail and wanting to be petted. He said he could see she was just scared by the way she kept ducking her head. She needed time to adjust to people. You had to understand this and learn to be friends on her terms.

It would be nice if people would accept us on our terms occasionally. Sometimes the demands that people make on us are so strong that we don't want to be friends. Sometimes we just want people to accept us for who we are, to understand us, to be our friend, and to do all of this on our terms.

It has often been said that a "real" friend is someone who knows all your faults and flaws and likes you anyway, someone who will tell you what you don't want to hear, or someone you don't have to explain yourself to. In a lifetime, it is rare and quite a privilege to experience true friendship and those who accept us on our terms.

⌘⌘⌘⌘⌘

"My mouth will speak words of wisdom;
the utterance from my heart will give understanding."
Psalm 49:3

APRIL 29
...ELIMINATING POST-IT-NOTES

"A little fire is quickly trodden out,"
- Shakespeare

⌘⌘⌘⌘⌘

Most of the time I love Post-it-Notes. What a great way to semi-secure messages to and from people, to record information immediately, or to organize things you want to organize.

Sometimes, they can and do overwhelm us. When you can't see a page of your daily planner for post-it-notes, you are overwhelmed. When they cover your desk so thoroughly that you can't tell what color the wood is, you are overwhelmed. When you can't find an important piece of information without peeling off 50 post-it-notes and re-reading each one, you are overwhelmed.

There comes a time when it is necessary to stop fighting this "overwhelming" battle. It is a time to eliminate those visible signs of being overwhelmed and out of control and get organized. It is a time to eliminate the temporary quick fix for a more permanent solution: being organized.

Post-it-notes eliminate immediate chaos; but when they are stuck to something for more than 24 hours, they begin to add more to the chaos that they were designed to eliminate.

Post-it-note Disorder or Syndrome can be a very formidable malady!

⌘⌘⌘⌘⌘

"But everything should be done in a fitting and orderly way."
1 Corinthians 14:40

APRIL 30
...REALIZING WE ALL HAVE AN "UNLIMITED CEILING"

"Knowledge of what is possible is the beginning of happiness."
- George Santayana

⌘⌘⌘⌘⌘

The other day I was driving to a client's office when I noticed it was a beautiful day. The sun was shining, and the temperature was warm. How warm, I wondered? I turned on the radio to listen to the forecast. "Temperature 70°; Clear skies; Ceiling Unlimited." Unlimited? I don't think the ceiling is really unlimited. It is probably limited to "as far as the eye can see."

I thought how nice it would be if people realized that they, too, had an unlimited ceiling as far as their life was concerned. Typically, most people achieve the same level as their parents in education, finances, and careers. They believe that this is their level of achievement. But there are some people who have never had limitations set for them. These people were encouraged to get a better education, save more money, and have a better career. These people were propelled on to a different life on a higher level by people encouraging their success and not setting limitations.

A friend of mine who is in the military told me of one training exercise which required people to get to the top of a 30 foot pole. The only possible way to do it was for one person to climb on the back of another, then a third person to climb on their backs, and so on. By each person being there for support, both literally and figuratively, the exercise was accomplished.

My mother did just that. She helped me climb that 30 foot "life" pole and go above and beyond. She told me she would never lie to me, and that there was nothing I couldn't do. And, you know what? I believed her. That is why I was the first in our family to go to college, to make a six digit income and to travel all over the world. I wanted to have the best I could possible afford and to blend a wonderful career with a happy and successful marriage. I believed I had no limitations, and whatever I could conceive and believe, I could achieve.

There is an old Arab proverb that states, "Dwell not upon thy weariness, thy strength shall be according to the measure of thy desire." I think that our personal ceiling of achievement is limited only in our mind's eye.

⌘⌘⌘⌘⌘

"With man this is impossible,
but with God all things are possible."
Matthew 19:26

MAY 1

...REALIZING WHEN YOU LOVE

"Tis never for their wisdom that one loves the wisest,
or for their wit that one loves the wittiest;
'tis for benevolence and virtue and honest fondness one loves people."
- Hester Lynch Piozzi

⌘⌘⌘⌘⌘

My husband and I were introduced by a mutual friend. At the time we met we were both divorced and weren't really anxious to jump into another relationship. We had specific criteria that each other met, liked dating, and settled into a comfortable relationship. In fact, we dated for about five years before we got married.

I knew I liked Stan but wasn't really sure I loved him, and having been marriage before, if I married again, I wanted to make sure that I liked and loved my partner. Stan was nice looking, thoughtful, educated, "really" understood computers, handy around the house, had a good job, and loved to cook. There was a lot there to like.

One day, something happened to make me realize I did love him and wanted to spend the rest of my life with him. It was summer, and I was at his house. Stan was mowing his grass which was almost knee high since it had rained for about a week (typical of Indiana). I was helping him by cleaning up his kitchen. I looked out the window as the sound of the mower stopped and saw him bent over chasing something through the grass. He finally caught whatever it was, and I went out to investigate. He walked across the yard with his hands cupped together, and I asked him what he had. He opened his hands, and there sat a little crawdad. He said, "The sun is drying up his water, and if I don't take him over to the pond, he'll die."

Most people wouldn't have even noticed the crawdad, let alone stop a mower, chase it, and carry it to safe water. A simple act to save one of God's lesser creatures turned into one of the biggest acts to impact my life. It was at that moment that I realized how much I loved this man for his care, concern, gentleness, and compassion. It hit me that not only was there a great deal about him to like, but there was also a great deal about him to love.

⌘⌘⌘⌘⌘

"And I pray that you, being rooted and established in love,
may have power, together with all the saints,
to grasp how wide and long and high and deep is the love of Christ."
Ephesians 3:18

MAY 2
...FINDING SUPPORT PEOPLE

"To serve is beautiful, but only if it is done with joy
and a whole heart and a free mind."
- Pearl S. Buck

⌘⌘⌘⌘⌘

We live in a new development. In our neighborhood are quite a few young families with small children. The children love to play in the lots where new homes have not yet been built as they go on some type of "hunt" or "expedition." Rocks seem to be of major interest — especially BIG rocks.

One afternoon two of the little boys found a partially exposed rock. They started digging with play shovels; and, before you knew it, they had their dads' shovels and were digging in earnest. The next time I looked there were six little boys and two little girls. Each had some type of tool, and all of them were digging. I watched and listened for quite a while. Their instructions to one another and the way they worked together was amazing.

My husband and I had to leave for choir practice; and, by the time we got home, it was dark, so we couldn't see what they had accomplished. The next morning, I looked out the dining room window, and there, removed from the earth, was a rock of impressive size.

One of the children certainly couldn't have done this alone. It took a support group of about a dozen children to accomplish this task.

I have been a member of many groups, and I know how much easier things are with others helping. A group of friends and I built a ten acre fence in less than a day. A study group I was part of made it through a two-year Masters Program together. A dining club I was a member of cooked wonderful meals together every month. Things are not only easier with support people; they are also more fun.

As I've mentioned before, Jesus had 12 disciples. King Arthur had the 12 knights of the Round Table. Each judge has a jury of 12. I don't know if groups are cheaper by the dozen, but they do seem to get a great deal accomplished and leave lasting memories.

⌘⌘⌘⌘⌘

"We wait in hope for the Lord;
he is our help and our shield."
Psalm 33:20

MAY 3
...LEAVING A MESS UNTIL LATER

"Delay is preferable to error."
- Thomas Jefferson

⌘⌘⌘⌘⌘

I give seminars to many corporations, teach for the university, create new programs and classes, write, take care of my husband and dogs, spend time with my family, and, in my spare time, I try to tackle housekeeping.

The house had gotten so dusty that an asthma sufferer could have an attack just by walking in the front door. I couldn't stand it any longer! I shut off the computer, put the dogs outside, and spent the better part of the day cleaning, polishing, dusting, uncluttering, sorting, and mopping. I even made a splendid dinner. After dinner, I recleaned the kitchen and sat down with my husband to watch TV.

About 8:30, he got hungry for some popcorn, and he wanted to know if I minded if he fixed some. I said no and asked him to please clean up the oil and the popper when he was done. He said sure, no problem.

After eating the popcorn, he fell asleep on the couch. When he woke up later in a daze, cleaning up the mess was the last thing on his mind, and he promptly went to bed.

The next morning, I put on my robe and headed downstairs to make breakfast in my newly and nicely cleaned kitchen and was greeted by the mess he had promised to clean up. Remembering all my hard work, I walked over to the counter, opened the cupboard and put everything back dirty, then proceeded to fix my breakfast.

There are times we all need to walk away from a mess, literally and figuratively. If it's a literal mess, it will wait; it will be there later. This is good plan of action because sometimes we are not in the mood to deal with things now! If it is a figurative mess, we need time to sort things out and determine our best approach. It's gaining the distance, it's taking the breath of fresh air, and it's dealing with things when we are prepared to deal with them thanks to a new perspective. [That afternoon, when I was could deal with it, I took the popper out of the cupboard, washed it, and put it away clean.]

⌘⌘⌘⌘⌘

"Let us then approach the throne of grace with confidence,
so that we may receive mercy and find grace to help us in our time of need."
Hebrews 4:16

MAY 4
...GETTING A GOOD NIGHT'S SLEEP

"Sleep is the chief nourisher in life's feast."
- Shakespeare

⌘⌘⌘⌘⌘

Typically, I'm not a mean person; however, there are two times in my life when I tend to be more mean than usual: when I'm sick or when I'm tired. Being sick arouses fear. You wonder if you will get well, if you will be disabled, or if you have something terminal. Anger is an easy substitute for fear.

Sleep is different. It's like water: you don't miss it until you don't have it. It is the pause that refreshes and rejuvenates, like water, and, like water, it is life giving. Exhaustion is a well that is drained, depleted and empty.

Sleep can be an escape from illness, sadness, and depression. It is a time of mental and emotional healing. It helps us re-weave when we become unraveled. It helps us regenerate what we have lost. It eases pain and soothes frazzled nerves. It removes us temporarily from the unpleasant. It is a time of protection from the elements we face during waking hours. It increases concentration and the power of our intellect. We all need a good night's sleep.

When I was travelling about seven months out of every year and dealing with overeating, red-eye flights, different time zones, and stress, sleep did not come easy, frequent, or sound. I truly was suffering from sleep deprivation. I became mean, short-tempered, and irritable. The lack of sleep kept me from being in three states I enjoy frequenting: The State of Grace, The State of Intelligent, and The State of Happiness.

The need for sleep is so ritualistic that I began to establish rituals to set myself up for a state of relaxation and sleep. A short evening walk with the dogs, a cup of flavored caffeine-free cappuccino, and a few pages of a good book. Finally, before I shut off the light I reminded myself of a line from one of Gloria Copeland's tapes: "The Lord doesn't sleep nor slumber, and there is no sense in both of us being awake."

In keeping to this routine, I set my mind and body in a mood for rest and sleep, and with a good night's sleep, I can face almost anything.

⌘⌘⌘⌘⌘

"Come to me, all you who are weary and burdened,
and I will give you rest."
Matthew 11:28

MAY 5

...LISTENING WITHOUT ANSWERING

"A man who listens because he has nothing to say
can hardly be a source of inspiration.
The only listening that counts is that of the talker
who alternately absorbs and expresses ideas."
- Agnes Repplier

⌘⌘⌘⌘⌘

People want to talk to you; most simply do not know how. They will use any excuse – even the weather. Many times they do not want a reply; just a head nod will do.

I was on my way back to Indiana from California. The airlines had strapped a piece of white sticky tape to my luggage handle that read "IND" so, hopefully, my luggage would end up in the same place I did. I had to change planes in Dallas/Ft. Worth. As I was dragging my luggage through the check point, the woman checking the baggage looked at the IND, then me and the IND and me and finally asked, "Are you from Indiana?" I nodded yes. She smiled and continued, "Don't you love the change of seasons there? Isn't October beautiful? I will never forget the October sky in Indiana! And the people; they are so friendly. Do you realize that they actually look at your face when they talk to you?" This woman was delighted in talking with me because of a piece of white sticky tape and because I nodded yes.

Listening doesn't always mean answering. Sometimes listening is a nod and a smile and a momentary bonding of two individuals who have come together for one brief moment in time. No answers are required. All that is required is acceptance. This type of listening is the art form; the ideal. It is devoid of thinking of a clever cliche, an immediate bottom line solution, or a oneupsmanship. It is listening for the sake of listening. It is making the other person's thoughts and ideas important and allowing his or her life and your life to cross paths and engage in the fellowship of mankind.

⌘⌘⌘⌘⌘

"He who has an ear, let him hear."
Revelation 13:9

MAY 6

...LIMITING TECHNOLOGY THAT DOES NOT SUIT YOU

> "The danger always exists that our technology will serve
> as a buffer between us and nature, a block between us
> and the deeper dimensions of our own experience."
>
> - Rollo May

⌘⌘⌘⌘⌘

I've always liked the phrase "doesn't suit you." It says a lot to me because I wear many suits. They are fitted, appropriate, and selected with a great deal of thought. Consequently, in my life, if something doesn't suit me, then it means to me that it does not fit, is not appropriate, or wouldn't be selected by me for me, my personality, or lifestyle.

Some technology and I are suited for one another. [For example, this laptop computer and I are fast friends.] I love my technological advanced kitchen aids, automobiles and planes. As with all things, there are some that lend themselves more to our needs than others.

Recently, I was asked by a university if I would be interested in facilitating some classes for an "on-line" MBA degree program. I responded that I would not. The people from the university were curious as to why. I told them that while I could see the benefit from this type of program that the philosophy behind it did not "suit" me.

My goal in life is to help people enhance their personal and professional development by being a better communicator. It is fine tuning the one-on-one in communication. How can we go into teams, organizations and groups thinking we can communicate well when we can't communicate one-on-one? It's the type of communication where you can see another human being's lips move and understand the spoken and the unspoken words. You can't do this "on-line."

It's important for us to know what technology "suits" us and our ethics and values. What we have passion for, we excel at and with. What we feel in our heart comes out of our mind in words that ring true to others. They, too, feel our passion. I have listened to speakers, and even done a few presentations myself, for which they or I was not suited. Each and all failed miserably!

Select what technology suits you, and the level of contentment and happiness you feel with yourself will far surpass any inconvenience that is created by those you eliminate.

⌘⌘⌘⌘⌘

"A little yeast works through the whole batch of dough."
Galatians 5:9

MAY 7
...CHANGING HORSES IN MID-STREAM

"The absurd man is he who never changes."
- Auguste Barthelemy

⌘⌘⌘⌘⌘

I know we have been told not to change horses in mid-stream; but if the horse you are on isn't going anywhere or, worse yet, going in the opposite direction of your chosen destination, just getting wet by changing horses in mid-stream is a small price to pay.

At the Indianapolis Entrepreneurship Academy I met many interesting people, some of whom became friends. One friend, Ruth Hamner, had started a company called Tapping Resources devoted to helping older women learn new skills to re-enter the workforce. She also started a support group and produced a dynamite newsletter.

Ruth's husband works for a telecommunication company, and due to local downsizing, they relocated to Raleigh-Durham. Ruth knew she was faced with the task of starting her business all over again. Before unpacking her office, she decided to get her new home in order, and one of her projects involved much painting. Through a series of events, she began to paint furniture and pictures on furniture and now she has more demand for her "painting" work than she has time to supply painted pieces.

One day while we were talking, she lamented the fact that she had – again – changed horses. I was amazed. She is successful, busy and happy in this new career.

We learn from all paths we take and from all horses we ride. Every now and then we learn that we don't want to be on a particular course, or that the horse we are on is not the right ride for us. When we dismount, we will get wet, may fall in swirling water, and expend some extra energy in finding a new mount. However, we will find the mount that is meant for us, dry off, and head off on a course we are happy to be taking.

⌘⌘⌘⌘⌘

"May the Lord direct your hearts into God's love
and Christ's perserverance."
2 Thessalonians 3:5

MAY 8
...BEING CAREFUL WITH CRITICISM

> "We are better able to study our neighbors than ourselves,
> and their actions than our own."
> - A. K. Thomson

⌘⌘⌘⌘⌘

For many years I worked with a guidance counselor who was very wise. She was more of a listener than a talker (a good trait for a guidance counselor) and had the habit of letting you hang yourself when you deserved to be hung.

I was teaching seventh graders at the time. One student was a girl who got on my nerves. I was in the teacher's lounge complaining about this girl. She was so prissy, couldn't ever get dirty, and her clothes and her hair had to be perfect. The boys even sharpened her pencils for her. I went on and on with my grumblings. I didn't realize the guidance counselor was letting me make my own noose. When I finished my tirade, she asked me if I knew why the girl was like that. An interesting question to which I hadn't given much thought. The counselor told me that the girl behaved that way because her mother was a lesbian, playing the male role, living with another woman. [This was something that you didn't talk about in the early 70's.]

Needless to say, I suddenly did the ever-popular paradigm shift about this child. Here I was – the adult, the educated, the teacher, the leader. Here I was - the biased, the embarrassed, the uninformed, the saddened. I, who was trained to help young people be all they could be, had been unable to get past the prissiness of a little girl. I would have been much better off if I had remembered the motto of the Cherokee: Grant that I may not criticize my neighbor until I have walked a mile in his moccasins.

I had lost sight of the fact that many people, especially those who are not responsible for their situation, are too often criticized when understood would be more appropriate. This was a situation that I have made a concerted effort to correct. I have learned that there are two types of criticism: constructive and destructive. Most of us lean toward the destructive. The "you're ugly and you'll always be ugly" type of criticism that gives you no place to go and no way to improve. With no options, we make no effort.

⌘⌘⌘⌘⌘

> "You, therefore, have no excuse, you who pass judgment on someone
> else, for at whatever point you judge the other, you are condemning
> yourself, because you who pass judgment do the same things."
> Romans 2:1

MAY 9
...SHARING ENTHUSIASM

"Nothing great was ever achieved without enthusiasm."
- Emerson

⌘⌘⌘⌘⌘

We all know that we all go through bad times at some point is our life's journey. The nice thing is that seldom are we all going through bad times at the same time. There is usually someone we can speak to who can lend an enthusiastic hand to help us out of our emotional abyss. Ruth is that type of friend to me. I can be in a pretty foul mood, call Ruth, listen to her go on -- and I might add at top speed -- and before you know it, I'm smiling ear to ear.

We all need at least one friend like Ruth. The type of friend who has such enthusiasm for life that it can't help but be contagious. This wonderful contagion helps us smile when we don't feel like smiling, laugh when we don't feel like laughing, and stand tall when we feel as if the weight of the world is on our shoulders. It allows us to be lifted from our emotional basement to the balcony.

Thank God for friends like Ruth who have enthusiasm, and more important, share their enthusiasm with others.

⌘⌘⌘⌘⌘

"And do not forget to do good and to share with others,
for with such sacrifices God is pleased."
Hebrews 13:16

MAY 10
...KID'S PLAY WORKS WELL FOR ADULTS

"The older I grow the more earnestly I feel that the few
intense joys of childhood are the best that life has to give."
- Ellen Glasgow

⌘⌘⌘⌘⌘

I was told at a conference on working with adults that adults are just babies
in big bodies. I certainly agree in my own case. I still have a thousand "little girl"
loves. One of my major loves is playing dress up, but, at my age, I call it
reorganizing my closet. Gina enjoys this, also.

We each have so many responsibilities at business and at home that we get
little chance to play. So, when we do have time, we play really hard! Every now
and then, when our husbands are out of town at the same time, we have a slumber
party extravaganza!

We start the day off early with brunch. We clean out closets and decide
what looks fabulous, what we can live without, and what needs to be accessorized.
We then go shopping for "must haves" and accessories. [Once I was given a T-
shirt with a 1960's Prom Queen photo on it with copy that read "Every morning I
get up and thank God for my ability to accessorize."] Our shopping spree is
followed by a high fat, high calorie dinner and topped off with desserts (you will
notice that desserts is plural).

During our "playtime" we laugh, we hug, and we are silly. Sometimes we
cry. We share. We giggle. Basically, we do all the fun stuff we did as little girls.
It's wonderful, and it's a break from being an adult.

⌘⌘⌘⌘⌘

"Blessed is the man who does not condemn
himself by what he approves."
Romans 14:22

MAY 11

...APPRECIATING "WOODWORK" FRIENDS

"To be capable of steady friendship or lasting love, are the two
greatest proofs, not only of goodness of heart, but of strength of mind."

- William Hazlitt

⌘⌘⌘⌘⌘

I'm reminded of an old song that states "Make new friends, but keep the
old; one is silver, and the other's gold." During life's journey I think we have two
other types of friends. The first is "staple" friends: those we'll have forever. The
second type is "woodwork" friends: those who come out of the woodwork every
now and then, and with whom we reconnect.

Quarterly, I send out a newsletter for my business. It contains information
I've researched on a new topic, what's going on in a specific industry, and bits and
pieces about improving communication. It shows my friends and clients that I'm
still in business, and it is a great way to keep in touch. An additional benefit of the
newsletter is that I never fail to get a call from several of my woodwork friends: the
people I want to keep in touch with but find doing so difficult because so much of
my time is filled with other priorities. We usually don't connect on the first call.
It takes several rounds of telephone tag through voice mail, but, eventually, we
connect.

It's wonderful to find out how they are doing, what is going on in their lives,
and reminisce. We usually make time for lunch and spend two pleasant hours
catching up.

The next quarterly newsletter mailing, the same thing happens with a
different set of woodwork friends. This coming out of the woodwork helps keep a
worn path between two people and provides the human shelter we all need in
good times and in bad.

⌘⌘⌘⌘⌘

"A man who has friends must show himself friendly."

Proverbs 18:24

MAY 12
...STOPPING BEFORE YOU REACH THE END OF YOUR ROPE

"The question should be, it it worth trying to do, not can it be done?"
- Allard Lowenstein

⌘⌘⌘⌘⌘

Having been forced to climb a rope in my high school physical education class, I know that hanging on to the end of a knotted, hairy, prickly, rough piece of hemp to save myself from falling is not one of the more pleasant things in life. Undoubtedly, somewhere along the line, we forget that hanging on to the end of our rope is not pleasant because too many of us too many times keep going and going until we have, again, reached the end of our rope.

Stan was attending a week long medical conference in Las Vegas. He said most of the attendees were taking their spouses, and he wanted to know if I would like to go with him. I said yes hesitantly.

The only time I had to spare was a three-day weekend. I realized I would be spending most of two of the days on flights. I was getting a section of the book ready for the printer, finishing up a class for my DBA (Doctorate of Business Administration), packing for a move to a new house the following week, and, the day after I returned home I had a three hour, one way drive to do a 9:00 am presentation for a client. Somehow, packing for the trip, sitting on a plane, being rushed to get so much done in a very short time, and returning phone calls while away didn't seem like much of a break! But I went to be with my husband.

It had been four years since we had gone on our last vacation. I had forgotten how refreshing "getting away from it all — or at least part" can be.

On Monday morning when I kissed my husband good-bye and headed for the terminal, all I could do was cry. I cried in the shuttle van, while checking in my luggage, while standing in line for my ticket, and during most of the flights home. I was crying because I was over-booked, over-worked, lonesome, worn out, unhappy, and, once more, at the end of my rope. Once more I realized I was hanging at the end of a knotted, hairy, prickly, rough piece of hemp. Why did I let it go this far — again?

How much happier we would all be if, when we realize we are running out of rope, we grab on with both feet and hands for a better hold and stop long before we get in that uncomfortable position that only comes at the end of our rope?

⌘⌘⌘⌘⌘

"Now is the acceptable time."
2 Corinthians 6:2

...CALLING IN FOR MESSAGES

"Goodness is easier to recognize than to define."
- W. H. Auden

⌘⌘⌘⌘⌘

I know I can live without a car phone; I just don't want to. I know I don't have to call in for messages; I just enjoy it. I know this luxury costs me money; I'm willing to pay.

The main reason I got my car phone was traffic. I would be going somewhere to do a presentation, get caught in traffic, and begin to stress out over not being able to make it on time. Hence, the phone. I might still be late; but if I could call, I would not be stressed because my client would know where I was and what had happened.

Another wonderful reason for having a car phone is to be able to call in for messages. As a presenter, you get yourself psyched up for the presentation. Adrenaline runs fast during the presentation. Then you hear the applause, and you know it's over. The rush of adrenaline leaves, and you bottom out. Calling in for messages (especially when you have some) is a great pick-me-up. You get that great call from a client finally booking a date for a presentation or a call telling you how much a client appreciated the work you did for their company or a call from someone who just got your newsletter and wanted to say "well done."

One day, after hearing four spectacular messages and hanging up with a huge smile on my face, I thought how nice it would be if there were many places to call in for good messages: a modern day gospel that puts a lilt in your voice, a song in your heart, and a bounce in your step. Good messages and the gospel have a lot in common; they both lift your spirits.

⌘⌘⌘⌘⌘

"I commend you to God and to the message of his grace,
a message that is able to build you up and to give you the inheritance."
Acts 20:32

MAY 14
...NOT LAMENTING A LOST CAREER

"Each individual has his own kind of living assigned
to him by the Lord as a sort of sentry post
so that he may not heedlessly wander throughout life."
- John Calvin

❏❏❏❏❏

Once I learned about goal setting and what you could achieve when you planned for things, I set my goals high. In the past fifteen years I have achieved much in my personal life, my education, my career, and my finances.

When I see how far I have come in a relative short period of time, I sometimes lament the fact that it had taken me so long to understand the way to achieve success. Like everyone else, I have had times when I wished I had been born rich and pretty and with the mind of a genius. I lamented the fact that I have had to learn all by myself and wondered where the people were who could have helped me years ago?

I also lamented the 14 years I spent in teaching. Where could I be now if I had focused on my career 30 years ago instead of 15 years ago? After much introspection, the answer is probably not as far as I am now.

In the 14 years I spent teaching I learned many things: patience with others, that all people are not gifted in the same areas, how to recognize when you are not reaching someone and try another approach, compassion for what others are going through, using humor when it it desperately needed, organization of new material, and much, much more.

It occurred to me that I had no need to lament those years I spent in teaching. It taught me things I could not have learned any other way in any other environment.

None of us should lament time spent in careers. We learn something from every endeavor, even if it is to learn what we don't want in the next career.

❏❏❏❏❏

"...his work will be shown for what it is,
because the Day will bring it to light."
1 Corinthians 3:13

MAY 15

...BECOMING A PLATE SPINNER

"Nothing is particularly hard if you divide it into small jobs."

- Henry Ford

⌘⌘⌘⌘⌘

When I was a little girl, my mother took me to the circus every time it came to town. I was always interested in the animal acts; I didn't care much about anything else that was going on. One act I found particularly boring, as a child, was the plate spinner. He tried to make it look as difficult and astounding as he could, but it always fell short of lions, tigers, and bears. Oh, my!

As an adult, I've had another paradigm shift. This time it's about the plate spinner. I now appreciate what he did and how truly astounding his act was. If we are to accomplish all the things in life we want to accomplish, we must become a plate spinner.

Gina and I once attended a healthy eating seminar, and after the four hours of instruction, we were determined to drink eight glasses of water each day and walk at least 30 minutes each day. We went home and cleaned out all the high fat items from the cupboard and then went to the store and bought all the low fat, low sodium and fresh items the healthy eating seminar leader listed for us. We made a spread sheet to count calories, fat and exercise time.

On a daily basis we were going to eat one banana, one apple, and one orange, and fish and sweet potatoes twice a week. It worked great — for one day.

I now realize we were trying to do it all at once. We couldn't, and so we failed miserably. What we should have done was start with one thing, just as the plate spinner starts with one plate. We should have started with drinking eight glasses of water a day, made it a hard and firm habit and then added walking 30 minutes each day to the schedule until that was also a hard and firm habit. The way the plate spinner gets all the plates going by spinning one plate well and then going on to the next.

Doing one thing well requires maintenance. While maintaining one thing, it is easier to start something new and be successful at both.

⌘⌘⌘⌘⌘

"The boundary lines have fallen for me in pleasant places;"

Psalm 16:6

MAY 16
...GETTING LOST IN NOVELS

"The practice of fiction can be dangerous;
it puts ideas into the head of the world."

- Anthony Burgess

⌘⌘⌘⌘⌘

In *Gates of Excellence*, Katherine Paterson wrote, "A great novel is a kind of conversion experience. We come away from it changed."

I grew up with novels. My mother saved her money; and when she had enough, she bought me a set of Encyclopedia Britannica. With this set of encyclopedias came 10 classics: *Black Beauty, Tom Sawyer, Huckleberry Finn, Connecticut Yankee, Lassie, Call of the Wild, Heidi, Little Women, Little Men,* and *Treasure Island.* These novels helped create a special bond between my mother and me. My mother had to work when I was little, so our special time together was at bedtime. She would get one of the novels out and read to me as I went to sleep. I would dream of horses and pirates and riverboats. She told me I became insistent about being read to. Even when I had the measles and couldn't have the lights on, I had her read by flashlight. To this day, we still talk about those classics. They're a very special shared memory.

I went to school knowing the classics. Each summer my mother signed me up for a new Book of the Month Club, and I began to read *Nancy Drew, The Hardy Boys,* and *Clara Barton, Student Nurse.* I found out I loved mysteries!!! I still have a complete collection of Agatha Christie.

I majored in English literature in college because I had developed a passion for the extraordinary worlds that novels create for the ordinary person. I could be in the Swiss Alps one week and on a Mississippi riverboat the next. I learned about having brothers and sisters when I was an only child. I developed a love for animals and what they give to human kind. I learned about the human experience of many people. I learned about overcoming adversity and being strong. And, most important, I learned to get lost temporarily in the imaginary world that these novels created.

The set of classics I received with the encyclopedia has long since turned to dust, but the memories and the worlds they created and my mind, which they expanded, will last my lifetime.

⌘⌘⌘⌘⌘

"Poverty and shame shall be to him that refuseth instruction."

Proverbs 13:18

MAY 17
...LOOKING DEEPER

"New ways of seeing can disclose new things: the radio telescope
revealed quasars and pulsars, and the scanning electron
microscope showed the whiskers of the dust mite. But turn the
question around: Do new things make the new ways of seeing?"
- William Least Heat Moon

⌘⌘⌘⌘⌘

I think we believe we are actually looking at something when we are really
only seeing. Seeing is the physical action; looking is the added attention of the
mind.

When I was single, I had an extended family of 11 single women friends.
We met through work connections and introductions from others. We got
together as a group about once a month for a very nice dinner and some
wonderful conversation. The more we saw one another, the more time we took
looking deeper at each other and what each had accomplished.

Agnes went to the women's prison once a week and discussed the women
in the Bible with many of the inmates. Phyllis had taken flying lessons and had
flown Highway 1 all the way to Alaska. Janet and Sharon also flew planes. Dottie
had taken a walking tour through Europe. Cheryl rode and showed jumpers in
international competition. Their lists of accomplishments could go on and on.
Here was a group of "ordinary" women who had done "extra-ordinary" things in
their lives.

You could see their age, the color of their hair, their facial structure. You
could see the physical. But it was only by looking deeper that you could
understand and appreciate that part of them — the non-visible part – that really
made them who and what they were.

⌘⌘⌘⌘⌘

"The spirit searches all things,
even the deep things of God."
1 Corinthians 2:10

MAY 18
...ESTABLISHED PLANTS SURVIVE

"Whatever is formed for long duration arrives slowly to its maturity."
- Samuel Johnson

⌘⌘⌘⌘⌘

There is something so special about day lilies. I love their colors, delicacy, and freshness. They make you feel cheerful just by looking at them. I thin them out each spring and share them with friends or start new beds. It's one way to share beauty with others in this world.

This spring while visiting our local nursery I saw a new shade of day lily. It was a cross between yellow and orange, and I fell in love. I took it home and planted it amid the white day lilies.

As is typical in Indiana, spring is a little "iffy." And sure enough, the evening I planted my new day lily, it frosted, and the new day lily died, but the white day lilies were fine; they survived the frost. I realized that it is the established plants that survive. Established plants are a little older. Their roots go a little deeper. They are a little bigger. They are a little stronger. They have survived hot sun, drought, frost, and freeze. They are alive because they are strong.

Occasionally, don't we bemoan what age and time have done to us? We complain of aches and pains and sagging this and that. They are just part of the aging process: the process that establishes us and allows us to survive. With each season we learn more. With each season we become a little deeper in thought and wisdom. With each season our hearts become a little bigger. And, with each season we become stronger and stronger. With each season we become survivors, and we will endure.

⌘⌘⌘⌘⌘

"Even youths grow tired and weary,
and young men stumble and fall;
but those who hope in the Lord
will renew their strength."
Isaiah 40:30-31

MAY 19
...NOT FALLING FOR CLICHES

"A dull old saw that everyone borrows but no one sharpens."

- Anonymous

⌘⌘⌘⌘⌘

Somewhere, someone, some time has developed a cliche for nearly each and every situation. Which cliche we use depends on the situation and how we feel about the person(s) involved.

If we need to take action on a situation, we can either "look before we leap" or remember "he who hesitates is lost." Depending on our trust level with a person who is going away for awhile, we can believe that "absence makes the heart grow fonder" or "out of sight, out of mind."

If we are looking at investing money, we can believe "waste not, want not" or "you have to prime the pump." Wherever, whoever, whenever, there is a cliche to fit the occasion.

Cliches sound so good — like sage – that we tend to believe them instantly. We believe them not understanding or being familiar with their opposing cliche.

Use cliches wisely. In their brevity they may impart years of wisdom in thimbleful doses, but, as with each coin or dog or story, there are always two sides.

⌘⌘⌘⌘⌘

"...let the wise listen and add to their learning,
and let the discerning get guidance —
for understanding proverbs and parables,
the sayings and riddle of the wise."

Proverbs 1:5-6

MAY 20
...LOOKING UP

"There is no way in which to understand the world
without first detecting it through the radar-net of our senses."
                                                    - Diane Ackerman

⌘⌘⌘⌘⌘

There are certain passages or measures in our music where our choir
director asks us to look up at the congregation. It is a connection we make, even
if it is with just one person, that gets them to think about the words and lets them
know that it is important for them to sing, also. It is a blending of not only notes
and voices but of spirits.

When your face is buried in the music you never know what impact you are
making. Your voice projects into the paper when it should project to the
congregation. You miss shared smiles and wistful thoughts, and you truly lose out
on seeing their appreciation for the music you sing.

We get letters from members of the congregation telling the choir how
much they enjoyed a particular piece, who and what it reminded them of, and how
it met the need or fulfilled what they were looking for that particular day. One
Sunday, when I was making my usual trip to the church office to turn in our
offering, the secretary behind the desk asked me why I was turning it in the office
and not in the basket. I told her the choir never gets the basket. She smiled and
responded, "The choir shouldn't have to pay money. You are so wonderful in
what you give to the congregation with your music that it is more than enough."
What a sweet thing to say!

Ursula K. Le Guin wrote, "It had never occurred to me before that music
and thinking are so much alike. In fact you could say music is another way of
thinking, or maybe thinking is another kind of music." By looking up at the
congregation, we blend music, voices, ideas, and thoughts.

⌘⌘⌘⌘⌘

"Each of you should look not only to your own interests,
but also to the interests of others."
                                                    Philippians 2:4

MAY 21

...LAUGHING AT THE PAST

"The past is our definition. We may strive, with good reason,
to escape it, or to escape what is bad in it,
but we will escape it only by adding something better to it."
- Wendell Berry

⌘⌘⌘⌘⌘

I've noticed that the past is difficult to laugh at when it is the present. In the present we are so concerned with image and embarrassment, that laughter over something we have done is usually the last thing on your mind.

I was raised in my grandmother's home. Our home consisted of my grandmother, mother, two aunts, two female cousins, and me. [Yes, seven women under one roof.] Being an old-fashioned house, there was only one, centrally located bathroom. [Yes, seven women under one roof with only one bathroom.] Privacy was hard to come by.

I think I was in the fourth grade: a very impressionable time in a young girl's life because she is just starting to mature. I had been in the bathroom during my time slot, and I had no idea that company, including my two uncles, had arrived. I jumped out of the tub, grabbed my dirty clothes in my arms, and began my mad dash for my upstairs bedroom. I was too far from the bathroom door to retreat gracefully. I was in the middle of the dining room before I realized I was standing stark naked in front of 11 people. And, in a very sophisticated fourth grade manner, I screamed, ran upstairs, and refused to come out of my room until all the company had left.

It took me a long time to laugh at this. Actually, I think I was in college before this became amusing. (Now this story is well known. I laugh at the circumstances just as others and know that I have learned humor and tolerance of myself.)

⌘⌘⌘⌘⌘

"Is not wisdom found among the aged?
Does not long life bring understanding?"
Job 12:12

...KNOWING MEMORY AND IMAGINATION ARE NOT THE SAME

"The memory represents to us not what we choose but what it pleases."
- Montaigne

⌘⌘⌘⌘⌘

Have you ever noticed that when people gossip they don't restrict themselves to the truth? Typically they take each story and embellish, elaborate, and expand it making it more entertaining and interesting.

I think memory is very similar. Didn't all of our parents walk at least 14 miles to school each day? And, with the retelling of the story, didn't the distance increase? Weren't the Christmases either Currier & Ives or National Lampoon with no in between? Weren't grandparents either sinners or saints? Wasn't our dog the prettiest, smartest, or meanest in the neighborhood? Memory is selective; we remember what we choose to remember and how we wish to remember it.

Time seems to have a way of changing memory into imagination. The funny becomes more funny, the tragic more tragic, and the outrageous more outrageous.

Imagination can lessen pain to the point of erasing it from our memory entirely. We remember broken bones and that we hurt, but we really can't remember the pain. Imagination stretches family happenings and humor to the breaking point. I think this is why so many family satires exist as entertainment.

Imagination is the artist that paints the memory for others to see. With time, memory and imagination become one.

⌘⌘⌘⌘⌘

"One man considers one day more sacred than another;
another man considers every day alike.
Each one should be fully convinced in his own mind."
Romans 14:5

MAY 23

...KNOWING YOU CAN PLAY ANY ROLE IF YOU HAVE THE RIGHT COSTUME

"Perhaps one never seems so much at one's ease as when one has to play a part."

- Oscar Wilde

⌘⌘⌘⌘⌘

Haven't you read many articles about being a good leader? How many articles have you read about being a good follower? There seems to be a plethora of the first and an absence of the second. This could be because the traits necessary to be a good leader are also the traits necessary to be a good follower.

Don't we all spout wonderful quotes on leadership? How many of us use quotes on "followership"? Are there any? Yes. The quotes you spout on leadership can be the same for followership.

No matter who we are, depending on where we are at any given moment, our roles can change. We just need to know what our costume is at that time. When I'm in front of an audience, I'm a presenter or leader. When I'm at home with my husband and step-children, I'm a wife and step-mother. When I'm with my mother, I'm her daughter. When I'm at home by myself with the dogs, I'm a kid or a puppy mom. When I'm on the phone with friends, I'm a friend.

Our costumes are in our mind as well as on our back. One of my mental costumes is that of status and education. Another mental costume is of validation and intimacy. Which of these traits are for leaders and which are for followers?

We take who and what we are and structure it to the audience and interaction at the time. As Bev Gallagher, a friend from church, said, "I can play any role; just give me the costume."

⌘⌘⌘⌘⌘

"Then you will understand what is right and just and fair —
every good path. For wisdom will enter your heart,
and knowledge will be pleasant to your soul.
Discretion will protect you, and understanding will guard you."

Proverbs 2:9-11

MAY 24

...HEARING THE MUSIC AND NOT JUST THE NOTES

"Music relates to sound and time
and so pictures the ultimate edges of human communication."

- Iris Murdock

⌘⌘⌘⌘⌘

As I have mentioned before, our church choir has some really impressive member. In addition to having wonderful voices, many of them are incredible musicians. Several members play piano. We have a husband and wife team who play in a string quartet, two flutists who play in a quartet, trumpeters, bell ringers, etc.

When our director picks a piece of music that would blend beautifully with additional instruments, he will ask one of the musicians to accompany us. The strings, brass, and tympani add so much to the sound.

One Sunday, the string quartet was playing with us. We were presenting "Jesu, Joy of Man's Desiring." The congregation was entranced, and so was I. In fact, I got so entranced and hypnotized by the sound of the strings, I kept missing the up-take from our director. I was hearing the music and not just the notes.

The individual notes make up the piece, but by themselves, the impact lessens. It takes all of the notes together to be effective. Just one voice from the choir does not have the same kind of impact as the full choir. Just one stringed instrument does not have the same kind of impact of the quartet.

It takes unity — pulling it all together — to get lost or entranced in the music not just the notes. Notes are momentary; music endures forever.

⌘⌘⌘⌘⌘

"How good and pleasant it is
when brothers live together in unity."

Psalm 133:1

MAY 25
...UNDERSTANDING SUCCESS IS BLENDING PASSION AND PRACTICE

"Only passions, great passions, can elevate the soul to great things."
- Denis Diderot

⌘⌘⌘⌘⌘

Because Corporate Masters, my company, has had a degree of success, I am asked to give presentations for many organizations on starting a speaking career. I give them techniques for keeping your voice healthy, camouflaging nervousness, organizing material, and getting yourself known in the community and corporations.

Although these points are very important, they are not the most important. The two points that are the most important in starting a presenting or speaking business is to 1) have passion for what you are saying and 2) practice, practice, practice.

I have asked my audiences to remember a time when people presented to them without practicing, and the presenter had to read their material word for word. What was the audience's interest level when the speaker never made eye contact with them and read in a monotone? Their interest level, as an audience, was probably the same as the interest level of the presenter: not too high. I also asked them to remember a time when they listened to someone present a subject that the presenter had no interest in or passion for. It's terrible, and most people, including the presenter, end up watching the clock waiting for the ordeal to be over. This is not good for repeat business, referrals, and letters of recommendation: three "must haves" for a speaker.

I ask my audience if anyone knows the old joke about how you get to Carnegie Hall: "Practice, practice, practice." That is how you learn to do anything well. Practice will help develop proficiency.

And, the passion? It is the blending of the mind and, more important, the heart. It can be seen, felt, and heard. It shows genuineness and commitment. It is the understanding of the information not just the information.

Words spoken with practice and passion remain long after the sound of the voice is gone.

⌘⌘⌘⌘⌘

"Commit to the Lord whatever you do,
and your plans will succeed."
Proverbs 16:3

MAY 26
...HAVING NO MEAN NO

"Courage is not a virtue or value among other personal values
like love or fidelity. It is the foundation that underlies
and gives reality to all other virtues and personal values."
- Rollo May

⌘⌘⌘⌘⌘

For being just a two-letter, one-syllable word, NO is very difficult to say at times. And even more difficult than saying it is sticking to it and having NO mean NO. To compound the matter, it is also a difficult word for others to understand. When others hear No, their mind usually registers a MAYBE.

Ben, my step-son, is a very gifted person in many areas including athletics. His athletic ability earned him a Football Scholarship to Purdue. Even if you are not a sports enthusiast (and I'm not), when you know someone who is playing on the field, the game becomes more interesting. I had the pleasure of watching him play for Purdue for four years.

There were a few games that I did not attend due to inclement weather. My career is my voice. I know that my voice will take wet, and it will take cold, but it will not take wet and cold together. When it was close to freezing and raining and I had a presentation to do the next week, I told my husband that I couldn't go. He would try to talk me into it, but I would still say no. [It took him a while to realize that most of my no's don't mean maybe.]

My husband was not as happy with me as when I did go to the games because we are not only married, but we are also best friends. He likes to have his best friend with him, and I am certainly glad of that. I did not like saying no, but I knew if I went, I would worry about getting sick. I'd be unhappy and angry with myself for going, then I probably would get sick. I would be angry with my husband because I wouldn't have been there if it weren't for him. This would not be a good relationship for friends or husbands and wives.

There are definitely times when NO has to mean NO. I have learned over the years to try not to speak in absolutes. There are times when I have made an absolute statement and ended up eating my words, and they were not very palatable. Most NO's are not everlasting; but if their use in a situation is of major importance to you, they must be considered.

⌘⌘⌘⌘⌘

"Be on your guard; stand firm in the faith;
be men of courage; be strong."
1 Corinthians 16:13

MAY 27
...HAVING FAITH IN THE FUTURE

"The future is plump with promise."
- Maya Angelou

⌘⌘⌘⌘⌘

I cannot begin to tell you how many conversations Gina and I have had about writing books. What can we write about? What do we have or know that makes us special? When will we ever find time? Who will buy it? How can we support ourselves while we are writing? Who can we share our ideas with? Etc. The list was endless. Finally, we had both started so many books and put them aside that we decided whatever it took, we would write a book.

We realized to have the time to write we were going to have to shut down part of our life temporarily. We became plate spinners, and the first plate became authorship. Our families and the people we worked with were notified, and to our pleasant surprise, they were more than willing to let us devote our time to our writing. At times they even showed interest!

The one question that kept coming back to us was could we make a living at this? We both had to have faith in our future.

For two business women, who had usually been sure of what they were doing, relying on something unsure was a new experience. We couldn't verify it, put it on a spread sheet, or forecast its future based on past results. It wasn't based on logic, conclusions, or bottom lines.

The faith in our future was based on the fact that "with God, all things are possible." We are His children, and He wants the best for us. We didn't need a psychic line or a crystal ball. We finally realized that we had what we needed to succeed: faith in our future based on the growth — spiritually and professionally — that we had achieved to date.

⌘⌘⌘⌘⌘

"'So there is hope for your future,' declares the Lord."
Jeremiah 31:17

MAY 28
...NEVER LOSING YOUR SENSE OF HUMOR

"Humor is an affirmation of dignity,
a declaration of man's superiority to all the befalls him."
- Romain Gary

⌘⌘⌘⌘⌘

When you grow up in a family of practical jokers, humor, although never common place, is a standard. The crazy things our family members have done to one another gives us something to talk about during the holidays, and it lets our friends understand why we are the way we are. We are a product of our environment.

My mother had the most dry sense of humor of us all. You could almost see the dust roll out of her mouth as she talked. You would hear her voice but couldn't actually believe that she had said what she said.

Her humor was not limited to lines; she played incredible pranks, also. The year I became a member of Job's Daughters I wanted a Job's Daughters' ring for Christmas. I made sure my mother knew this. My hints were well taken, and she bought me the black onyx ring I wanted. Now, she couldn't just put it in a ring box, wrap it, and put it under the tree. No, not my mother. She bought a box of Cracker Jacks, opened the paper the prize was wrapped in, took out the prize, put the ring in the wrapper, put the wrapper in the box, wrapped the box, and put it under the tree.

When anyone asked me where I got my Job's Daughters' ring, I had to respond, "Out of a box of Cracker Jacks."

Laughter and humor are for enjoyment, healing, memories, and appreciation.

⌘⌘⌘⌘⌘

"The uneven ground shall become level,
and the rough places a plain."
Isaiah 40:4

MAY 29
...LOVING AND LEARNING FROM GOD'S CREATURES

"Nothing but the forms of our virtues and vices,
wandering before our eyes, the visible phantoms of our souls."
- Victor Hugo

⌘⌘⌘⌘⌘

The other day I was listening to a radio talk program. A woman was talking about animals and pets, and she made a point I had never consciously thought about before. She said that we, human beings, are the only creatures that take in other creatures to care for. In the animal kingdom, each creature tries to eliminate as many other creatures as possible to help assure themselves and their offspring of a better chance of survival.

My husband and I have two semi-pet ducks. The female, whom we called Granny, had an injured foot when she first came to our house. She had a terrible time walking. She would just hobble and drag her injured foot. The drake, whom we called Bubba, would stand and guard her as she ate and slept. He was doing all he could to help her make it. We, too, were doing all we could do to help her survive. We built a shelter with rocks, trees, and shrubs and put out cracked corn and fresh water for them every day.

The following spring we were looking out the back window and coming down the hill was a pair of mallards. The female was limping. It was Granny and Bubba. They were looking for corn.

At the time we were trying to give Granny an extra hand, I was going through chemotherapy. One day, when Stan was watching Bubba stand guard over Granny as she was eating, he said, "You know, he is trying to take care of her while she is hurting like I'm trying to take care of you."

By learning to take care of God's creatures we learn to take care of one another. By being kind to God's creatures we learn to be kind to one another. By sharing a life with a creature that loves unconditionally maybe we, too, will learn to love less conditionally.

⌘⌘⌘⌘⌘

"For everything God created is good,
and nothing is to be rejected if it is received with thanksgiving."
1 Timothy 4:4

MAY 30
...LESSENING SORROW WITH COMPASSION

"Teach me to feel another's woe, To hide the fault I see;
The mercy I to others show, That mercy show to me."
- Alexander Pope

⌘⌘⌘⌘⌘

As mentioned before, I had breast cancer and had to go through surgery, chemotherapy, radiation therapy, and hormone therapy. I'm way past my two year mark, and I have hair, eyelashes, eyebrows, and fingernails again. Life is good.

My husband, a medical professional, knew from past experience some of what I was going to have to go through. The most difficult part of the whole ordeal was the chemotherapy. Internally, you are sick most of the time, and you are so tired. But the external changes are so visible. If the darkened eyes and skin aren't enough to give away your state of health, the hair loss certainly is.

We had been married for only two months when this occurred and were still in the honeymoon stages of our relationship. Image is always more important in the beginning.

It was the week before Christmas, and my hair had started coming out by the handfuls. I was truly devastated at the thought of having to spend Christmas in a wig. Feeling sorry for myself, I was sitting in front of the bathroom mirror crying. My husband walked in, put his hands on my shoulders and asked what was wrong. Through tears I said, "I don't want you to wake up each morning and see me bald." He squeezed my shoulders, smiled, kissed me on top of my head and said, "But, honey, you wake up seeing me bald every morning."

I burst into a flood of tears — not over the sorrow of losing my hair — but at the compassion of his remark. His love and compassion for me and what I was going through had lessened the sorrow I was feeling for myself. It reminded me of a line quoted by Virginia Woolf, "Learn to make yourself akin to people...But let this sympathy be not with the mind — for it is easy with the mind — but with the heart, with love towards them."

Yes, I made it through the chemotherapy. With love — and compassion — all things are possible.

⌘⌘⌘⌘⌘

"Finally, all of you, live in harmony with one another;
be sympathetic, love as brothers, be compassionate and humble."
1 Peter 3:8

...KNOWING WHEN WE MUST DO MAINTENANCE

"Man is the only animal for whom his own
existence is a problem which he has to solve."
- Erich Fromm

⌘⌘⌘⌘⌘

Maintenance means to keep into existence. We want to live to its fullest,
but in order to live life to its fullest, there is part of our life that must be
maintenance.

There are two types of maintenance. There is basic maintenance like
bathing, eating, cleaning and changing the oil in the car. This will continue
throughout our lifetime. Then, there is the type of maintenance that is a
temporary concentration while we are busy getting from one place to another.
These are the things we do to pay the bills and exist while we are working on a life
we enjoy living – not just existing. This type of maintenance is the part-time jobs
we take on or full-time jobs we do to keep us out of debt while we find the career -
- not job — we are after. It's the late nights of studying for an advanced degree to
go on with a different career. It's the late nights of taking care of the house
because you can't get it cleaned during the day. It's the weekends of cooking and
freezing so that you and your family will have something good to eat during the
week. This type of maintenance is the 18 hour days we are willing to put in
temporarily to get where we want to be and become who we want to become.
This second type of maintenance is paying dues. It is linked to ambition.

There is an old Danish proverb that states, " He who would leap high must
take a long run." For something to run long, it takes a lot of maintenance.

⌘⌘⌘⌘⌘

"This is a trustworthy saying. And I want you to stress these things,
so that those who have trusted in God may be careful
to devote themselves to doing what is good.
These things are excellent and profitable for everyone."
Titus 3:8

JUNE 1

...SEEING OTHERS IN NEED – AND HELPING

"How far that little candle throws his beam!
So shines a good deed in a naughty world."

- Shakespeare

⌘⌘⌘⌘⌘

I had left teaching and had taken a job at a medical equipment company. I wanted to get into marketing, and this firm told me if I would be the secretary for three months and learn the business, I could then go into marketing. So, I did.

When you are seated at the front desk, you get an opportunity to see people come and go. A woman came in to interview for a job. She did her interview and then walked into the lobby where I sat. I watched her. She walked toward the chair in front of my desk as if she were in slow motion. She gradually bent at the knees and set her purse on the chair. Then, just as slowly, she stood up and tugged at the hem of her ill fitted, newly purchased suit jacket.

I looked at her face and saw fear, sadness, and near desperation. I knew this woman was hurting. She was in need – of a friend, a life, a future. As she stood there, suspended in time, I thought that she seemed to be missing from her own life. She was disconnected.

I knew I could not let this pass. I needed to reach out to her and try to reconnect and bring her back to this world. Without thinking, I said, "Hey! My name is Suzanne. Do you want to have lunch?" She looked at me in amazement through the most incredible, luminous eyes I had ever seen and nodded yes.

At that moment I had no idea where this impulsive act would take us. I am certainly glad I committed this act because it has taken us to a wonderful friendship. "A friend in need is a friend indeed."

⌘⌘⌘⌘⌘

"The King will reply, 'I tell you the truth,
whatever you did for one of the least
of these brothers of mine, you did for me.'"

Matthew 25:40

JUNE 2
...TREATING OTHER TO A SPECIAL TIME

"All good things which exist are the fruits of originality."
- John Stuart Mill

⌘⌘⌘⌘⌘

Treat is a "special delight or pleasure." I think the key word here is "special."
It's not something that has to be done; it's an extra.

Stan and I have two good friends, Denise and Harry, who were relocated to
Illinois. Prior to their move, they lived across the street. We had impromptu dinners
together, went to concerts, helped each other out when there was a need, took cooking
classes together, and spent holidays together. They took care of our dogs when we
were out of town. We truly miss them and our everyday interaction.

Once they were settled in their new home, they ask if we would come over for a
weekend. It was tough to work in an entire weekend away. We were preparing for a
wedding and a graduation. We had both been working hard and travelling. A drive to
Illinois was just what we needed now. The weekend we were to go finally rolled
around, and almost begrudgingly, we packed the car, loaded the dogs, and headed out.

Our friends knew what a busy and stressful time we were having, so they
planned nothing for us to do. No sight seeing, dining out, running around – nothing.
It was heaven. They have a gorgeous home set in a woods. We sat on their deck and
watched the birds, rabbits, and deer. We ate every meal in and enjoyed every bite for
Denise is a wonderful cook. We played pool, watched TV, read, played with the dogs
and just sat and talked.

What a special treat this was. They knew what we had been going through and
gave us just what we need. Denise and Harry are very special people. They, by just
being who they are, are a treat in themselves, and they gracefully share themselves with
others.

⌘⌘⌘⌘⌘

"My command is this:
Love each other as I have loved you."
John 15:12

JUNE 3
...KEEPING HOPE ALIVE

"Strong hope is a much great stimulant of life
than any single realized joy could be."

- Nietzsche

⌘⌘⌘⌘⌘

Mythology was one of my favorite subjects to study and to teach. To me it was fascinating to imagine that the reason the sun shone each day was because Apollo was driving his golden chariot across the sky. Listening about the earth rotating on its axis waned in comparison.

One of my favorite stories was about Pandora. Her name means "all gifted." She had been a bride that was a gift from the gods who were secretly trying to punish mankind. Her dowry was a small jeweled box that she was to keep but never open. Since Pandora had all gifts, including curiosity, and the box was her dowry, she opened it. Before she could close the lid, out flew evil tiny winged creatures. Pandora had released evil into the world. When she realized what was flying out of the box, she slammed the lid closed. Listening intently, she heard, still contained in the box, a very weak flutter of wings. Again, being curious, she opened the lid and out flew "Hope."

Whether we want to admit it or not, hope lives within all of us. It's that little pilot light that keeps body and soul alive and going even in the darkest times. It's the inner knowing that whatever we are going through, it will not last forever. Hope is in every heart beat and every breathe and is just as necessary for our survival. When we cease to hope, we cease to live.

Hope is a good thing.

⌘⌘⌘⌘⌘

"'For I know the plans I have for you,' declares the Lord,
'plans to prosper you and not to harm you,
plans to give you hope and a future.'"

Jeremiah 29:11

JUNE 4
...APPRECIATING SILENCE

"Silence is as full of potential wisdom and wit
as the unhewn marble of great sculpture."
- Aldous Huxley

⌘⌘⌘⌘⌘

When I was in college, I had to read *Brave New World* and *1984*. They were novels that predicted what could possibly happen in futuristic societies. Both books left strong impressions on me. Every now and then I hear or see something that reminds me of something I read in one of those books.

One day I had heard just one sound too many. The loud commercials, barking dogs, ringing telephone and fax, screaming parents, screaming kids, honking horns, screeching brakes, and construction noise were just too much. I had to put a stop to it. I was truly at the point of not being able to hear myself think.

I got in my car, drove to one of the parks, and listened to nothing but the beautiful birds and running water. It was bliss.

This scene and sound of bliss reminded me of the futuristic novels. In this predicted future, people were not allowed to be alone, and there was constant noise: no peace of mind and no getting in touch with what was going on in your head.

Silence is golden and precious and, many times, hard to come by. Peace of mind also brings peace of heart and soul. It is the personal reflection time just as we have in church during silent prayer. Silence produces both calm and creativity. We need our silence to survive.

"I work out of silence, because silence makes up for my actual lack of working space. Silence substitutes for actual space, for psychological distance, for a sense of privacy and intactness. In this sense silence is absolutely necessary." Radka Donnell.

⌘⌘⌘⌘⌘

"But the Lord is in his holy temple;
let all the earth be silent before him."
Habakkuk 2:20

JUNE 5
...CULTIVATING LOYALTY

"Nothing else than an accord in all things, human and divine,
conjoined with mutual good-will and affection."

- Cicero

⌘⌘⌘⌘⌘

I wanted a dog desperately when I was in junior high and high school. I was the lonely ugly duckling, and I wanted something that would love me unconditionally. My mother got me a Shetland Sheepdog. I named him Ichabod Crane. (I'm a Washington Irving fan). I loved this dog with all my heart. He was my companion and friend.

One night the gate was not locked properly, and Ichabod got out. I came out the next morning and called for him. He did not respond. Finally, I saw him in front of the gate. His beautiful white chest and side was a mass of bloody fur. He opened his eyes and what seemed like a tear ran down his face. He wagged his tail once and closed his eyes. I knew someone had shot him.

I ran in and called my mother. She came home immediately, and we took him to the vet. The vet shaved off his fur and, after looking at him, told me there was nothing he could do. It is difficult to stitch up a dog for they rip out the stitches. The vet said the bullets could have lodged in his ribs; and in that case, he would survive.

I carried Ichabod home and made him a bed on the landing. I hand fed and watered him. I carried him out to go to the bathroom. I sat by him on the stairs for hours, petting him, and trying to get him to know how much I loved him. At the end of one week he was still alive — and improving. His fur was growing out. He could get up on his own. He could eat on his own.

Ichabod must have realized I had saved his life and must have decided that he would do whatever he could to save mine. He never left my side at home. He traveled with me, ate with me, sat with me, walked with me, and slept with me. When strangers came to the house, he sat between them and me. He would not allow anyone to touch me. There was a bond between us that was as strong as iron.

He was as loyal to me as any one or thing could be. I grieved at his passing. I had lost not only my dog but my friend and companion. I missed him, his faithfulness, and his companionship.

Cultivate loyalty. Be loyal and let people and things count on you. It comes back.

⌘⌘⌘⌘⌘

"But the fruit of the Spirit is love, joy, peace, patience, kindness,
goodness, faithfulness, gentleness and self-control."

Galatians 5:22

JUNE 6
...ELIMINATING THREE UNIMPORTANT WORDS

"There is a world of difference between a strong ego,
which is essential, and a large ego — which can be destructive."
- Lee Iacocca

⌘⌘⌘⌘⌘

In my presentations on becoming a more effective communicator, I try to get people to eliminate the words **I**, **me**, and **my** from their vocabulary. Not only are they unimportant, but they are also self centered; and when you are interacting with other people, being self centered is one of the last things you want to be. You want to be other people centered or group centered.

When I was taking classes in self-defense, our instructor told us that if we were being attacked or mugged, never to yell "Help." Help means "I'm in trouble," and there are many people who won't care if you are in trouble. You are to yell "Fire." Fire means "we're in trouble," and that's a whole different ballgame.

One Sunday during the sermon, our minister made an interesting point. He said the world's greatest documents did not contain the words **I**, **me** and **my**. The world's greatest documents are everyone focused. Don't we say "give **us** this day **our** daily bread," "**we** hold these truths to be self evident," "**our** fathers brought forth" and "**we**, the people"?

I, me and my are rather insignificant in this world. If we want to bond with others and interact with others, we must be everyone focused.

⌘⌘⌘⌘⌘

"Do not seek revenge or bear a grudge against
one of your people, but love your neighbor as yourself."
Leviticus 19:18

JUNE 7
...DONATING TIME TO OTHERS

"The charity that is a trifle to us can be precious to others."
- Homer

⌘⌘⌘⌘⌘

I make it a point to do three "free" presentation each year. I know there are some organizations out there that would like for me to come in and speak but lack the funding to hire me. Doing the "free" presentations is one way I try and give back to others.

To donate means "to present as a gift." When you give, you typically do not expect to get anything back at that time. It is amazing, however, that when you give, you usually do get back. I cannot begin to tell you how many speaking engagements I have gotten as a result of a "free" presentation. People in the audience hear me and pass my name along to other organizations, and the business comes in.

One that lives in my memory was the "free" engagement I did for an ABWA chapter. A woman in the chapter had heard me speak at one of the hospitals. She went back to her chapter and told them about me. They were very interested. She called and asked if I would speak to them. She told me they didn't have any money, but they would buy my dinner. Her solicitations were so sincere, I finally agreed to speak to her chapter. They were a very warm group and seemed very appreciative. To my surprise, the women in the chapter got together and wrote a letter to their national headquarters requesting that I be asked to speak at the next national convention. It worked! This "free" presentation lead to my speaking at my first national convention.

⌘⌘⌘⌘⌘

"In everything I did, I showed you that by this
kind of hard work we must help the weak, remembering
the words of the Lord Jesus himself said:
'It is more blessed to give than to receive.'"
- Acts 20:35

JUNE 8
...KNOWING FOR SOME THAT LOVE IS DOING

"Only the action that is moved by love for the good at hand
has the hope of being responsible and generous."
- Wendell Berry

⌘⌘⌘⌘⌘

Men live and love in a physical world. I'm not talking about just a physical relationship; I'm talking about all aspects of their life. Basically, it has been a physical world for them since birth. The games they play as little boys are physical. The humor is physical humor such as pranks. Their life has always been doing.

For women, whose world and love is more emotional, understanding how someone who lives in a physical world thinks and reacts takes a little focused thought.

It is easier for men, in general, to show that they love you rather than say that they love you. For men love is doing. It's shoveling the drive out from under the snow; it's running the vacuum when you are busy; it's holding you for a long evening. The words may not be there, but the feeling is.

When Stan does something special for me, like vacuuming down the stairs, I tell him I love him, too. When he went with me to every doctor's visit and chemotherapy injection, I knew that was his way of showing he loved me without ever saying a word. When he plays some silly practical joke on me, I know he is showing me how much he loves me.

Knowing how someone loves you is just as important as knowing that someone loves you.

⌘⌘⌘⌘⌘

"God is not unjust; he will not forget your
work and the love you have shown him as you have
helped his people and continue to help them."
Hebrew 6:10

JUNE 9

...BEING INFECTED WITH OTHER'S LAUGHTER

"The most wasted day of all is that on which you have not laughed."
                                                                    - Chamfort

⌘⌘⌘⌘⌘

My husband has a laugh – almost a giggle – that is absolutely infectious. Just hearing and seeing him laugh puts everyone is a good mood. One time he had an entire plane of people laughing – not because they knew what he had done – but because they had heard him laugh.

With his daughter Sarah, Stan and I were headed to Orlando. [Every couple of years we try to theme park ourselves to death.] The flight attendants had gone through the plane serving us breakfast. Stan is a big "cut up" around Sarah; and when the two of them are together, they are constantly doing something. He had a small amount of scrambled eggs on his plate. He put them on his fork and asked Sarah if she knew the "correct" technique for flipping food. He pulled the tines of the fork back as if he were going to really flip the eggs. The tines of the fork were slippery; they slipped out of his fingers, and eggs went flying – ending up in the hair of a woman sitting three rows in front of us.

Sarah and I were shocked. We had the silver dollar eyes and dropped jaw. Not really believing what he had done, Stan started to laugh. His laugh started with a slow exhale. His apple cheeks began to glow; his entire face turned red. He put his hand over his mouth, doubled over, tears rolled down his cheeks, he wheezed, and out came this laugh/giggle. He usually does this for two or three minutes. He can't stop himself.

The row behind us heard him. The row across from us and in front of us heard and saw him. They began to laugh. And, then the next row and the next row and so on. People were shouting "What'd he do?" and kept on laughing. Even the flight attendants came up to us to see what was going on. I whispered what had happened. They laughed, and one went up and pulled the eggs out of the lady's hair.

What amazed me was that most of the people didn't know what had happened. They were laughing at the infectious sound of laughter.

I guess this is what they mean when they say "laugh and the world laughs with you."

⌘⌘⌘⌘⌘

"A happy heart makes the face cheerful,"
                                        Proverbs 15:13

JUNE 10
...BEING STONE CUTTERS

"The right word and the right accent."

- Joseph Conrad

⌘⌘⌘⌘⌘

Many years ago, someone was explaining how important it was to keep at something if we wanted it to happen. It's called tenacity. The example they used to explain the significance of being tenacious was that of a stone cutter.

A stone cutter will take a block of stone and hammer away at it 100 times without ever seeing any visible difference. On the 101st stroke, the stone falls in two, and the stone cutter finally sees the results of the labor of his work. It wasn't just the final 101st stroke that made the difference; it was all of the 101 strokes that made the difference. Without each one of them, the stone would have never fallen in two.

With many things in our life we need to be stone cutters. We need to continue to hammer away at something to make a difference and to create the results we want to create.

It's difficult for us to continue when we don't see any immediate visible change. We are all so used to immediate gratification. But just by being persistent, we can make changes with some of the most difficult things we have to encounter: the stones of our lives.

⌘⌘⌘⌘⌘

"Therefore, my dear brothers, stand firm.
Let nothing move you. Always give yourselves
fully to the work of the Lord, because you know
that your labor in the Lord is not in vain."

Corinthians 15:58

JUNE 11
...MAKING DISGUSTING JOBS FUN

"We must like what we have when we don't have what we like."
- Roger De Bussy-Rabutin

⌘⌘⌘⌘⌘

There are some jobs in this world that are just not what they are cracked up to be. Dusting, cleaning toilets, and folding underwear come to the forefront of my mind. And then there are some jobs that are just down right disgusting!!! The more you can make disgusting jobs fun, the quicker they go by, and the less you mind doing them.

When you have two dogs, your yard will be full of what my husband likes to refer to as "land mines." Cleaning up "land mines" is one of those disgusting jobs, so I have tired to make it less disgusting. Do you remember the guards' song in *The Wizard of Oz*? It went "Yo, hee, oh; yo, hee, oh." Well, when I have my little pooh bucket and pooh shovel, I go around the yard singing, "Yo, hee, oh; pooh patrol." The dogs are used to the song and follow behind me wagging their tails. My husband and my neighbors think it's pretty funny, and the job goes a little bit faster.

I take pleasure in throwing all the dirty clothes down the stairs while yelling "laundry shoot" — especially when the dogs are sitting on the landing and end up with underwear on their head. There is joy in making up songs for the dogs while I take them for a walk. I raise my metabolism as I dance with my feather duster. I have fun pretending I'm driving a tank when I'm bouncing along the field on the tractor, or yelling "Got ya, ya little sucker" when I'm pulling up weeds.

We all have to do some disgusting jobs. They do not go away. But, by trying to find a way to make them less disgusting, they, in turn, will become less disgusting.

⌘⌘⌘⌘⌘

"Restore to me the joy of your salvation
and grant me a willing spirit, to sustain me."
Psalm 51:12

JUNE 12
...KNOWING HUMOR IS NOT UNIVERSAL

"Clumsy jesting is no joke."
- Aesop

⌘⌘⌘⌘⌘

Have you ever wondered why some jokes fall flat? I have. Doing a little research and having a little understanding of people, I believe it is because humor is a very personal thing. It is not only a matter of what the joke is about, but it is also a matter of who is telling the joke to whom.

An Irishman can tell me an Irish joke, and I usually think it is pretty funny. I would probably not find it quite so funny if a non-Irish person told me an Irish joke. Italians tell jokes to Italians. Lutherans tell jokes to Lutherans. Blondes tell jokes to blondes. Democrats tell jokes to Democrats. Men tell jokes to men. Women tell jokes to women. We don't seem to mind when someone like us is telling a joke about us. It seems to be the mixing that causes the problem. We seem to have more insight and tolerance for our own. Humor makes fun of things; many of these things we hold dear. What a group of two may find funny, someone in a group of twenty will take offense. Humor can be caustic and cynical; two things we are not always in the mood for.

In college, a friend and I were sitting facing each other at a table in the woman's lounge. We were talking about one of our fellow classmates who had just gotten the lead in a play. This girl was not a favorite with us. She was not very pretty and overly dramatic about everything. I can't remember what the play was, but a monkey played one of the leading characters. My friend, in a moment of humor, said she would only go to the play if this girl was playing the part of the monkey. We started to laugh. I dropped my pen and bent over to pick it up. When I sat up, my friend was not laughing any more. She was pale. I asked her what was wrong. She mouthed that the girl we were talking about was sitting right behind us.

Humor is situational, emotional and personal. It is not always effective. It is not always funny. Humor can hurt and embarrass others and us. Humor, like beauty, is in the eye and mind of the beholder. We need to always keep this in mind; and because I will always remember how I hurt this girl's feelings, I know I will.

⌘⌘⌘⌘⌘

"Do good, O Lord, to those who are good,
to those who are upright in heart."
Psalm 125:4

JUNE 13
...WATCHING EXPENSES

"He is not poor that hath not much,
but he that craves much."
- Thomas Fuller, M.D.

⌘⌘⌘⌘⌘

Expenses! Aghhh! More going out than you have coming in! Don't you hate it? I do and did and will. It's the extravagance of our over-indulgence at a price we cannot afford to pay.

I went to college on government loans: the type of loan that you don't have to pay back until you have been graduated and working for three to six months. I got out of school, got a job, and began paying back my debt. Through the electronic grapevine, major department stores heard about me. Since the government had loaned me money, I must not be a big risk; so, let's give her credit cards. And they did. I had credit cards for every major department store in town and all the catalog stores. I used them — and not wisely. Before I knew it, I was in major debt. My second year in the "real" world I had to get a consolidation loan. I was in hock up to my elbows after working only one year!

And what was I in debt for? Ten pair of jeans, not one. Ten pair of black shoes, not one. Ten gold necklaces, not one. Things that were on sale that I couldn't live without. Things that I had to have to keep up with someone else. Things that were "in" this year.

What I discovered was I usually wore just one favorite pair of jeans, and the rest lay on the closet floor. I wore my favorite necklace and left the others in the drawer. I had nothing to go with the sale items. I ended up not speaking to the people I was once trying to keep up with, and the "in" things were out the following year.

I began to shop more wisely. I bought one or two of what I really loved; and when it or they wore out, I got another one. I was always in style, pretty chic, and within a budget.

I should have listened to the advice of Sir Henry Taylor. "The art of living easily as to money is to pitch your scale of living one degree below your means."

⌘⌘⌘⌘⌘

"Moreover, when God gives any man wealth
and possessions, and enables him to enjoy them,
to accept his lot and be happy in his work — this is a gift of God."
Ecclesiastes 5:19

JUNE 14
...WEARING SUNGLASSES WHEN IT IS TOO BRIGHT

"Most people want security in this world, not liberty."
- H. L. Mencken

⌘⌘⌘⌘⌘

Did you ever wonder what we would do without sunglasses? For someone, like me, whose eyes are light sensitive, I would not be doing very well.

Sunglasses filter out harsh light. They keep me from squinting and putting lines on my face. They keep others from knowing where I am looking. They help prevent strain on my eyes and making them weary. They help protect my eyes against strong wind, dirt, and dust. They keep my eyes from being burned. They eliminate glare. I don't know what I would do without my sunglasses.

There are many events in my life that I am unprepared for, and I wish I had some type of glasses that would protect me from life's harshness just as my sunglasses protect my eyes from the sun. I need protection from the worry of life that puts lines in my face just as the sun does. There are times when I am so hurt and confused that I do not want others to see how I am looking or where I am looking. There are days that make me so weary that I feel as if I cannot take one more step, and I need to hide this weariness from others. There are times I need a shield to protect me from the harsh, strong winds of life that try to batter me down. There are times when I have been burned in relationships and careers until I am raw. I need protection from this, too. And, there are times, when what I am looking at is such a strong, stark image, that it hurts my heart as well as my eyes.

We not only need sunglasses for the eyes, but we also need sunglasses for the soul: a pair of protective glasses that shield the soul from life just as the sunglasses shield the eyes from the sun. Soulglasses. Faith.

⌘⌘⌘⌘⌘

"We wait in hope for the Lord;
he is our help and our shield."
Psalm 33:20

JUNE 15
...APPRECIATING GRANDMOTHER'S WISDOM

"Nine-tenths of wisdom is being wise in time."
- Theodore Roosevelt

⌘⌘⌘⌘⌘

My grandmother was a "HOOT." She was a six foot tall, blue-eyed blond who looked like Queen Helga and had the temperament of King Thor. She wore spiked patent leather heels every day just to clean house and walk to the store. She was gifted with an incredible sixth sense; she always "knew." She was pregnant 14 times and lost 9 babies in childbirth. She had the physical strength of 10 women her size. Once, when the garage was on fire, and my mother was trapped inside, she took an axe and chopped down a wall to save her. She had the emotional strength of — I don't even know what to compare her to. She raised five children through the Depression, and she raised her children alone because Grandfather was an engineer on the New York Central and always gone. She played any piece of music by ear on her Baby Grand Piano. She named her pet rooster Liberace and was asked to be on "I've Got A Secret," but she wouldn't because she loved Liberace too much.

She never went to high school, and this woman had more "earthy" wisdom and humor than most people with terminal degrees. Whatever you asked her or wanted to discuss with her, she had an answer that always sounded like sage.

When one of her sons passed away, she made the comment, "Ain't none of us gonna get out of this life alive." Once, when I was dating someone she didn't like, she gave me her definition of love: "Love is like the morning dew; it would just as soon fall on a pile of horse manure as it would a morning glory." She always taught us to start off any situation with a kind heart because "you could slide further on excrement than you could on sand paper."

If we were playing cards on the dining room table and she lost, it was because she could never play cards on a lace tablecloth. When you were picking blackberries or raspberries with her, she made you whistle; that was the only way she knew that you were picking more than you were eating.

My grandmother taught me what it meant to be strong. She taught me the definition of matriarch. She gave me wisdom, insight, and ideas that I refer to everyday, and this wisdom was not something you could learn from a book. It was the wisdom of a hard life and survival. It was the mixture of laughter and tears that I am glad she shared with me for it has helped make me what I am today.

⌘⌘⌘⌘⌘

"...the price of wisdom is beyond rubies."
Job 28:18

JUNE 16
...GIVING SURPRISE GIFTS TO OTHERS

"Surprise is the greatest gift which life can grant us."
- Boris Pasternak

⌘⌘⌘⌘⌘

When Stan and I were dating, we went through many situations which I suppose were intended to make or break our relationship. One such situation revolved around a vacation.

We all know that vacations are pretty expensive. Stan wanted to go on a nice vacation with Sarah, his daughter, and me. A week in Orlando sounded great to all of us. He looked into prices. A week at the hotel/suite was going to be about $1,000 for the three of us, and by the time you throw in meals and airfare, it was more than he could afford. He was disappointed.

I asked him why I couldn't provide the airfare. I explained that with all the travelling I had done I had several "frequent flyer" tickets, and I could exchange them for three free round trip tickets. He just stood there and looked at me. Finally, he asked, "You mean you would give my daughter a free ticket?" I couldn't believe this statement!

I responded, "No, you are right. I couldn't possibly give a ticket to you and Sarah. I would rather have them in a safety deposit box, just lying there until they expire, not bringing any joy or fun to anyone, including me. No, you are right. I had just better keep those tickets where they are." He sighed and said, "Point well taken." We went to Orlando and had a wonderful time and brought home wonderful memories. It was through the giving of these tickets that I received fun and memories. It was through giving that I received.

"A cheerful giver does not count the cost of what he gives. His heart is set on pleasing and cheering him on to whom the gift is given." Julian of Norwich.

⌘⌘⌘⌘⌘

"Every good and perfect gift is from above,
coming down from the Father of the heavenly lights,
who does not change like shifting shadows."
James 1:17

JUNE 17
...HELPING CATERPILLARS BECOME BUTTERFLIES

"The important thing is this: to be able at any moment
to sacrifice what we are for what we could become."

- Charles Du Bos

⌘⌘⌘⌘⌘

Ruth, my wonderful, impulsive, upbeat, high energy friend, was in town the other day. This was a special treat because she and her husband had been relocated to Raleigh/Durham. We don't get a chance to see one another often, but when we do, it's always special and gives me a new perspective on life.

Ruth had been a corporate person for probably 30 years; and when you are as unconventional as Ruth, that is really a long time. After her marriage, she decided to start her own business, *Tapping Resources*. She was very successful in her own corporate arena.

When her husband and she moved, they bought an older home that needed a little work, so she began painting. She took painting classes. She bought old furniture, refurbished it, and painted it. And, by painting it, I mean pictures of Noah's Ark, landscapes, children's dinosaurs, etc. They are incredible. When she came back to town, she brought her "picture book" of the pieces she had done. I could not believe how detailed and beautiful they were. Ruth is a Grandma Moses.

She now wears jeans not suits. She hangs out at antique stores not office parks. She spends her day painting not typing. And she LOVES it!!! Ruth has become a butterfly.

During our caterpillar stage, we can get around but not fly. We are not exactly ugly, but then we aren't exactly pretty either. People watch us to see how cold the winter is going to be, but they take no joy in our beauty.

Ruth went from doing what was expected of her to what she loved. She went from the demands of others to the demands of herself. She went from the familiar to the unfamiliar. Her effervescence is contagious. You see the happiness and self-actualization on her face and hear it in her voice. I never thought it was possible for her to be more impulsive and upbeat than she was, but she is.

If you ever have a chance to help create a butterfly, please do. Just being around their beauty will be reward enough.

⌘⌘⌘⌘⌘

"And Jesus grew in wisdom and stature,
and in favor with God and men."

Luke 2:52

JUNE 18
...BENEFIT FROM OTHER'S EXPERIENCES

"No one over thirty-five is worth meeting who has not something
to teach us, — sometimes more than we could learn ourselves, from a book."
- Cyril Connolly

⌘⌘⌘⌘⌘

My undergraduate degree is in English Literature. I love novels, short stories, biographies. What new and exciting worlds are on those pages! I not only wanted to major in English, but I also wanted to attend a college where the instructors were way above average. I attended Indiana Central University (now the University of Indianapolis).

The instructors in the English Department were fabulous. The head of the department was the most intelligent and dearest man I have ever known. He had barbecues every fall, and the English majors would go over and help rake leaves. He had a Halloween Party each year. The only requirement for attending was we had to come as book titles (i.e. you could pretend you were pregnant and come as *Great Expectations*). My German Literature professor had been an interpreter at the Nuremberg Trials. There always seemed to be a sadness behind this pretty, frail woman. She was very private. My French Literature professor had received the Le' Quadagare from DeGaulle for leading wounded troops through enemy lines. He had Sunday evening dinners and painted wonderful word pictures for us of the French countryside. My Romantic and Victorian Literature professor worked for the French Underground during WW II. Her parents were missionaries in China, and she opened her home to us and shared her history and antiques. My American Literature professor was graduated from the University of Edinburg and told us wonderful stories about Scotland.

It's not often you can get a dual education. I did. I learned about the world's great literature and about the world. No where else could I have received this dual education. Certainly not only in books. This was real. These wonderful people were not only sharing their knowledge but also their lives. These shared stories live on in me, and I, in turn, share them with others. We benefit in generosity.

⌘⌘⌘⌘⌘

"Praise the Lord, O my soul;
and forget not all his benefits —"
Psalm 103:2

JUNE 19
...DEALING WITH LIFE'S UP'S AND DOWN'S

"There is no gathering the rose without being pricked by the thorns."
- Fables of Bidpai

⌘⌘⌘⌘⌘

Gina and I had been friends for quite some time when we realized our lives ran a very similar course. Some of the similarities were we had both made major career changes, lived through an unhappy, unsuccessful marriage, maintained strong religious beliefs, and came from a rural background, and there were hundreds of minor things.

We have had our ups and downs. The nice thing is when one of us was up, the other was down; and when one was down, the other was up. Our lives not only run parallel, but they also see-saw.

We were in Chicago at a trade show. I was up. I was travelling to new places, eating at very fancy restaurant, dating a man who had a lot of money and spent it on me, and enjoying it all. Life was good! Gina, on the other hand, was in the pits. She hated her job, her ex-husband, and her life, in general.

We had just gone back to our hotel. She had been crying about how rotten life was at this moment, and I just sat there and listened while she enumerated all the things that she hated. I didn't know how long I would have to listen when, suddenly, I got a break because she had to move her car. She put on a "Good Times" sweatshirt and headed out. A drunk tried to make a pass at her in the elevator, and two greasers tried to pick her up in the parking lot. She came back in from the cold and snow all wet and crying louder than ever. I figured the best thing I could do was pretend I was asleep; so I did.

She threw herself on her bed making a lot of noise. [I know she knew I was faking sleep.] She started in with greater furry than before about all she hated and all that was going wrong. Finally, she ended by saying, "And, on top of all this, my best friend's life is going wonderful!" I couldn't help it; I started to laugh hysterically.

Several months later, she was up with a new marriage, a new home, a new career, etc. and I was in an abyss with my career and relationships. This time we spent one evening together in my kitchen. She was trying to talk to me as I sat cross-legged in the middle of the kitchen floor sobbing, crying, and refusing to get up or ever do anything again.

The teeter-totter has never been my favorite ride. Usually, when you head for the ground, you hit with a jolt. The only nice things about the jolt is that it helps propel you upwards. Since we have to have the downs, thank the Lord for the ups.

⌘⌘⌘⌘⌘

"Though I have fallen, I will rise. Though I sit in darkness, the Lord will be my light."
- Micah 7:8

JUNE 20
...KEEPING VISIBLE REMINDERS

"The past is our definition. We may strive,
with good reason, to escape it, or to escape what is bad in it,
but we will escape it only by adding something better to it."
- Wendell Berry

⌘⌘⌘⌘⌘

Sometimes we marry for the wrong reasons. I know I did. I married to be independent of my family. After the marriage, I realized this must have been what my grandmother meant when she talked about going from the "frying pan into the fire." I had married a man who was stingy, emotionally retarded, and embarrassing.

I was married for four years. For three and one-half, I was miserable. I knew I had to get out. I also knew I didn't want to move back in with my mother, and I didn't have enough money to live on my own. So, for three and one-half years, I bit the bullet. In addition to my full time job, I got a part time job and paid off all my debts, saved as much money as possible, and got a small apartment. I was on my own. I was determined from that day on to live a new life.

I wanted a visible reminder to remember that things could be worse.   As soon as I got more on my feet financially, I took my wedding ring to a jeweler, had it melted down into a nugget, put on a chain, and wore it around my neck for years. It was a visible reminder to me that I would never settle for less than I wanted ever again. It was a visible reminder to guard against being vulnerable, being caught, and being taken advantage of. It was a visible reminder to look for happiness, prosperity, and true love. It was my visible reminder to always go towards something not away from something.

Visible signs are important to us. They help keep us focused. They are a personal sign for us that is as easily recognizable as the McDonald arches and "no shirts, no shoes, no service" symbols and much more important.

⌘⌘⌘⌘⌘

"By faith we understand that the universe was formed at God's command, so that what is seen was not made out of what was visible."
Hebrews 10:3

JUNE 21
...FINDING YOUR OWN COMFORT ZONE

"What nature requires is obtainable, and within easy reach.
It's for the superfluous we sweat."

- Seneca

⌘⌘⌘⌘⌘

Our comfort, whatever it is to us, is self-nurturing. It is self-care. It is essential. Comfort is warm, safe, cozy, cheerful, kind, cuddly, and soothing. This is why comfort is essential.

We all need to be very clear about what comforts us. What can we wrap ourselves in, like the big comforter, that helps each of us take care of ourselves? What can we add to our day to make us comfortable or able to be comforted?

I have a very special comfort for each of the five senses. I have focused on the senses for they are what take the external stimuli and internalize them. We have so many disrupters that irritate the senses: the sound of car horns, the touch of someone we don't welcome, the smell of garbage, the taste of spoiled food and the sight of hideous things happening around the world. This can be our daily intake. We need a counter-balance to keep our lives in sync.

What comforts me are the sound of hearing someone read the Beatitudes, the touch of my dog's silky coat, the smell of cinnamon, the taste of chocolate, and the sight of the ducks and geese flying overhead. The warmth and coziness of a fire, the soothing water of the Jacuzzi, the safeness of my husband's arm around my shoulder, the cheerful laughter of a friend, the kindness of a gentle word, and the cuddly feeling of blankets keeping you warm in the winter are also a comfort zone.

We desperately need comfort. With so many major things bringing stress into our lives, isn't it amazing how little it takes, sometimes, to bring comfort to our lives.

⌘⌘⌘⌘⌘

"Praise be to the God and Father of our Lord Jesus Christ,
the Father of compassion and the God of comfort, who comforts
us in our troubles, so that we can comfort those in any
trouble with the comfort we ourselves have received from God."

1 Corinthians 1:3-4

JUNE 22

...KEEPING YOURSELF SAFE

"To multiply the harbors does not reduce the sea."
- Emily Dickinson

⌘⌘⌘⌘⌘

This is another "Murphy Story." As you remember, Murphy has taken it upon herself to be my protector. I am very glad this is her mission.

It was the first warm, sunny day of spring, and I could hardly wait to get outside. I put on my old clothes, got my gardening tools and the dogs, and headed out to the back yard. As I was pulling weeds, Murphy began barking wildly. I look up to see a man in his 20's walking toward me. When he saw Murphy (90 pounds of big, mean, barking black dog), he stopped. With eyebrows raised and standing very close to Murphy, I asked if I could help him. He said no; he was just walking to the road to wait on someone. He stood there and kept watching the dog. Finally, he said she was very pretty and asked if he could pet her. I told him not if he wanted to leave here the same way he came. She kept jumping and barking. He must have become annoyed or scared because he walked back the same way he had come.

I called my husband, who, in turn, told me to call the police. I did, and three policemen showed up in five minutes. They praised my dog, took a description and went in search of the man. They came back in 30 minutes and told me they could not find anyone. I thanked them for their work. When they started to leave, I said, "You know what really makes me mad? I realize that without this dog I'm not even safe in my own backyard."

We tend to judge others as ourselves, and when we are open, honest, and kind, we assume that everyone else is, also. Most are, but not everyone.

We must risk in this life, but we must make sure that our risks are calculated for probable success not failure. If we risk foolishly, it can cost dearly, even to the point of loosing our lives.

⌘⌘⌘⌘⌘

"The eternal God is your refuge,
and underneath are the everlasting arms."
Deuteronomy 33:27

JUNE 23
...BEING A THURSDAY'S CHILD

"The toughest thing about success is that you've got to keep on being a success."
- Irving Berlin

⌘⌘⌘⌘⌘

I'm a Thursday's child. Do you remember the old poem?

Monday's child is fair of face,
Tuesday's child is full of grace,
Wednesday's child is full of woe,
Thursday's child has far to go,
Friday's child is loving and giving,
Saturday's child has to work for its living,
But the child that is born on the Sabbath Day
Is good and kind in all God's ways.

And, I certainly have come a long way and still have a long way to go. I have always believed that if we stop heading for a destination, we cease to live.

I started my career teaching. I then went to working in corporations and finally to having my own company. Even through hard times, I have enjoyed the evolutionary process because, as with the evolution of all things, we only get better and better. When I think of the hard times, I'm reminded of my aunt who painted beautiful porcelain plates. The plate always started out dull and insignificant, but after the plate was put into the fire, it shown bright and clear, the colors jumped at you, and you had something that was worthwhile and lasting. It was the heat of the fire that caused the transformation.

Just as everyone is Irish on March 17, everyone is a Thursday's child. We all have a long way to go. We don't just want to exist; we want to live. We want to be involved in the process or game of life and not always sitting on the sidelines. Evan Esar said, "You can't do anything about the length of your life, but you can do something about its width and depth." That is what being a Thursday's child is all about - -regardless of what day of the week you were born.

⌘⌘⌘⌘⌘

"...and let us run with patience the race that is before us."
Hebrews 12:1

JUNE 24
...KNOWING SOME EVENTS ARE GREATER THAN PEOPLE

"The vain should be wise, for a giant is sometimes strangled by a fly, and there are times when towering giants stumble into pitfalls, and lions fear sheep."
- Berechiah Ven Natronai Ha-Nakdan

⌘⌘⌘⌘⌘

Some of the events in our lives are so big, have so much magnitude, that they are more memorable than the people involved. Ask yourself these questions:

Who was the captain of the Titanic?
Who was the pilot of the Heindenberg?
Who dropped the bomb on the USS Arizona?
Who was the architect of the Empire State Building?
Who developed the television set?

Good or bad, these are huge historical events that have made impact on the world. It was the event, in itself, that was important; the people involved – each one -- played a significant role, but were so overshadowed by what had happened, their role was secondary. The events were immortal; the people were not. There are events in our lives we are only a part. We are a cog in the wheel, a tool used in the construction. Even though the event could not have happen without us, the event took precedence.

All life cannot be lived on vanity, self-importance, and arrogance. Blowing your own horn soon develops a cacophony that grates on the ears. Patting yourself on the back repeatedly causes muscle strain, and you will become short-winded constantly puffing out your chest.

Take comfort in the thought of being a "part of something." I have helped build fences and raise barns. I have collected toys for underprivileged children. I have been 1 of 10 people to ride a 10-seater bike. I am only one alto in a 75 person choir. I take joy in each of these activities even though my name is not listed, and I am not recognized. What I have done will be remembered long after I am forgotten.

When the event is bigger than any one person, take pride in being part of the event. This is where the satisfaction lies. Letting our vanity get in the way makes us look as foolish as the rooster who thinks the sun rises just to hear him crow.

⌘⌘⌘⌘⌘

"What does the worker gain from his toil? I have seen the burden God has laid on men. He has made everything beautiful in its time. He has also set eternity in the hearts of men; yet they cannot fathom what God has done from beginning to end."
Ecclesiastes 3:9-11

JUNE 25

...KEEP DATING ALIVE -- EVEN AT 50 YEARS OLD

"They that have had it have slipped in and out of heaven."
- James M. Barrie

⌘⌘⌘⌘⌘

My husband and I had been so busy that we only sat down to have dinner together one night in six weeks. That's one night out of 42; not a very good average for a couple. We had just over-scheduled ourselves to the point of not being able to spend time together. We were both irritable and snapping at each other over stupid little things. We knew this had to stop. This was one of the problems we had experienced in previous failed relationships.

We decided every two weeks, whether our schedules were busy or not, that we would have a "Big Date Night." Our first BDN was fun and refreshing. We had dinner at a very nice restaurant, saw "The Lost World," and then went to Finale's for dessert. At the movie we got one big drink with two straws and a bucket of popcorn. We held hands and laughter and acted like kids.

When we get married, we select the one person with whom we wanted to spend the rest of our life. Why, then, do we get so busy that we never spend time with them? Aren't we doing the opposite of what we set out to do?

It is by spending time with one another that we grow, know one another better, and create a relationship that is lasting.

⌘⌘⌘⌘⌘

"If you have any encouragement from being united with Christ,
if any comfort from his love, is any fellowship with the Spirit,
if any tenderness and compassion, then make my joy complete
by being like-minded, have the same love, being one in spirit and purpose."
Philippians 2: 1-2

JUNE 26
...KNOWING WE ARE ALL FALLIBLE

"The discipline through which we advance."
- William Ellery Channing

⌘⌘⌘⌘⌘

Don't we all have moments when we think we are infallible and can do no wrong? I have, even if they are shorted lived. Don't we have moments when we know soooooooo much that we don't have to ask others for advice? I have. And, when we get into situations like this, don't we just tell and demand and yell. I do and then end up looking foolish!

I had only been driving a couple of years, but I knew it all. I had just had my car serviced. I had some errands to run, backed the car out of our very long drive way, put it into Drive, and it wouldn't go. I could back it up, but I could not get it to go forward. I was so mad at the service station people. It was their fault. They had messed up and, boy, was I going to tell them!!! I called them and started screaming. The man just listened to me. When I had stopped long enough to take a breath, he asked me if I had released the emergency brake. Hum!

My mother and I had just purchased a new refrigerator/freezer. She wanted this special freezer with adjustable shelves because she made tall elaborate frozen desserts. About a month after the freezer was delivered, ice started building up in the bottom. My mother was furious! She called the appliance store and demanded they come out right now and fix the freezer. A man arrived that afternoon, and after he took a chisel and mallet and chipped the ice out of the bottom, he found a cherry stuck in the drain. A cherry that had fallen off of one of my mother's frozen desserts. Hum!

A friend bought a new "big screen" TV. It was installed while she was at work. She could hardly wait to get home and turn it on. She rushed home after work, turned the TV on, and nothing happened. She plugged and unplugged the cord. She jiggled the plug. She tried other outlets. Nothing worked. They had delivered damaged goods. She was irate. She called the appliance store and screamed at them. She wanted them out there now! The man came out, looked around, and flipped the wall switch. Instant programs. Hum!

I don't know about you, but I have finally realized I'm not infallible. I need to tell people the situation and ask them for their help. I like eating eggs, but I don't like wiping them off my face.

⌘⌘⌘⌘⌘

"If one falls down, his friend can help him up.
But pity the man who falls and has no one to help him up!"
Ecclesiastes 4:10

JUNE 27
...CHOOSING FRIENDS WISELY

"Friendship is a strong and habitual inclination in two persons
to promote the good and happiness of one anther."
- Eustace Budgell

⌘⌘⌘⌘⌘

I'm sure we all remember the story of the Ugly Duckling who turned into a Swan. I've always thought of myself as that ugly duckling who, hopefully, has made it to swandom. When I entered puberty, I was tall, fat, and miserably shy. I had few friends in junior high, and most of them turned out to have different agendas, so we lost track along the way to high school.

I wanted friends. Friends who were pretty and popular, so I could feel as if I were pretty and popular, too. I found two. They were both popular and pretty. They had nice homes, nice cars, and nice clothes. One even had a cabin on a lake and invited people up to spend the weekend. For a while, life was great. I had reached swandom. I was invited to parties and went to games, etc.   One Friday night after a football game, the three of us piled into a car and left the high school. We drove around Tee Pee and Steak 'n Shake one time, and then we headed to my home. My friend said her mother told her she had to be in early. Fine with me.

On Monday morning in study hall, the girl setting next to me asked my why I wasn't at the sock hop with my two friends. I didn't know what to say. The pain I felt was so intense I was numb. It was my survival mechanism. When study hall was over, I passed my two friends in the hall. They smiled and said "Hi." I looked back at them and asked them if they had had a nice time at the sock hop on Friday night. It was their turn to not know what to say. This was the longest and most miserable day of my high school life. I went home broken, sad, lonely, and unpopular -- again. With one sentence I was back to being the ugly duckling.

We must choose our friends wisely. They must be our friends because they like us and want to be with us for the right reasons. When we choose people to be our friends and the friendship is solely based on how they make us feel better about ourselves, it will not last. How we feel about ourselves must come from us. If good feelings come from others, they have the opportunity to take it away. This is what happened to me. It was a very hard lesson for me to learn, but one I learned well and never forgot. Choose your friends wisely and for the right reasons.

⌘⌘⌘⌘⌘

"The truth will make you free."
John 8:32

JUNE 28
...MAKING YOUR OWN CINDERELLA WORLD

"Stories that never run out of edition."
- Anonymous

⌘⌘⌘⌘⌘

As most of you are now aware, we have two dogs. One is a retriever. She stares at the birds constantly, and I know she would like a real Dove Bar. The other is a terrier, and, like all terriers, when you let her out, her nose hits the ground tracking.

Next door is an empty field that we try desperately to keep the terrier out of. We are not always successful. There is one spot she always heads for, and we didn't know why until recently. There is a rabbit nest there. The other day, before we could stop her, she ran as fast as she could to the nest. Unfortunately, the baby bunnies were outside — and helpless. Before we reached her, she had killed two of the babies. We tried to save the others from her. The next morning we found them dead, also.

I was just sick at heart. I called my mother for consolation. She began to explain that CoCo was a terrier and that was her instinct to survive in the wild. I began to cry more in earnest and told her, in my mind, I knew this. My heart hurt. I then told her I wanted that perfect "pink and white" world she told me about when I was a child. I wanted everything to end "happily ever after." I wanted the Cinderella world.

My mother, always intelligent and always having incredible wisdom about life, replied, "When you get to be an adult, you have to make your own Cinderella world."

⌘⌘⌘⌘⌘

"But be glad and rejoice forever, in what I will create,"
Isaiah 65:18

JUNE 29

...UNDERSTANDING THE PURPOSE OF TWINGES

"Wounds heel and become scars. But scars grow with us."
- Stanislaw Lec

⌘⌘⌘⌘⌘

Recently, a "woodwork" friend and I had lunch. We had a wonderful lunch chatting and catching up on old times and where we were now. Her work was going well, and she told me that her personal life with her husband had improved tremendously. I say improved because many years ago he had had an affair with a woman he worked with. She said things were going much smoother, and she was usually able to trust again.

I ask her what she meant by "usually." She said sometimes when she was out of town, and her husband said that he was going to be home all evening, she would call, and no one would answer. She likened it to a broken ankle she had a long time ago. She said, "You think it is all healed, and you will have no more problems with it, but then you step on it wrong, and you immediately get that twinge of momentary pain that brings the all memories back again."

We all have these twinges. We see someone we have maligned, and we twinge. We see someone who once broke our hearts, and we twinge. We use a once broken bone under stress, and we twinge. We read or hear a story that reminds us of something that happened to us long ago, and we twinge.

I think I understand the purpose of twinges. Twinges are to stop the hurt we may do to ourselves and to stop the hurt we may do to others. Whether it is a physical twinge to a bone, joint or muscle or an emotional twinge to the soul, heart or conscience, it makes us stop momentarily to think of what we have done or may do to ourselves or others.

Although uncomfortable at the moment, twinges are a necessary protection to us and others.

⌘⌘⌘⌘⌘

"I gain understanding from your precepts;"
Psalm 119:104

JUNE 30
...HELPING OTHERS OUT OF BAD SITUATIONS

"Remember that you are all people and that all people are you."
- Joy Harjo

⌘⌘⌘⌘⌘

This story is going to sound "made up," but you are going to have to trust me; it's real! No one could make up a story like this. It was the week after Thanksgiving, and Gina and I were working a trade show at McCormick's Place in Chicago. And, as most winters in Chicago, it was cold, snowy, and icy.

My friend was having a bad time both personally and professionally. Her company scheduled her to share a room with another sales person. Their co-existence was miserable. Every day at the Trade Show my friend was holding back tears. Finally, I went to her and asked what was the problem. Tears finally fell as she said she didn't know if she could take going back to her room with this person for three more days. I told her I was in a Double Room by myself, and she was welcomed to come and stay with me. She immediately looked relieved. We decided to move her stuff that night after we had attended a reception.

We took the bus to her hotel, packed her stuff, loaded her car, and headed off down Michigan Avenue. Her car was about 10 years old and not in very good shape. Half way to our destination the car quit. Here we sit in high heels, evening dresses and evening coats. The car is loaded with luggage. We are three blocks from my hotel. It is cold, snowy, and icy. Everyone is honking at us. We have one recourse. I get out of the car in this hideous weather that I certainly was not dressed for and pushed her car down Michigan Avenue. [You can't make this stuff up.]

We get to the corner. I push the car to the curb, and we unload the car. I picked up all the luggage I could and said, "Let's go." Gina was just standing at the curb crying again. This was just "one more straw" for her at the wrong time. I'm cold and miserable and again tell her to come on. She said through tears, "What is someone steals it?" I said, "It's insured; let's go." She said, "What if someone hits it?" I said, "It's insured; let's go." However, this time I said it a little louder. Finally, she picked up her luggage, and we walked three blocks to my hotel.

The rest of the week went much better for her because she was more relaxed and for me because I had a friend to spend time and laugh with.

It's nice to know that the Good Samaritan set all of us this example years ago.

⌘⌘⌘⌘⌘

"But a Samaritan, as he traveled, came where the man was;
and when he saw him, he took pity on him."

Luke 10:33

JULY 1

...BEING CONFIDENT WITH YOUR OWN STYLE

"The style is the man himself."
- Georges Buffon

⌘⌘⌘⌘⌘

Several years ago I attended a two day conference at a local university. One of the attendees was a tall thin woman with short auburn hair. The first day of the seminar she wore a belted sweater and long flowing skirt. The second day of the conference she wore leotards, a short wool skirt and suit jacket. This woman was definitely comfortable with her own style. I admired her because, at this particular point in time, I was not comfortable with my style. I was wearing structured business suits to everything — and hating it.

Her name was Michelle, and she and I became friends. We have a wonderful time when we meet. At one luncheon, I broke down and told her how I admired her comfort with the way she dressed. She reminded me of another friend, Sherry, who worked in the military. Sherry always wore flowered dresses with suit jackets and knit separates. I told her, also, how much I admired her. She said she had finally gotten comfortable enough with her self and her skills to be whom she was. She didn't want to have to dress like a man or a floozy to get the job done.

I have finally developed my own style. Denim is my main ingredient. I love long straight dresses, jog suits, and non-traditional suits. Pins and scarves are wonderful accessories. Elastic waistbands are heaven. Thigh high stockings take precedence over pantyhose any day.

It is so gratifying to discover your own style and live in it. You are comfortable, and you project it. From season to season, styles may change, but once you find your style, it is here to stay.

⌘⌘⌘⌘⌘

"Above all, clothe yourselves with love,
which binds everything together in perfect harmony."
Colossians 3:14

JULY 2

...KEEPING A SAFE DISTANCE

"Bad is never good until worse happens."
- Danish Proverb

⌘⌘⌘⌘⌘

I know, even before I even start to tell this story, some of you will be astounded at the stupidity connected with it.

I was in my early 20's living with my mother. We had a small pony farm in Greenfield, Indiana, and a lovely house. One of my favorite things was our fireplace. It was the first time we had a working fireplace. I'd sit in our family room, evening after evening in the dark, just watching the light from the fire and listening to the crack of the wood.

I had had a pretty stressful week. All I could think about was the fireplace. I went home, changed clothes, fixed supper and went into the family room to relax. I went out to get wood. I hadn't realized it had been raining all day, and the wood was too wet to burn. But, I would not give up. I brought the logs in, wadded up newspaper and tried to start the fire. The paper would burn up, but the logs would only smoke and sizzle.

I was mad! I wanted my fire! I figured just a little bit of gasoline wouldn't hurt. I went out to the garage with a small paper cup and filled it with gasoline. I came back into the house and threw the gasoline on the logs. I was a little worried about what might happened when I lit the logs, so I got on my hands and knees low on the floor and threw the lighted match on the logs.

Thank the Lord I was down on the floor! Flames shot out of the fireplace up to the ceiling. The hair was burned off my arm, and my eyebrows were singed.

What a really stupid thing to do. I could have set myself and our house on fire. I had not kept a safe distance. I had not kept any distance. Distance sets us apart from things, and there are definitely dangerous situations and people we should keep a safe distance from.

When I was training horses, I learned that if you saw a horse was about to kick you, you took a step toward it, not away from it. You were bound to get kicked, but by being close, you were less likely to be severely hurt.

Whether we are far enough away to avoid long range attacks or close enough to create a short striking distance, we must always try and keep a "safe" distance.

⌘⌘⌘⌘⌘

"When I thought, 'My foot is slipping,'
your steadfast love, O Lord, held me up."
Psalm 94:18

JULY 3
...NOT FEELING HELPLESS

"Help yourself, and heaven will help you."

- La Fontaine

⌘⌘⌘⌘⌘

I came from a family that lived on schedules and time frames. I knew that if you said dinner would be at 6:00 pm then you were to be there at 6:00 pm and ready for dinner. My husband and step son "hang loose." Time and schedules don't have the same meaning for them as it does for me. Dinner for them is some time between 6:00 pm and midnight.

I don't like it when I am at the whim of other's time. I feel helpless, and I hate that. Ben's new wife, Jill, is the same way I am. We have had long talks about these men and their ideas of schedules and our ideas of schedules. I think the best advice I have given Jill is to always have something to do. When you are at the mercy of someone else's time frame and must wait on them, that nasty old helplessness kicks in and often leads to stress and anger: not two emotions that are high on my list.

I always have things to do — columns and newsletters to write, letters to get out, even books to read. If I get hungry, I'll eat. I have a car phone, so I can even run errands and meet people places. The result of not feeling helpless is happiness. I'm happy to see them, to be with them, to share part of their life. I'm not sullen, sarcastic, or screaming.

We all get along much better because we have learned each other's definition of time. And, we have learned that when time is an important issue, we conform for the sake of the situation.

Helplessness leads to anger, rage, and frustration. Happiness leads to cheerfulness, good humor and a kind heart. It is an easy choice for me.

⌘⌘⌘⌘⌘

"Be renewed in the spirit of your mind."

Ephesians 4:23

JULY 4
...KNOWING WHEN AND WHEN NOT TO BE INDEPENDENT

"Independence? That's middle class blasphemy.
We are all dependent on one another, every soul of us on earth."
- George Bernard Shaw

⌘⌘⌘⌘⌘

Independent! I could hardly wait. As do most people, I had to test my independence. I independently bought a pair of high heels, and without any instruction, fell off them and sprained by ankle. I independently tried to shave my legs, and without any instruction, cut my leg from my knee to my hip. I independently tried to make Shrimp Creole, and without any instruction, served it with raw shrimp. I independently tried to operate a computer, and without any instruction, lost documents and hours of sleep. Sometimes, independence isn't all it is cracked up to be.

We all seem to follow a pattern of dependence, independence, dependence. We spend the first 16 to 18 years of our lives being dependent on adults for everything. We just cannot wait until we are our own boss, set our own hours, do things our own way and take orders from no one. So, we get what we want. We are independent. We will count on no one. We will listen to no one. We can do it all ourselves.

This attitude begins to change when one mistake or error in judgement follows another and another and another. We don't know how to cook, to manage our money, to do laundry, or to manage our time. We can't get a piece of furniture up the stairs by ourselves. We don't understand why our car knocks. We miss our family. We are lonely. We finally realize that we don't know much of anything or can't do much of anything by ourselves.

Once we have experienced the cold, cruel world, having someone to talk to us, guide us, hug us, instruct us, help us, and hug us becomes very important. Being dependent doesn't seem so bad any more.

We don't come into this world alone. I am amazed at the number of people who think they can go through this world alone.

⌘⌘⌘⌘⌘

"Trust in the Lord with all your heart
and lean not on your own understanding;"
Proverbs 3:5

JULY 5
...KEEPING THE DEVIL BEHIND YOU

"One is always wrong to open a conversation with the devil, for, however he goes about it, he always insists upon having the last word."

- Andre Gide

⌘⌘⌘⌘⌘

When my Grandmother, Mother, Aunt June or I are having a rough time, all of us say the same thing: "Satan, get thee behind me!"

It's something my Grandmother started. I don't know where she came up with the idea, but we are all glad she did. Sometimes bad things get in our way, and I'm not talking about small things like splinters – I'm talking large things like railroad ties. It seems their purpose is to trip us up, take our attention off the good, and make us loose contact with the Lord. The devil is in front of us blocking our path to success.

By telling the Devil to get out of our way and behind us, we are keeping our paths clear and headed in the right direction, not tripping over things, and keeping our focus and contact with the Lord.

It is always desirable to have unpleasant things over with, out of the way, and behind us.

⌘⌘⌘⌘⌘

"Get thee behind me, Satan."

Luke 4:8

JULY 6
...GOING ONE DAY AT A TIME

"The best thing about the future is that it comes one day at a time."
- Abraham Lincoln

⌘⌘⌘⌘⌘

What Abe Lincoln said has always been a comfort to me. Because we do not know what the future will bring, it's nice to have it delivered a piece at at time.

One day, my college friends and I were talking about the future. Many said they wished they could see into the future. I qualified my wish. I would like to be able to set into the future but see the good things – only – that were going to happen. Personally, if I knew what the bad things were and when they were going to happen, I'm not sure I could take it. The death of loved ones, the loss of friends, breast cancer. These events are hard enough to go through at the time they occur; I certainly wouldn't want to spend time anticipating their arrival.

I, like most, love the play **Hamlet.** My favorite line is not "To be or not to be." My favorite line was said by Claudius, who was Hamlet's uncle and a military strategist. He said, "When troubles come, they come not single spies, but in battalions."

I have had my share of "battalion" days. They are inevitable for all of us. The nice thing about these "battalion" days is that they, also, come just one day at a time.

⌘⌘⌘⌘⌘

"So do not worry about tomorrow,
for tomorrow will bring worries of its own.
Today's trouble is enough for today."
Matthew 6:34

JULY 7

...BEING HIGH TOUCH

"Better to be without logic than without feeling."
- Charlotte Bronte

⌘⌘⌘⌘⌘

I remember a time when a Liberal Arts Degree was the degree to have. Having a background in art, music and literature, plus your major, helped make you a well-rounded person. When we lost the Race for Space, the free world determined that we were way behind in the fields of math and science; so, we were all suppose to specialize, and a liberal arts degree became a thing of the past. High tech was in, and high touch was out.

I agree that we need technology, but it should be an "in addition to" not a "substitution for." Our high touch skills are what relate us to one another. By de-emphasizing or eliminating high touch, we lose our inactive ability — our ability to be a part of the human race.

Right now some people can go for 24 hours without interacting with others. They sit at a computer screen all day. They send messages by e-mail. They walk through a gerbil tube to their car. They drive home looking out through tinted windows with no one seeing in and grab dinner at a drive-thru. After driving to their bank of mailboxes, they pull up in front of their home, hit the garage door opener, drive in, hit the button one more time, the door goes down, and they are safe and secure from the rest of the world. Some people have alienated themselves with the aid of technology.

The pendulum is swinging back again, and high touch is being looked upon in a new light. Soft skills have value again. We are realizing that people are not doing business with companies; people are doing business with people in the companies, and each one of us need these soft people skills to be successful.

Our ability to be effective in this world is how well we communicate one to one — high touch.

⌘⌘⌘⌘⌘

"If I rise on the wings of the dawn,
if I settle on the far side of the sea,
even there your hand will guide me,
your right hand will hold me fast."
Psalm 139:9-10

JULY 8
...FINDING YOUR OWN THERAPY

"The end and reward of toil."
                                        - James Beattie

⌘⌘⌘⌘⌘

Therapy is defined as "healing power or quality." I find the mixing of these two terms very appropriate. There is quality in therapy, and there certainly is healing power.

It's important for us to have something that we can do that is therapy. Therapy heals us from the stress and daily wear and tear and brings some quality to our life.

Mine is wall papering. I love to wall paper. I'm the person who wallpapers the inside of the closets. When I run out of walls at my house, I go to other peoples' houses and wall paper. I don't just stop with wallpapering; I do the entire decorating package. I put up wall paper borders, make wreaths, put matching mats in pictures, make pillows, cover stools and settees, hang towels, cover waste baskets and light switches, make flower arrangements, and on and on. I transform a room. I forget about the stress of life and have this wonderful aesthetic quality added to help glorify my life. I have achieved self-actualization.

Self-actualization is the pinnacle of our lives. It is essential to a happy existence. It blends what we love to do with the skills we have and creates an environment in which we take pride. Rising to this level helps bring us joy and happiness, helps create quality in our lives, and helps us heal from the wear and tear of life.

⌘⌘⌘⌘⌘

"Come unto me, all ye that labor and
are heavy laden, and I will give ye rest."
                                        Matthew 11:28

JULY 9
...KNOWING SOME THINGS ARE MORE EXCITING AT A DISTANCE

"Distance has the same effect on the mind as on the eye."
- Samuel Johnson

⌘⌘⌘⌘⌘

For 14 years I not only taught high school English, but I was also the yearbook sponsor. The yearbook staff had its own darkroom, and we took, developed, and printed about 80 rolls of film each year. Because most of my staff was involved, in some capacity, with the football program, I took most of the football pictures. The lens I used was called a "macro-zoom." On one setting it could get a clear picture of an eyeball, and on another setting it could get a clear shot of something 80 yards away.

At one particular game, I had a freshman staff member on the side lines with me. When you are looking through a lens, you can't tell how close people really are; so, your assistant's job is to watch through "real" eyes and tell you when people are getting too close.

It was near the end of the fourth quarter. The score was tied. We had the ball. The play was taking place on the opposite side of the field. I had the camera set on the far setting. I told me assistant I was going to try and take a series of shots, and if the two teams got within 20 feet of me, her job was to tell me they were near. One of our players had the ball, broke free of the defensive line, and was on the move. The straight way to the goal was blocked, so he began running our way. I keep pulling the lens in taking one shot after another. I wanted to get a shot of him making the touchdown. I knew my assistant was watching out for me, so I kept my eyes and the lens glued on the players.

What I did not realize was that my assistant was so excited over the game that instead of watching out for me and the distance the players were coming to me, she was yelling, jumping up and down, and cheering the players on.

The next thing I knew, the camera went flying out of my hands, and I was on the ground with two of our players and two of the opposing teams players. The wind was knocked out of me, and I couldn't breath. The team physician had to come over and help get me breathing again.

It was quite an exciting game. It was the first time I was actually in a football game. And, while I enjoy football, I found out I do prefer it at a distance.

⌘⌘⌘⌘⌘

"For in him we live and move and have our being."
Acts 17:28

JULY 10
...HAVING COURAGE TO EXPRESS AN UNPOPULAR OPINION

"One must judge men not by their opinions,
but by what their opinion have made of them."
- Georg Christoph Lichtenberg

⌘⌘⌘⌘⌘

I do not care for Thoreau or Bach. It doesn't mean that they are not wonderful in their own right. It simply means that I do not care for them. I have my reasons, and, for years, I would try to explain and justify why. Sometimes, I would be in "sophisticated" circles, and they would express their love for Thoreau or Bach or someone else I was not particularly fond of. I would try and remain silent so that I did not have to express an unpopular opinion (i.e. loving the simplicity of Strauss or the wit and wisdom of Mark Twain). I was very frustrated. I did not like the fact that I had silently agreed on something that I did not believe. It must just be the principle of the thing.

I don't try and justify any more. I have learned, over the years, that we all have reasons why we believe what we believe. That is what makes them our opinions.

Now, if asked, I tell people my opinion, and if asked why, will give the reasons. My goal is usually not to sway but to enlighten. I believe just as Charles A. Dana stated: "Fight for your opinions, but do not believe that they contain the whole truth, or the only truth."

⌘⌘⌘⌘⌘

"Do not be wise in your own opinion."
Romans 12:16

JULY 11

...SEEING THINGS IN A NEW LIGHT

"All good things which exist are the fruits of originality."
- John Stuart Mill

⌘⌘⌘⌘⌘

Running a darkroom literally makes you see things in a new light. First of all, everything in the darkroom is seen in a red glow. It's that eerie, sur-real effect. Things are not as clear as they would be in white light. Second, everything is seen in reverse. Whatever is white in the picture you shoot is black on the negative, and whatever is black in the picture you shoot is white on the negative.

Nothing in this world is seen the same way. Even if one event is witnessed by many people, you will have as many interpretations of the event as you have people.

If negatives in the darkroom are a total reverse of what is taken, I'm sure it is reasonable to assume that people can understand things in the total reverse of what they were meant to be. We speak of two sides of every coin and two sides of every issue.

This is the 180 of life, and our understanding lies somewhere in between the two points. Our ability to see things in a new light relies heavily on our ability to put ourselves on a different point, a position other than the one we are comfortable with, of this continuum.

⌘⌘⌘⌘⌘

"For with you is the fountain of life;
in your light we see light."
Psalm 36:9

JULY 12
...UNDERSTANDING THE DIFFERENCE BETWEEN BEING LONELY AND BEING ALONE

> "Solitude is as needful to the imagination as
> society is wholesome for the character."
> - James Russell Lowell

⌘⌘⌘⌘⌘

I dated the same man for seven years. The better I got to know him, the more certain I was that I would never marry him. This was for one reason: he could not spend time with just himself.

I love time to myself, by myself, and for myself. I can't survive without solitude. I am not lonely; I am alone.

He, on the other hand, always had to be doing something. He had to attend some opening, meet with friends, play golf, have friends over, go to socials, go to movies, go to dinner, and have a constant companion. He did not enjoy being alone for he was lonely. Alone is "to be apart from other people." Lonely is "dejected by the awareness of being alone." One heals; the other hurts.

I have often wondered if people that constantly have to be with someone else cannot stand the idea of being with just themselves? They seem to be absent from themselves; and until they learn to be comfortable with who they are, I don't think they will be truly comfortable with others. With no time to spend with just ourselves, we do not know who we are. Mary Sarton described loneliness as "poverty of self."

My husband and I both need our "alone" time. Because I work many evenings, he has time at night by himself, and I have time by myself during many days when he is at his office. Because in our aloneness, we know who we are, and we come to each other more secure, confident, and comfortable with self and with each other.

⌘⌘⌘⌘⌘

> "Be at peace among yourselves."
> 1 Thessalonians 5:13

JULY 13
...KNOWING THE PURPOSE OF ORDER

"Good order is the foundation of all things."
- Edmund Burke

⌘⌘⌘⌘⌘

Whatever it was, my Grandmother had an expression for it. She was very much the strong, conservative, orderly Southern Baptist. Order was key to her life. If you inadvertently or deliberately left something laying out, some expressions you might hear were:

A place for everything and everything in its place.
Waste not, want not.
If you take it out, put it back.
Keep thy house, and thy house will keep thee.
If you open it, close it.

For a woman who raised as many children and grandchildren as she did, and did it alone because her husband was always on the road, the order she needed must have provided her with structure. This order allowed her to spend less time on cleaning and more time with her children. Instead of having to look for everything, she saved time by knowing where everything was and that it was in a state of good repair.

I appreciate this lesson of order now that I have my own business. When you present to many companies on many topics, being able to pull files, lay your hands on letters of agreement, make meetings, tailor make for each client, and keep up with invoices is essential. You cannot do all of this without order.

My order is computer based while my grandmother's order was a box of 3 X 5 cards. Regardless of our system, we both have order.

"A schedule defends from chaos and whim. It is a net for catching days. It is a scaffolding on which a worker can stand and labor with both hands at sections of time. A schedule is a mock-up of reason and order — willed, faked, and so brought into being." Annie Dillard.

⌘⌘⌘⌘⌘

"But everything should be done in a fitting and orderly way."
1 Corinthians 14:40

JULY 14
...ENJOYING BEING A "STRATUS DWELLER"

"The heavens call to you, and circle around you,
displaying to you their eternal splendours,
and your eye gazed only to earth."

- Dante

⌘⌘⌘⌘⌘

My office is in my home, and I love having it there. It allows me the luxury of filling dual roles of working at a business and keeping a house. It is also low – almost no – overhead. That is great for business.

Most of the time I meet my clients at their office. Occasionally, clients will want to meet off-site to discuss my presentations or a specific issue they do not want to have overhead. Consequently, I need a meeting place. My meeting place is The Skyline Club. It is a dining club on the 36th (top) floor of the AUL building. Its roof is glass. The view overlooks the city. The food is marvelous. The service is extraordinary.

Every time I go to the club, I think about an episode of Star Trek. Spock and Kirk were on a planet with only two classes of people. One class, the lower class, worked underground in the mines. The other class of people lived in the clouds and called themselves "Stratus Dwellers." The Stratus Dwellers just seemed to walk around looking good, thinking wise thoughts, and enjoying life.

At The Skyline Club, I'm a Stratus Dweller. I'm in the clouds when I'm on the 36th floor. I'm looking good; I'm thinking – hopefully – wise thoughts for my clients; and I am definitely enjoying life.

Whatever we use for our get-a-way, it's nice to have occasions when we can remove ourselves from the mines and be part of a special society. A society and a place that allows us an atmosphere to improve ourselves.

The Skyline Club is my overhead in more ways than one.

⌘⌘⌘⌘⌘

"But our citizenship is in heaven."
Philippians 3:20

JULY 15
...NEVER KNOWING WHO WE MAY TOUCH

"All credibility, all good conscience,
all evidence of truth come only from our senses."
- Nietzsche

⌘⌘⌘⌘⌘

As I have mentioned before, students teach us many things. For about five years, I taught 7th grade. They are unpredictable in this difficult stage between childhood and puberty, and they are still fairly uninhibited and very egocentric.

The teachers spent their free period in the faculty lounge. On one particular day the "free period" was almost up, and the teachers got ready to head back to class. I mentioned that I had to go get another pencil ready. One of the teachers asked why. I said that little Johnny Jones never had a pencil when he came to class. The other teachers looked surprised and remarked that he always had a pencil when he came to their class. I was confused. We couldn't possibly be talking about the same Johnny Jones, but we were.

Johnny walked into class, put his books down, and headed for my desk. As usual, he asked if I had a pencil he could use. I told him his other teachers said he always had a pencil when he came into their classrooms. He hung his head and admitted this was true.

I asked him why he borrowed a pencil from me every day. He said, "Because your pencils always smell so good." I didn't respond; I just handed him a pencil. He smiled and went back to his seat.

I don't even remember what hand lotion I used, but I do remember him sitting at his desk, happy, with this inexpensive perfumed piece of wood.

We never know who we will touch, literally or figuratively, or what type of impact we will make on someone's life. Touching someone else's life helps us go beyond ourselves and change the world in small ways. I often wondered if little Johnny Jones remembers that pencil he borrowed every day. I also wonder what impact that had on his life. I'm assuming since he asked for it — everyday — it had some type of impact.

Our hands and our touch are our extension to others in this world, and, hopefully, what people remember from our touch are gentleness, kindness, and caring.

⌘⌘⌘⌘⌘

"You have blessed the work of his hands,"
Job 1:10

JULY 16
...RELYING ON CRUTCHES WHEN NECESSARY

"'This not enough to help the feeble up.
But to support him after."
- Shakespeare

ⵝⵝⵝⵝⵝ

I had the experience of relying on crutches for three months during the ice and snow of winter. I have to admit I didn't like them. I'm glad I had them, but I didn't like them. They were awkward, hurt my arm pits, slowed me down, and were difficult to manage — especially on ice and snow. But I do realize that without them I would have been down and out for three months of my life. This would have been the worse of these two evils. When we need crutches, we are glad we have them, but we don't like the physically restraints that crutches put on us.

Many times in our lives we have to rely on mental or emotional crutches. We don't like this either, but we are just as glad to have these mental and emotional crutches as we are to have the wooden crutches when we need them. To have someone hold us when we cry, to take over and make decisions for us when we are not able to reason, to run interference for us, or to do for us when we cannot do for ourselves. These are the crisis times in our life. It doesn't matter if the crisis is mental, emotional, or physical, in all cases we need a little extra help for a short while.

Whether our crutches are the wooden kind you lean on or the shoulders you lay your head and cry on, what a blessing it is to have them to help us over the rough times until we can mentally, emotionally and physically stand on our own.

ⵝⵝⵝⵝⵝ

"But I have had God's help to this very day,
and so I stand here and testify to small and great alike."
Acts 26:22

JULY 17
...LOOKING UP FOR THE CUT OFF

"There is music wherever there is harmony, order, or proportion."
- Thomas Brown

⌘⌘⌘⌘⌘

We have approximately a 100 person choir. When that many people are assembled to sing, you definitely need a director to help keep everyone together. Our director is very specific about the uptake and the cut off – especially the cut off. It sound amateurish to hear people ending words at different times. We probably all remember times when we have heard a group singing, and everyone ends together but one person. The sound of the one person stands out and sounds awkward and unprofessional. If the end of lines, measures, and chords are in unison, and the t's, p's, d's, m's and n's are enunciated at once, the impact on the audience is awesome. The room once filled with the sound of 100 voices is now filled with the sound of silence. What a dramatic contrast!

I think it would be great, regardless of what we were doing, if we always had someone to look to for the cut off. Someone who would point out to us when we had screamed too much, talked to much, criticized too much, cried to much, nagged too much, or told too much. Someone who would point out to us it was time to shut our mouth and give the world a break with our silence.

I think we do. We just have to look a little higher and listen a little harder for this director and his cut off.

⌘⌘⌘⌘⌘

"For this God is our God for ever and ever;
he will be our guide even to the end."
Psalm 48:14

JULY 18
...ESTABLISHING GUIDELINES

"Nothing in life is as good as the marriage of true minds
between man and woman. As good? It is life itself."

- Pearl Buck

⌘⌘⌘⌘⌘

I had been dating a man for about seven years. [Once in a bad marriage, you don't want to jump into things too fast.] For at time this relationship had been fun and exciting, but, after a while, it grew rather stale and boring. I told Gina I was just tired of seeing this man; he was not what I was looking for. She asked me what I was looking for. I said, "OK; I can establish criteria. Here's what I want. I want a man who doesn't do drugs, doesn't drink heavily, isn't emotionally or physically abusive, doesn't have small children to raise, doesn't have 14+ co-dependent relationships, isn't looking for a meal ticket, has a good job, doesn't want a mother, is my intellectual equal, comes from the same small town farming background, likes simple things, loves animals, and is cute." I figured I might as well list them all and be very specific. This type of person couldn't actually exist!

Gina was looking at me. Finally she said, "I have someone I want you to meet. He is looking for someone like you. If I set up a blind date, would you go out with him?" I thought it would be a free meal, so, why not.

My first date with Stan was on October 31st. We dated for several months, and on Valentine's Day of the next year, he said he wanted us to just date one another and see if we had a true working, living, loving relationship that would stand the test of time. Evidently we did because we are now married, and short of winning the lottery, we couldn't be much happier.

It's important for us to set guidelines. If we don't ask for or state, specifically, what we want, how can we ever recognize it when it comes our way. Our guidelines are our map that gets us to the right place. They are our credo that we need to share with others so they know where we stand.

I am so grateful that I established my guidelines and shared them with Gina. If I had not, I would have never met Stan or be married to this wonderful man. My grandmother always told me to dream big because you were just as likely to get that as a small one!

⌘⌘⌘⌘⌘

"Therefore shall a man leave his father and his mother,
and shall cleave unto his wife, and they shall be one flesh."

Genesis 2:23-24

JULY 19
...KNOWING WHEN "RETAIL THERAPY" IS HELPFUL

"Only within the moment of time represented by the
present century has one species —man — acquired
significant power to alter the nature of his world."

- Rachel Carson

⌘⌘⌘⌘⌘

I have an unusual sense of humor in the fact that I can find something humorous in most situations. I tell people it is my way to survive some of the things in life that I had to deal with but would have preferred not to.

After my second surgery and my diagnosis of breast cancer, my husband and I were talking about how to proceed. You do have an option of when you want to do what. So, we decided the best course would be chemotherapy followed by radiation therapy followed by hormone therapy.

Every time we talked about the therapies, the pain on my husband's face was intense. Being in the medical field, he knew, more than I did, what I was going to go through. I knew I had to break this pain; so, my sense of humor came to my rescue. I asked, "Didn't they tell you about the fourth type of therapy they want me do to?" Naturally, he said no. I said, "Retail therapy. The more I shop, the quicker I'll heal."

He just stood and looked at me for about 60 seconds. Then, he threw up his hands, turned around, and walked away telling me that I was impossible to deal with. I followed behind him detailing how much money I needed to spend daily, and even though he was still going on about me being impossible, I knew he was smiling. Following him, I could see his ears go up when he smiled.

I think retail therapy is an reprieve for all people. The mall is pretty and smells good. There are no problems for the moment. An escape. And whether it's an actual trip to the mall to escape life for awhile, a humorous escape from the pain of the moment, or a prayerful escape from the worries of the world, sometimes it works.

⌘⌘⌘⌘⌘

"Know that I am with you and will keep you wherever you go."

Genesis 28:15

JULY 20
...KNOWING WHERE I STAND

"The real world is not always easy to live in. It is rough; it is slippery.
Without the most clear-eyed adjustments we fall and get crushed."
                                                              - Clarence Day

⌘⌘⌘⌘⌘

I can't make it to every choir practice. Few of the members can. This is the
reason we practice songs for three or four Sunday services each Thursday evening
of choir practice. On June 29, 1997, we had a ground breaking service for the
church's new addition. The choir was scheduled to lead the congregation outside to
the expansion site. There was a flatbed trailer setting where the new choir loft
would be. We would climb up on the flatbed and sing "Upon This Rock."

I could not be at the Thursday night rehearsal for the ground breaking
ceremony; consequently, even though I knew the song, I wouldn't know where to go
or stand. I turned to Debbie, whom I stand next to, and said, "I can't be here
Thursday, but I will be here on Sunday. Please just save me a place and show me
where I stand."

I was thinking how nice knowing where you stand would be. Just tell me or
show me where I stand. I don't want to make decisions today; just do it for me.
We don't **always** want people to tell us where we stand; but, on those special
occasions, when life is too confusing, it sure would be a nice luxury to have.

⌘⌘⌘⌘⌘

"I will strengthen you, I will help you."
                                    Isaiah 41:10

JULY 21

...PRAISING COMMON SENSE

"No one tests the depth of a river with both feet."
- Ashanti Proverb

⌘⌘⌘⌘⌘

Most people don't give a lot of credence to common sense. It's taken for granted all too often. Many times common sense comes with trial and error, but, for some who lack common sense, even trial and error isn't enough. My mother, bless her heart, was given extra in the areas of mathematics and mechanics and less in the area of common sense.

My mother and I had just bought our first new house out in the country. We were so happy because it had so many things we wanted – especially a real live log-burning fireplace. We used the fireplace every cold weekend. We had used it on a particularly cold Friday night. The next morning I got up and told Mother I would clean out the fireplace when I got back from the store. [I really wanted her to leave everything alone. Mother wants to help because she means well, but she doesn't always use good common sense. My wonderful mother, wanting to help me by going to the store, drove my new 5-speed through the wall in the family room because she thought the shift pattern was the same as on a 4-speed. Because she thought my toast looked too light, she turned the toaster to DARK! The toaster, which sat below a roll of paper towels, ignited the roll of paper towels and set the kitchen on fire.]

As I came over the rise in the road, I saw all the doors and windows were open and smoke was rolling out of the house. The dogs were running in and out of the house, and the neighbors were standing there watching the spectacle.

Mother had decided to help me after all. She knew it would be easier to suck the ashes out of the fireplace with the sweeper than shovel and carry them out in a bucket. She did not realize there were live coals in the ashes which set the sweeper on fire which set the rug on fire which caused smoke damage to most of our brand new house.

I love my mother. I love her mathematical and mechanical ability. I do wish, at times, that she had more common sense. Of all of our senses, we shouldn't take the "common" one for granted. Our common sense is our base on which much of our other abilities are built.

⌘⌘⌘⌘⌘

"Who is wise and understanding among you? Let him show it by
his good life, by deeds done in the humility that comes from wisdom."
James 3:13

JULY 22
...HAVING AN ALTER EGO

"You are who you are because of your ego."
- John Cassavetes

⌘⌘⌘⌘⌘

We all have different egos or personalities that come out at different times. In front of my audience, I try my best to appear composed, knowledgeable, and articulate. At home with my husband, I'm a wife and step-parent who shares in the lives of others. At home alone with my four-legged children, I'm a "puppy mom" who crawls on the floor, talks in a sing-song voice and acts silly chasing the dogs around the yard yelling, "I'll be getting you now."

If you have known me only as I am in front of my audience, you would be amazed finding out about these alter egos I have. When you walk into our home, you know immediately, by the way I have it decorated, that I'm not just a businesswoman. The floors and cabinets are butterscotch maple. The furniture is cushy leather. The design is Country French. The key colors are forest green and burgundy. Each room has a needlepoint pillow I have done. The pictures have long silk ribbons as hangers. An occasional teddy bear or bunny will grace a chair, and antique toys are properly displayed.

This is my alter ego. My soft side; the other side of me, that is privy to a select few. It is the genuine me where I am at home and at peace.

I love having this home and this alter ego. Our alter ego, what we would consider to be our true self, is where we go to relax, be safe, and enjoy ourselves.

⌘⌘⌘⌘⌘

"Remember that it is not you that support the roots,
but the roots that support you."
Romans 11:18

JULY 23

...DOING WHEN YOU DON'T FEEL LIKE DOING

"In the arena of human life the honours and rewards
fall to those who show their good qualities in action."

- Aristotle

⌘⌘⌘⌘⌘

It was one of those days! I had been the "Clutz of the Day". I had stubbed
my toe, tripped on rugs, banged into door frames, gotten tangled up in the
sweeper cord, stepped on one of the dog's tail, and suffered a paper cut. I was
going to improve my mood by ordering this little adorable tea bag holder on
QVC; but, by the time I got around to ordering it, it had sold out. This reduced
me to tears. I had to run errands, and, to finally top my day off, I got stuck in the
world's largest construction traffic jam. I was so angry. Nothing was going to go
my way this entire day. Aggghhh!

I was sitting in a line of traffic trying not to lose my mind. I glanced to my
left, and there, on a side road, sat two guys in a truck loaded with cardboard
boxes. I don't know how long they had been there, but I do believe I saw
cobwebs on the boxes in their truck. I knew I should let them in line, but I was so
angry I didn't feel like being nice or kind to anyone. Then I thought, "In this line
of traffic what difference is one more car going to make?" So, when I got near
them, I waved them in line.

This was the best things I could have done for it made my day go much
better than I would ever have expected. They were so overjoyed that I let them in
line that they didn't stop just with a wave of thanks. They raised their arms up to
heaven as if they were receiving blessing. They kept blowing me kisses. They
clasped their hands in prayer. They did these things over and over.

I sat behind them and laughed and laughed. I forgot about the paper cut,
the sold out tea bag holder and the line of traffic, but I wouldn't have been able to
forget or let go of my anger and frustration if I had not decided to be kind to these
two men in the pick-up truck.

It was George Eliot who wrote, "Our deeds determine us, as much as we
determine our deeds."

⌘⌘⌘⌘⌘

"God will give to each person according to what he has done."

Romans 2:6

JULY 24

...NOT SPEAKING JUST FOR THE MOMENT

"A liar should have a good memory."

- Quintilian

⌘⌘⌘⌘⌘

My family and I loved to vacation in Gatlinburg, Tennessee. We loved the national park, the shopping, the mountain streams, the restaurants, and the mountain crafts. We went there every fall, its most beautiful season. I was in junior high when we first started going to Gatlinburg, still pretty uninhibited, and I enjoyed talking to the Cherokee Indians.

One of the old Indians that people could have their picture taken with was particularly interesting, and he used to explain the Cherokee philosophy. One of the points he made really hit home with me. He told me that the Cherokee find a liar to be a very brave and unusual person. Why? The liar is afraid of other men but not afraid of God. They soothe the mortal and short lasting, and they anger the immortal and ever lasting. They speak for the moment.

Speaking for the moment gets us into one lie after another. It is the "tangled web we weave;" and when things start unraveling, we can do little to stop the process. The only thing worse than lying is getting caught lying.

I don't know how many times I have told someone that I couldn't attend their gathering because I was going out of town; and then they called my house to leave a message, and I answered the phone. I stuttered and stammered and sounded incredibly stupid making up other lies from illness to mechanical difficulties. And, I know the other person knows I'm lying.

I have learned as I have aged that it is better just to tell people I'm tired and need to rest, or I have work to do. It may not be what they want to hear, but I'm not lying, or worse, getting caught in that lie. When you don't speak for just the moment, each moment of your life becomes easier to live.

⌘⌘⌘⌘⌘

"Even in the case of lifeless things that make sounds,
such as the flute or harp, how will anyone know what tune
is being played unless there is a distinction in the notes?"

1 Corinthians 14:7

JULY 25

...BEING IN THE RIGHT PLACE AT THE RIGHT TIME

"The best thing we can do is to make wherever we're lost in/
Look as much like home as we can."

- Christopher Fry

⌘⌘⌘⌘⌘

In a previous career, I had a job that required me to do a great deal of traveling and entertaining. We were holding a conference in New Orleans at the Hyatt. It was the night of our company's awards dinner. I had arrived at the dining room early to check things out and realized I had left the certificates for the attendees in my room. Knowing that the attendees would be arriving soon, I had to hurry back to my room.

Now, I was wearing a long strapless black lace gown. I picked up the front of the gown in my arms and ran for the elevator. [I must explain that the Hyatt in New Orleans adjoins the football stadium. This was Saturday night, and the next day the New York Jets would be playing the New Orleans Saints.] I pressed the elevator button, the doors opened, and there stood an elevator crammed full of New York Jets. They were so young and so cute, and I just stood there staring at them. Seeing my indecision, they smiled (some winked) and asked me to come on in. I took a deep breath, smiled and said there wasn't enough room. They began backing up and said they would make room. I said, "Oh, no thanks. I've never been in a glass elevator with a football team, and I just wouldn't know what to do." The door closed, and I heard them laugh.

This incident always brings a smile to my face. How often do you have the opportunity to see an entire squad of a football team let alone have the opportunity to ride in an elevator with them. It sure couldn't have been planned. You just had to be in the right place at the right time. Unfortunately, this was one opportunity I was not equal to! Go, Jets

⌘⌘⌘⌘⌘

"In his heart a man plans his course,
but the Lord determines his steps."

Proverbs 16:9

JULY 26
...MAKING A "MAJOR" WRONG MOVE

"A small demerit extinguishes a long service."
- Thomas Fuller

⌘⌘⌘⌘⌘

We accidentally make many wrong moves during our life time. Most of them are small, and we can recover easily from them. However, some of the moves we make are wrong and major, and they do make lasting changes that we must accept.

When Murphy was a puppy, like most puppies, she loved everyone. She would see a new person and almost nothing could hold her back. She would wiggle in circles, lick them, and roll on her back to get her belly scratched. She ran to greet the postal carrier and the UPS people. They petted her and made over her. She loved everybody! Murphy also likes to run; she will always be a chaser. It makes no difference if it is dandelion fluff, leaves, or semis. If it moves, she will run for it.

One morning we were out on the deck. It was very early; I didn't think anyone would be around, so I didn't hook her up to her lead. I walked into the house to get my coffee. She saw a jogger; and before I could catch her, she ran over the hill after him. I screamed her name, but it was too late. The jogger saw her coming and evidently was afraid. He picked up a log and hit her with it. He hit her so hard that she kept crying out loud and came back walking to the side to favor her ribs.

That was the one "major" wrong move in Murphy's life. Her personality changed from that moment on. She is still friendly to the people she knows, but she does not trust any stranger. When someone new approaches her, she bares her teeth and growls, and she means business. I must always be on guard with her.

It has made me very sad to see this once loving animal become so shy and scared around people that she becomes mean in order to protect herself. It has also made me view some people differently. When I see people who are mean or scared, I can't help but wonder if they, too, were once wonderful people who had been clubbed. In many situations, one "major" wrong move is all it takes.

⌘⌘⌘⌘⌘

"He heals the brokenhearted
and binds up their wounds."
Psalm 147:3

JULY 27

...FINDING A COACH

"The real leader has no need to lead — he is content to point the way."

- Henry Miller

⌘⌘⌘⌘⌘

When I was teaching school, all the teachers used to get together once a week and play volleyball. The basketball coach headed up one team, and the football coach headed up the other. I loved playing every position except server. It always hurt my hand and wrist to serve. My coach knew this, and every time it was my turn to serve, he'd say "Just one." Then, if I had to serve a second or third time, he's say "Just one more." Now, I knew what he was doing, but I have to admit, it worked. I kept thinking just one more time. Coaches are invaluable.

The first time I met Susan Bixler and Lisa Scherrer I was at a pretty low ebb of my life. It was summer and hot, and I was wearing a wig because I had lost all my hair during chemotherapy. I was tired, and I had spent so much time focusing on my health that I had lost direction with my business. I was down emotionally and professionally. I needed to hear "just one more time" from someone. On the advice of a friend, I went to Susan's and Lisa's training at The Professional Image Institute in Atlanta. It was the first time I had been by myself for nine months. I went to Atlanta early, took off the wig and for a day held up in the hotel room to try and get back in touch with myself.

I went to the training session and met Susan, Lisa and six other wonderful women. The first day we spent listening and viewing slides. The second day we had the opportunity to interact with and get to know one another. When it came my turn, I told them, in a very matter of fact manner, what I had gone through and why I had come to the training. I passed out brochures and told them about my business and who my clients were. From that moment on, I heard wonderful things from everyone. They told me how much they admired my strength, my entrepreneurial endeavors, my faith, etc. The verbal shot in the arm they gave to me was just as valuable as any chemical injection I had received.

The world has had many great coaches or leaders. Jesus had disciples. King Arthur had knights. We have bosses, family, and friends to guide, lead and inspire. I am very thankful I had the opportunity to meet Susan and Lisa and the other attendees. We still keep in touch; and when I receive a note or get a call from any one of them, I know I can do almost anything "just one more time."

⌘⌘⌘⌘⌘

"Since you are my rock and my fortress,
for the sake of your name lead and guide me."
Psalm 31:3

JULY 28
...SAYING THANK YOU FOR ALL THINGS

"A blessing we give to one another."
- Robert Reynolds

⌘⌘⌘⌘⌘

When words have 100's of definitions, our understanding of words is based upon our definition and interpretation of words. We have so many interpretations and definitions to choose from, we must decide what meaning suits our purpose — today.

Words not only deliver a direct message, but they also deliver an underlying message: the meaning behind the actual words. To give you an example, let's look at the direct message and the underlying message behind two very simple words we use daily: Thank you.

If someone walks up to you and compliments you on your beautiful hair, and your response is, "The last time I had it cut they didn't get it even on the sides. It needs a touch up, and the ends are split. It's really oily in the crown, and ...." These are the words you are saying, but it may not be what the other person is hearing. What they may be hearing is, "Boy, you are pretty stupid, aren't you? How dare you compliment me on something I know is not true. We can't be friends. I don't want to work with you. I don't want to develop a relationship with you because you are just stupid." [Aside: This person will never compliment you again.] However, if someone compliments you on your hair, and you respond with "Thank you," what they may be hearing is, "I like what it is you have to say. You and I could probably be friends. We could work together and even develop a personal relationship because I like what it is you have to say."

Saying "thank you" creates a bond with others. It shows the world we are proud of who and what we are. It shows we have self-confidence. It shows we can meet the world head on. And, most important, it shows the world we are grateful to God for all the gifts we have no matter how trivial they may seem.

⌘⌘⌘⌘⌘

"Enter into his gates with thanksgiving, and into his courts with praise."
Psalm 100:4

JULY 29
...NOT ALWAYS HAVING TO KEEP SCORE

"The most important thing in the Olympic Games is not
winning but taking part .... The essential thing in life
is not conquering but fighting well."
- Baron Pierre de Coubertin

⌘⌘⌘⌘⌘

For four years almost every Saturday in the fall, my husband and I drove to Purdue and other college campuses to see his son play football. The atmosphere was exciting and fun. The crowds, street vendors, band, Purdue Pete, the wave, sitting with the other parents and riding the "Boiler Maker Special" all added to the festivities.

Purdue's scoreboard was pretty spectacular. It showed time outs, yards rushing, yards passing, pictures of the players in action, scores, the school fight song, etc. You knew who was winning and who was losing because someone was keeping score. In our life, there are many things for which we need to keep score. We need to know who is ahead and who is winning. But not in all things.

When we begin to keep score in relationships, we are wrong. If we get upset and argumentative over who made the bed more this month or who took the trash out more times this month or whose car was driven more times this month, we will begin to alienate ourselves from one another. Yes, we need to share responsibilities, but we need to realize because of our schedule – this month – maybe we can't make the bed, cook, or take out the trash the same number of times we did last month. Next month, we may be back on schedule, and our spouse or significant other may be a little pressed for time.

Quantity is important, but it should not always win out.

⌘⌘⌘⌘⌘

"Do nothing out of selfish ambition or vain conceit,
but in humility consider others better than yourselves."
Philippians 2:3

JULY 30

...FORGIVING THOSE WHO DON'T LIKE US

"The highest and most difficult of all moral lessons."

- Joseph Jacobs

⌘⌘⌘⌘⌘

As we discussed in one of the January entries, seasoned speakers know, the instant they walk into the room, who in the room is taking exception to them or what they are presenting. We don't know why they are taking exception to us; we just know they are.

At a training session for speakers, we discussed this issue, and we came up with some interesting reasons for this attitude. We could possibly look like someone who dumped them in high school and made life a "teenage hell on earth." We could possibly look like an in-law who is currently making their life miserable. They could just hate our topic and be forced to attend. Or, they could be suffering from a lack of sleep or constipation. We just don't know why. The important point to remember is just to get by these people.

Early in my career, I did a presentation for a local Chamber. The room was set up in a U-shape. I watched the attendees as they entered. There were two women, I spotted as they walked in, that did not want to be there. They sat in the center of the back row glaring at me with folded arms. They did not take one note, laugh at one joke, or nod in agreement at any time. They spent the two hours trying their best to make me uncomfortable by whispering to one other each time I made a major point. And, they were the first ones out the door.

It was a long two hours, and I spent a great deal of that time hating these two women. This situation, although uncomfortable, was not a waste for I did learn several things from this experience: 1) Hating people doesn't change their attitude ab out you, and 2) if someone walks into a room disliking you, they probably won't like you any better when they walk out of the room.

All we can do is let go of the situation and forgive others for not liking us. We don't like everyone; we can't expect everyone to like us. We must hope that those we dislike will try to forgive us just as we will try to forgive those who dislike us.

⌘⌘⌘⌘⌘

"Be kind and compassionate to one another,
forgiving each other, just as in Christ God forgave you."

Ephesians 4:32

JULY 31

...KNOWING HOW SOMEONE FEELS

"Only that which is deeply felt can change us."
- Marilyn Ferguson

⌘⌘⌘⌘⌘

"I know how you feel." How many times have each of us said that? And having said that, how many times do we really know how someone feels.

I was scheduled to have six injections when I was going through chemotherapy. I was told that with six injections, along with the other forms of therapy, I had a 95% chance of being a survivor. I made the decision to do chemotherapy. The injections started in December, one week before my birthday, and were to end in March/April. The injections were every three weeks. For one week you felt like the walking dead, for one week you just felt sick, for one week you felt pretty good, and then you had another injection. I managed to stay on a good time schedule, and I counted the days until the last injection. After the fifth injection, I became very sick. My body turned red and itched horribly everywhere I had skin. Welts started. My tongue swelled. I couldn't see. I was terrified.

I was sent to an allergist. He said it was quite possible I was having a reaction to the chemotherapy and that I might want to postpone the last injection. I went through some serious thought and finally concluded that my body was telling me I had had enough. I truly thought I would die if I did the last injection. So, I opted out.

My husband, who is in medicine, was worried. He called the oncologist and told him what I had decided. He wanted to know what the percentages were with five injections. It was 92-93%. Stan said he didn't know what to say to me. The oncologist talked with him and said, "You think you know what you may do, and I think I know what I may do, but we don't sit in that chair — she does. We do not know how she feels." That was good enough for my husband.

The night we knew the chemotherapy was over, my husband reclined in his chair. He fell into a coma-like sleep. Nothing could wake him. Yelling, shaking him, nothing. I sat up until 3:00 am just watching him sleep and making sure he didn't stop breathing. I think all the stress he had endured during the surgeries and chemotherapy left him, and he collapsed. I believe that the only thing harder than going through chemotherapy would be watching someone you love go through it. No, my husband did not know how I felt, and I pray he never will. I, on the other hand, did not know how he felt, and I pray, too, that I never will.

⌘⌘⌘⌘⌘

"He who has prepared us for this very thing is God."

AUGUST 1
...BEING ENTERTAINED BY A MOCKING BIRD

"The merry minstrels of the morn."
- James Thomson

ℋℋℋℋℋ

I do most of my writing sitting in the family room recliner next to the fireplace. Instead of four office walls, I look out the windows and watch the dogs and see the flowers. It is a moment of mental refreshment. I can throw clothes in the wash and watch supper bake. The phone and the television are there, so, all in all, it's a pretty good location.

I do have a special secret reason why I like to sit in this chair by the fireplace – I can hear a Mocking Bird. Mocking Birds typically sit on top of chimneys because it is warm. And my own, personal Mocking Bird sits on my chimney during the day and entertains me. One minute he sounds like a Robin, and the next minute he sounds like a Sparrow. Occasionally, he meows like a cat or barks like a dog. Sometimes I go outside to look at him while he sings. Every minute or so he jumps straight up in the air, twirls around, and drops back down to the top of the chimney. He's a hoot, and listening to him and watching him never fails to bring a smile to my face.

There are few, if any, of us that can be all things to all people. The Mocking Bird probably comes as close as anything can. I think that is why it is a sin to kill a Mocking Bird. By killing this one bird you are silencing the voices of 100's of birds and eliminating the joy that this one small creature can bring to each person — especially the one who sits in the recliner next to the fireplace just to hear the Mocking Bird.

ℋℋℋℋℋ

"For everything God created is good, and nothing
is to be rejected if it is received with thanksgiving,
because it is consecrated by the word of God and prayer."
1 Timothy 4:4-5

AUGUST 2
...LOVING SPECIAL POSSESSION

"Every possession and every happiness is but lent by chance
for an uncertain time, and may therefore be demanded back the next hour."
- Schopenhauer

⌘⌘⌘⌘⌘

Murphy loves balls. She chases them, chews on them, catches them and steals them from the other dogs in the neighborhood. She has quite a few balls: the typical tennis balls, soft balls that squeak, balls with jingle bells inside, and this big, ugly, stupid-looking, dog-spit covered yellow gum ball.

Originally, she had an orange one, but she ripped it to shreds and was devastated. I'd throw the pieces away, and she would drag the pieces out of the trash. Consequently, I went back to the pet store and got her a yellow gum ball. It was the last one.

It is her "special" prized possession. She sleeps with it, carries it in and out of the house with her, places it by her bowl while she eats, refuses to let CoCo near it, rolls on it, holds it in her paws when she lays at the top of the stairs, and even tries to take it on our walks.

It is her constant companion. If it has rolled under the couch, she whines until we drag it out. If she has misplaced it in excitement, she walks the house looking for it until she finds it. When we travel, she will carry her own gum ball into the car to make sure she has it with her on the trip.

I have no idea what has made this ball so special; I just know that it is special. It must be like my teddy bear was to me when I was a child or my laptop computer is now that I am an adult. We all have those special "prized" possessions: lockets with pictures or wisps of hair, toys, pressed roses, wedding invitations, first cards sent from a loved-one or a trinket from a grandparent. It's not the object; it's the memory associated with the object.

I shudder to think what will happen when the yellow gum ball finally meets its doom. I shudder to think what will happen to each of us when we lose our special "prized" possession.

⌘⌘⌘⌘⌘

"Thanks be to God for his indescribable gift!"
2 Corinthians 9:15

AUGUST 3
...HOLDING FOR JUST A MINUTE

"How much of human life is lost in waiting!"
- Emerson

⌘⌘⌘⌘⌘

The other day I was trying to complete some phone calls. I was trying to hurry because I had a meeting I was to attend, and for some reason, with every call I made, I heard "would you please hold for a moment." Now, this is not a question because they say it and then press the button. I didn't even get a chance to say No, as if that would do any good anyway. I was very frustrated, and I couldn't stop thinking how my callers must feel when I say the same thing to them.

We always seem to be in a rush; and when we have anything thrown in our way that slows us down, we do get frustrated. Not only that, but when we feel as if we are not being treated special or given attention or slighted, it affects our interaction with the person on the other end of the phone. I suppose we think, "Why should I be kind to them when they have not been kind to me?" We sigh and are determined to treat others the same way. Not a good scenario.

I know holding for just a minute is a way of life for most people and most businesses. Maybe a better approach would be to tell others, briefly, what is going on and then ask them if they care to hold or get their number and call them back. This little bit of special attention sets up a better interaction and relationship with people: something I think we all desire.

⌘⌘⌘⌘⌘

"For God alone my soul waits in silence."
Psalm 62:1

AUGUST 4

...WALKING A MILE IN SOMEONE ELSE'S SHOES

"Only the wearer knows where the shoe pinches."
- English Proverb

⌘⌘⌘⌘⌘

In teaching adult education classes for a university, I have had the opportunity to meet many interesting people. They differ in age, gender, occupation, race, culture and religion, but even with all these differences, they have two major things in common: they bring with them wonderful stories and the benefit of real life experiences.

A few weeks ago, I started a new class. I walked in and looked at the students. They were nicely dressed, professional looking educated adults who sat there as a group waiting to begin class. One of the first exercises we do to get to know more about one another and to get each person to realize they all have something to share is to tell of an event that had an impact on their life.

Now, this nicely dressed, professional looking group of educated adults began to tell stories about growing up with an alcoholic father, having to be a mother to sisters and brothers because the real mother wasn't there, having a mastectomy due to breast cancer, being sent from one foster home to another, and having a two year old daughter die. I was stunned. Who knew that stories and experiences like this were under this "I've got it together" exterior.

Situations like this often remind me of one of the philosophies of the Cherokee Indians: "Grant that I may not criticize my neighbor until I have walked a mile in his moccasins." Without more insight and understanding of people, it is so easy to look at them and think to ourselves "What do you have to worry about? You don't have a care in the world."

We all have our own cares and our own load of sticks that make us what we are. Only by listening and taking a few "verbal" steps in another's shoes will we ever even begin to understand what they have gone through.

⌘⌘⌘⌘⌘

"Understanding is a fountain of life to those who have it,"
Proverbs 16:22

AUGUST 5
...KNOWING THE DIFFERENCE BETWEEN LUCK AND BLESSINGS

"The man who glories in his luck
May be overthrown by destiny."
- Euripides

⌘⌘⌘⌘⌘

My grandmother, a person strong in her beliefs, was very superstitious to the point that there were even some words she would not let you use.

She would never allow us to use the word "luck." We always had to use the word "blessings." Luck came from the devil. Blessings came from God. Luck was something you could make yourself, but blessings were a gift. We were not lucky; we were well blessed. Luck was "dumb," and you couldn't depend on it. Blessings were the gifts that were bestowed on you every day of your life. Luck was chance — something you just fell into. Blessings were purposeful. And, luck is singular, and blessings is plural.

Remembering her philosophy and her view of these words, I have gone through life telling people I was well blessed. When I hear someone say they are lucky, without thinking, I parrot her words: well blessed not lucky. And when I explain to people how she described these words, they, too, usually agree that they would rather be the beneficiary of something that was a purposeful gift of God bestowed on them in multiples every day of their lives.

⌘⌘⌘⌘⌘

"God, our God, has blessed us."
Psalm 67:6

AUGUST 6
...HAVING A "GET OUT OF JAIL FREE" CARD

"It is the heart always that sees, before the head can see."
- Thomas Carlyle

⌘⌘⌘⌘⌘

Every now and then, my husband will bring me a bouquet of flowers. I love the flowers and my husband even more for bringing them home unsolicited. One time when he brought flowers home, Ben, his son, was here, and I heard my husband remark to Ben that the flowers were his "get out of jail free card."

He figured by bringing home the flowers unsolicited that when he did something he probably shouldn't have done or something that might make me upset, I wouldn't say anything to him because he had brought home so many flowers. Flowers on no special holiday or occasion meant to him that I shouldn't be angry with him and give him a break. A get out of jail free card.

We all step on peoples' toes from time to time, and most often, we don't do it deliberately. When we do step on toes, how nice it would be for all of us to have this "free" card that was concrete proof of our affection for them.

Knowing in advance how much someone cares for you can certainly lessen any suspicions, pain or misunderstandings in our daily, sometimes careless and hurried, interaction.

⌘⌘⌘⌘⌘

"Love one another. Just as I have loved you,
you also should love one another."
John 13:34

AUGUST 7
...DREAMS DO COME TRUE

"If you have built castles in the air, your work need not be lost;
that is where they should be. Now put the foundations under them."
- Henry David Thoreau

⌘⌘⌘⌘⌘

I read every novel I could find about horses. I watched every horse
centered show. I listened to all the documentaries about horses. I read all the
training books. I collected statues and pictures of horses. I love horses!

My mother knew how much I loved horses, and she said she was sorry we
didn't live in an area where there was room for horses. Even though we didn't live
in a place that we could have horses, I never stopped dreaming of owning one.

My mother got a new position at Eli Lilly, and, as chance would have it, the
man she worked for had a horse farm. She mentioned to him how much I loved
horses, and he said to bring me out some Sunday. She did, and this man, Smitty,
her boss, and I became great friends. I went out every Sunday. I mucked stalls,
built fence, trimmed feet, curried and washed the horses, made harness, and
learned to train horses.

I had done this Sunday ritual for two years. It was Christmas time, and
Mother brought home a white box tied with a red ribbon. It was from Smitty to
me. I opened the box and inside was a certificate of ownership to Buck Creek's
Jo Jo, and my name was listed as the owner.

I went out to see him. There, next to his mother, Lord Admiral's Honey
Bee, was a blood bay with a white star and two white socks. He was three days
old, had on a sheep's halter because he was too little for a pony's halter, and had
long spindly legs and an attitude (he was one of the son's of King of Belgium, the
Number One Living Sire), and he was mine.

I cried as I wrote this entry. I remember all he meant to me, and I'm so
sorry he is gone — for now. He had a bad foot disease, and I had to have him put
to sleep.

Receiving Jo Jo as a Christmas present is always a reminder that there are
Santa Claus's all over this world and to never stop dreaming, no matter what your
age, because dreams do come true.

⌘⌘⌘⌘⌘

"All things can be done for the one who believes."
Mark 9:23

AUGUST 8
...UNDERSTANDING THAT HOLIDAYS CHANGE

"Custom reconciles us to everything."
- Edmund Burke

⌘⌘⌘⌘⌘

It was spring, and a group of students and I were talking about the holidays. The students ranged for Old Boomers to Young X'ers, and it was interesting to me to see how differently we viewed the holidays.

This one young mother was telling how this Easter was the first Easter her daughter was aware of the Easter Bunny and Easter Egg Hunts. She said her daughter loved to hunt the eggs, and ever since Easter Sunday, her daughter wanted her to hide the same eggs so she could find them again. This had gone on for three weeks.

The look on the Boomer's faces was one of disgust. The X'ers didn't understand and said, "What?" The Boomers asked how they could stand to have three week old boiled eggs around. The X'ers laughed. The eggs weren't boiled; they were plastic.

The generations go from Boomers to X'ers; interpretation of holidays go from the "way we use to do things" to "how we do things now;" and eggs go from boiled to plastic. Times change.

⌘⌘⌘⌘⌘

"'For my thoughts are not your thoughts,
neither are your ways my ways,' declares the Lord."

Isaiah 55:8

AUGUST 9
...LETTING OTHERS TEACH THEMSELVES VALUABLE LESSONS

"Life is a succession of lessons which must be lived to be understood."

- Emerson

⌘⌘⌘⌘⌘

My husband is notorious for letting others teach themselves valuable lessons or, as he would say, letting others hang themselves.

I had received an invitation to a "black tie" affair at Lilly Endowment. I called my husband and told him we needed to attend because I was one of very few women to receive an invitation. He agreed, and we went.

As we emerged from the elevator on the second floor, we were greeted with a very long receiving line. We began the gauntlet. Talking to different people about different things at different speeds, my husband had gotten ahead of me. About half way through the line, we ran into a political candidate. He greeted Stan, my husband, warmly, and said how nice it was to see him again, it had been so long, what was he doing now, and on and on. The politician said how great it was for Stan to get an invitation. [I must point out here that he didn't know Stan from Adam. He was being politically correct.] Stan let him go on and on; and when he stopped long enough for someone to get a word in, Stan stepped to the side, pulled me forward and said, "Thank you for your kind words, but you have made a mistake. The invitation was to my wife."

The look on his face was one of devastation — and possibly shock. You could tell the taste of shoe leather was not agreeable to him. By assuming one thing and slighting another, the man had made a fool of himself. Marie De France stated, "The fool shouts loudly, thinking to impress the world."

⌘⌘⌘⌘⌘

"And this is my prayer, that your love may overflow more and more with knowledge and full insight to help you to determine what is best."

Philippians 1:9-10

AUGUST 10
...PLAYING IT BY EAR

"To do easily what is difficult for others is the mark of talent."
- Henri Frederic Amiel

⌘⌘⌘⌘⌘

One of the most unbelievable and disgusting talents my grandmother had was her ability to play any piece of music by ear. She was the most auditory person I have ever known. All she had to do was hear a piece of music once, and she could duplicate it note for note.

For someone who struggled through a series of piano teachers and hours of practice, to have a grandmother with this talent was demoralizing. No matter how long I practiced, it never sounded as good as anything she had heard just one time and reproduced. She was a natural, and she took it very much for granted.

Most of us have to work hard at what we accomplish; and when we reach a certain level of completion, we are very proud and happy because we know what we have gone through to attain this level of achievement. We have reached a level where we have done the very best that we can.

Although I can not play by ear, I did reach a level where I had done the very best I could. I took more pride in what I had achieved than my grandmother took for her natural ability.

When things come too easily, as playing by ear, you don't take as much pride in your accomplishments as you do when you have combined some talent and a lot of hard work. For most of us, success and achievement lie in the effort we have expended to get to our desired level.

⌘⌘⌘⌘⌘

"But each man has his own gift of God,
one has this gift, another has that."
1 Corinthians 7:7

AUGUST 11
...ADDING VALUE

"Every time a value is born, existence takes on a new meaning;
every time one dies, some part of that meaning passes away."
                                                    - Joseph Wood Krutch

⌘⌘⌘⌘⌘

In a class I was teaching on communicating within organizations, one person was complaining that her employees added little value to the organization. I asked her to tell me a little about her employees, and she began to describe a group of people who were survivors of down-sizing having low morale and less motivation. Many were doing twice the work with the same pay. If anyone commented about the morale, they were told that they should just be glad that they had a job.

I told her that I could probably tell from her description why they added little value. She asked why, and I said, "I don't think you can add value if you don't have value."

Value is "a fair price or return for goods and services and worth in usefulness or importance to the possessor." When we treat or are treated in such a way that we begin to think that nothing we do, have, or are is of value or worth and that we are not useful or important, how can we possibly be expected to add what we don't have.

When we want that extra added value to our products, shouldn't we want the same from our fellow man? And, to have this added value human being, shouldn't we be helping each one of them see the value they have to contribute?

James Hilton said, 'Surely there comes a time when counting the cost and paying the price aren't things to think about any more. All that matters is value — the ultimate value of what one does." And I would like to add, "of what one is."

⌘⌘⌘⌘⌘

"Such confidence as this is ours through Christ before God."
                                                    2 Corinthians 3:4

AUGUST 12
...KNOWING WHEN TO SWITCH TO DECAFE

"Peace is not a passive but an active condition, not a negation
but an affirmation. It is a gesture as strong as war."
- Mary Roberts Reinhart

⌘⌘⌘⌘⌘

I have heard the expression "switch to decafe" so many times, and the more I hear it, the more I know it is true. We get so wired and involved with what we are doing, we have to know when to pull away and take a break.

I can get rather involved when I write. I get "on a roll" and don't want to quit. But the more I write, the more I notice the stories come a little slower, I delete a little more, and I get a little more frustrated. When I finally get to the point that my body is stiff from sitting in one position too long, I know it is time to quit or switch to decafe.

This is when I take the dogs for a walk or sit in the back yard swing. I get something to drink, read a short piece in a magazine, breath in a lot of fresh air, and try to get the brain cells rejuvenated so that I can go back to writing.

Knowing when you have had enough and need some down time is essential. I think the best analogy from this "old farm girl" is rotating the crops. You can't continue to grow the same crop in the same ground because it depletes the soil of the same minerals, and the crop gets weaker with each season.

You have to make changes, rotate crops, or switch to decafe if you want to stay vital, effective, and productive. A short break, which many would regard as a waste of time, is the best thing you can do for relief of an overloaded mind.

⌘⌘⌘⌘⌘

"Blessed are the peacemakers:
for they shall be called the children of God."
Matthew 5:9

AUGUST 13
...SINGING A CAPPELLA

"To put up with...distortions and to stick to one's guns
come what may—this is the...gift of leadership."
- Mohandas K. Gandhi

⌘⌘⌘⌘⌘

One of the most difficult and challenging singing contests I was in was an a cappella contest. The song I sang was "Clouds." The first and last notes were the same, but there were many high and low notes in the middle of the song. A pitch pipe was blown to give you the beginning note. You sang the song; and when you had completed the piece, the pitch pipe was blown again to see how close you were to the first note. You were on your own from beginning to end; and if you wanted to be successful in this competition, you had to focus on that one "right" note.

When we begin a project, it is easy to get side tracked: to go up and down the scale of notes of what we are doing. It becomes difficult to know if we will end up where we intended. We start off on the right note, and only by maintaining an incredible focus and staying in tune can we end up on that same right note.

It would be nice to have a person blow the pitch pipe periodically and keep us in tune when we were just a flat or sharp away from where we should be when coming back home was a short distance. Most of our life, we do not have this person. It is up to us, alone, to make sure we end up where we want to be.

⌘⌘⌘⌘⌘

"But when he, the spirit of truth, comes,
he will guide you into all truth."
John 16:13

AUGUST 14
...RESCUING WHEN YOU CAN BE A RESCUER

"Often we can help each other most by leaving each other alone;
at other times we need the hand-grasp and the word of cheer."
- Elbert Hubbard

⌘⌘⌘⌘⌘

I'm terribly near-sighted. For something to be clear, it has to be from the length of my arms in. I don't wear my glasses around the house or yard because I know where everything is, and I assume I won't be falling over things.

The other day I was taking one of my "switch to decafe" breaks. I let the dogs out in the front yard and just sat on the porch watching the dogs and letting my mind rest. Across the street I saw movement and could vaguely tell it was a small child riding on a bicycle. I went back to watching the dogs. I heard a commotion, and from the sound I could tell that the child had fallen off his bike. He wasn't crying hard, so I assumed it was the sympathy cry to get his mother to come running, but his house was shut up tight, and no mother came running.

Finally, I focused more on what he was yelling than the fact that he was yelling. It was "Help." I got up off the porch, walked down the street and asked what was the matter. He said, "I need scissors." I went back to the house, got the scissors, and headed back down the street. His shoe lace had come untied, and it was wrapped around the pedal and caught in the chain. His little foot was pulled down into the side of the bike, and he looked really uncomfortable.

I cut the shoelace off the bike, unwrapped it from the pedal, helped him up and told him to go home and let his mother have a look at him. He did. Five minutes later, his mother came running over to my house thanking me for rescuing her son. When the father came home that evening, he also came over and thanked me. They were even telling the other neighbors about the incident. I'm the Neighborhood Rescuer.

I know we can't rescue everyone. We are lucky to be able to rescue ourselves most of the time; but when we do have the opportunity to lend someone a helping hand, we should. We will be setting up a cycle of kindness, and you can't go wrong with that.

⌘⌘⌘⌘⌘

"I will strengthen you, I will help you."
Isaiah 41:10

AUGUST 15
...WHEN A COVER UP WON'T DO

"Customary use of artifice is the sign of a small mind, and it almost always happens that he who uses to cover one spot uncovers himself in another."
- La Rochefoucauld

⌘⌘⌘⌘⌘

When you have two dogs that live in the house with you, as with anything or anyone who lives in a house, accidents do happen. My husband and I, and our home, have been the victim of theses accidents: broken vases, stolen pieces of meat, disemboweled teddy bears, destroyed flower arrangements, and the mysterious disappearance of loaves of bread, sticks of butter, and one half a pumpkin pie. But these were not the worst.

Murphy got a bladder infection, and the poor little thing had to eliminate as many as 20 times a day. One day I had to do an all day presentation for my client, and I was not available to let her out. When I came home, I was greeted not only by the two dogs but also by the smell of strong dog urine. I walked into the living and dining rooms, and there on the carpet were about 10 yellow stains. I almost cried. I got out the carpet cleaner, ionizer, deodorizer, etc. and scrubbed and scrubbed. But to no avail. The smell was not only in the carpet, it was also in the carpet pad. I was just covering up, and it wasn't working. The carpet and pad needed to be replaced.

As I've gone through the accidents in my life — being unkind, hurting people's feelings, not taking good care of my pets or things — I also tried to cover up. But that didn't work either. Just as I needed to replace our carpet, I also needed to replace the hurt, the unkindness, and the carelessness with something clean, honest, and new. With many things we do in our lives, cover ups will just not do.

⌘⌘⌘⌘⌘

"There is nothing concealed that will not be disclosed, or hidden that will not be made known."
Matthew 10:26

AUGUST 16
...APPRECIATING LIFE'S LINGERIE AND UNDERWEAR

"Timeliness is best in all matters."
- Hesiod

⌘⌘⌘⌘⌘

I love to go to the department store and wishfully and wistfully gaze at the beautiful lingerie. I say wishfully and wistfully because there is no way that most of these beautiful pieces of lingerie are going into my wardrobe. With my bra size, I fall more into the underwear category, not lingerie.

My bras are made with wire. This is the material I have built fence out of. It criss-crossed my front and back and sides. It has wide straps. It had three inch wide pieces of elastic. It comes in three basis colors — black, white, and beige. It lifts, binds, separates, minimizes, and holds in place. Even though it is very functional, it is not very attractive. Instead of dressing to feel feminine, I feel as if I am dressing to engage in some type of military assault.

There are things in our life that for some reason just don't fit: a particular clothing style for the season, a person that we can't gel with, a job, a vacation. They may not fit forever; it just may be a matter of timing.

Even though whatever it is doesn't work for us at this time doesn't mean we can't appreciate it at a distance, wait for a time when it is more appropriate, or appreciate it for someone else. Everything fits into someone's life at some time.

I know that someday someone will come up with pretty lingerie for the full-figured woman, long skirts will be back in style, new friends will come into my life, and my husband and I will find someone the dogs like so we can take a nice vacation alone; but, until these things do happen, I will wishfully and wistfully think of the times to come.

⌘⌘⌘⌘⌘

"To every thing there is a season,
and a time to every purpose under the heaven."
Ecclesiastes 3:1

AUGUST 17
...NOT ALWAYS BEING FIRST

"The wave pushed ahead by the ship."
- Leon Tolstoy

⌘⌘⌘⌘⌘

While doing a presentation for a corporation, I saw one of the most wonderful cartoons someone had photocopied and put on a public bulletin board. The name of the cartoonist was not visible, so I cannot give this person credit for this wonderful cartoon.

It was two deer standing on the edge of a cliff looking down at a very steep drop. Behind these two lead deer, through clouds of dust ,was a large herd of wildly galloping deer running at top speed after the leaders. One of the lead deer looks at the steep drop, the galloping herd behind him, and then at the other deer and says, "I don't want to lead anymore."

The rock and the hard place. Need I say anything else?

⌘⌘⌘⌘⌘

"For I, the Lord your God,
hold your right hand."
Isaiah 41:13

AUGUST 18
...MAKING LITTLE THINGS MATTER

"We must not, in trying to think about how we can make a big
difference, ignore the small daily differences we can make which,
over time, add up to big differences that we often cannot foresee."
- Marian Wright Edelman

⌘⌘⌘⌘⌘

Soon after my husband and I had started dating, he went back to school to get his
MBA. He is a wonderful writer and can create great "word pictures" to make his points, or he
can cut to the bottom line and give a very clear matter-of-fact "this is the way it is done"
explanation.

Because my undergraduate degree is in English Literature and Grammar, he
asked me to proof his papers for grammatical correctness. It was a small thing to request, so I
did. Seldom did he have any errors. He just felt better turning in his papers knowing that I had
proofed them.

After a long two years, he finished his course work and started his final paper.
Again, I helped proof it. His paper was accepted, and he received his MBA. When he
received his graded paper, he planned a surprise for me.

I came home one evening, and on my dining room table was a bouquet of roses
and his paper turned to the dedication page. He had dedicated his paper to me. He stated that
he could not have made it through the long two years without my help; but, more than my help,
he could not have made it through the long two years without my encouragement.

What I did for him was a little thing, and what he did for me was a little thing, but
we have both benefited immensely from each other's small kindness. The act may have been
small, but the memory is larger than life and will last forever for both of us. It has helped us lay
a foundation of kindness, helpfulness, and caring for each other.

⌘⌘⌘⌘⌘

"According to the grace of God given to me,
like a skilled master builder I laid a foundation."
1 Corinthians 3:10

AUGUST 19

...APPRECIATING RESOURCEFULNESS

"The bold are helpless without cleverness."
- Euripides

⌘⌘⌘⌘⌘

I, like most people in this world, hate moving. One of the biggest reasons I hate moving is because we moved so much when I was young. My grandmother was one of those rare individuals who loved moving and moved us about every two or three years.

When my husband and I were engaged, we decided that it would be best for both of us to have a clean start away from "household" memories, so we both sold our present homes, built a new home, and moved again.

Ben, Stan's son, was helping us with the move. We did fairly well getting all things loaded until we came to the hutch. This hutch was not mover friendly. It's one piece of heavy solid maple. We tried putting it on the dolly, but it was too wide, and the legs were at an awkward slant. Ben couldn't figure out how we were going to get it in the van. I stood there thinking, and then I remember seeing a long 2 x 8 in the garage. I got the 2 x 8, put it on the dolly, put the hutch on the board, and we rolled it in the van.

Ben complimented me many times over for being so resourceful. I thanked him and explained that I wasn't as strong as many people. I had always worked beside men, and they expected me to do my share. Because I lacked the physical strength of some of the men, I had to become more resourceful.

Resourcefulness arises out of necessity.

⌘⌘⌘⌘⌘

"And God is able to make all grace abound to you, so that
in all things at all times, having all that you need,
you will abound in every good work."
2 Corinthians 9:8

AUGUST 20
...ALLOWING ROOM FOR GROWTH

"To mature is to go on creating oneself endlessly."
- Henri Bergson

⌘⌘⌘⌘⌘

When we built our home, we decided to eliminate a patio and build a deck. My husband met with the builders and explained that we would like a deck that was away from the house so that we could put a flower garden between the house and the deck. This way we could view the flower garden from both the deck and the house.

We could hardly wait to get the garden blooming. We planned the garden and began planting. We put in phlox, lamb's ears, day lilies, rock cress, four o'clock, and many things I can't remember the names of. We read all the directions on how close to plant the bulbs and seedlings, but, begin over-anxious and not listening to advice, we over planted everything. The second year, when things really took off, there was no room for growth.

We spent the next year working even harder than we did the previous year when we first planted the garden. We spent hours digging up and separating seedlings, replanting them in other areas, and giving them away to the neighbors.

We had to work twice as hard because we did not allow for growth. We had forgotten that things, and people, expand with growth. We all take that slow steady path to maturity and expand our boundaries.

We must always leave enough room for each person to bloom and shape themselves. To achieve their full growth. To experience the rites of passage. And, to become.

⌘⌘⌘⌘⌘

"When the complete comes, the partial will come to an end."
1 Corinthians 13:10

AUGUST 21
...LOVING TO REMEMBER

"What God gave us so that we might have roses in December."
- James M. Barrie

⌘⌘⌘⌘⌘

I think that all families are dysfunctional to one degree or another. I know ours was and is. As a matter of fact, during the holidays we sit around and try to figure our which one of us is the most dysfunctional. We laugh knowing that although we have had our share of rough spots, there are many wonderful things we remember about our childhood.

We had large vegetable and herb gardens that we worked during the summer, and I have many happy, funny memories of the work. When we picked blackberries, my grandmother would make you whistle. This was the way she made sure you picked more than you ate. She had a huge front porch, and after we picked green beans, we would sit on the front porch in big white, cold metal rocking chairs and snap beans for canning. We would also sit in those metal chairs on summer nights when it stormed. They always felt cool; and after so many long hot summer days, that was a great feeling.

My mother had to work when I was growing up. I spent the week with my grandmother, but weekends were for my mother and me. We dressed alike in white cardigan sweaters, pearls, gloves, and handbags. Every Saturday, we rode the bus downtown and had lunch at Ayres Tea Room. Ayres Tea Room was definitely "kid friendly." Each week, I got to pick a prize out of the treasure chest and eat a Cheerful Charley Luncheon followed by a Snow Princess Dessert. All the family attended Garfield Baptist Church, and every Sunday after church, we went to Howard Johnson for Sunday lunch and to partake of 1 of 31 flavors. On Sunday afternoons, we would put my dolls in their buggy and walk to this big woods at the end of the street and have picnics.

I love to remember those times. They certainly have helped me deal with some of the rough spots. I remember a line from a poem that reminds us that memory is a gift of God that death can never destroy. I like to think of memory that way. The deep impression that each detail leaves is seldom forgotten. It is the mental diary that we carry around with us. Memories help keep us, our happiness, and our hearts alive and well.

⌘⌘⌘⌘⌘

"Remember the former things, those of long ago;"
Isaiah 46:9

AUGUST 22
...CHANGING WITH THE SEASONS

"Nature taking up its option on the world."
- Leonard L. Levinson

⌘⌘⌘⌘⌘

When we built our first house, we chose the design of a white Cape Cod with black shutters and a red door. All the gardens are yellow and lavender, and on the pillar by the front door we hung decorative flags. We changed the flag for each season and special event. In January we hung a cardinal flag, February – a heart for Valentine's Day, March – a 4-leaf clover for St. Patrick's Day, April – a bunny for Easter, May and June – summer flowers, July — our national flag, August and September — fall flowers, October – a pumpkin, November – a turkey, and December — a Santa for Christmas. A flag represented each season, and I changed them just as the seasons changed.

The flags aren't the only things that change; we all change just like the seasons. In spring, we become impetuous and light-hearted. In summer, we appreciate the sun, long days, and slowed pace. In fall, we cuddle and begin storing up for the winter months. And, in winter, we hibernate from the cold and snow and wait for spring.

Mentally and emotionally, we also go through a change of seasons. We have times when we shut down or withdraw and times when we bloom and blossom. Just as we live through each season that passes, so shall we live through each stage of our lives. For however long our falls and winters seem, we shall always have springs and summers.

⌘⌘⌘⌘⌘

"Let us not become weary in doing good, for at the proper time we will reap a harvest if we do not give up."
Galatians 6:9

AUGUST 23
...SEEKING LIFE IN GOD'S WORDS

"It furnishes good Christians an armor for their warfare, a guide
for their conduct, a solace in their sorrows, food for their souls."
- Gaius G. Atkins

⌘⌘⌘⌘⌘

I was scared and stressed when I was going through chemotherapy.
Reading the Lord's words was my main source of comfort. I spent each morning
reading about the strength of the women in the Bible. During the day I worked as
hard and as long as I could just to make sure I was exhausted and could sleep at
night.

My aunt knew I spent a lot of time in my car, so she gave me several sets of
tapes. One tape was Gloria Copeland's "God Wants You Well." On this tape,
Gloria told many wonderful stories, and one in particular will always remain in my
mind.

It seems that during WW II and the Bombing of London, local residents
congregated at the same fall out shelters every night. They got used to seeing one
another there. The group in one of the neighborhood shelters realized that one
woman, whom they were used to seeing each evening, was not there. The group
sadly assumed she had been killed. One day, another woman from the shelter
saw the "missing" woman on the street and asked her why she had not been in the
shelter each night. The "missing" woman said, "A long time ago, my mother told
me that the Lord does not sleep nor slumber, and there is no sense in both of us
being awake."

On some nights, when sleep was hard to come by, I would remember those
words and the words of the Lord. There was life and calmness and healing in
those words.

⌘⌘⌘⌘⌘

"The word is a lamp unto my feet, and a light unto my path."
Psalm 119:105

AUGUST 24
...SEEING ONE'S EYES

"That which tells what the heart means."
- Judah L. Lazerov

⌘⌘⌘⌘⌘

I attend many meetings. It keeps me informed of what is going on in the community, helps me make new business contacts, and also helps me make new friends. Because I usually attend these meetings by myself, I look for a lunch partner with whom I may talk. I usually enter the dining room early, find a table and sit and watch the other attendees enter.

It is my habit to look people in the face and smile at them. I saw one woman enter, and I looked up at her and smiled. She said, "You have such a kind face. May I sit next to you?"

You can make wonderful friends just by looking them in the eye and smiling. I think it is because you are actually looking at them — not past or through them. You are seeing them as real live human beings, not as a non-entity. Our eyes are the mirror to our soul, and it is so comforting when others see not only that we are but also who we are.

⌘⌘⌘⌘⌘

"The light of the body."
Matthew 6:22

AUGUST 25
...SHARING LOVES IN ONE'S LIFE

"If wisdom were offered me with the proviso that I should
keep it shut up and refrain from declaring it, I should
refuse. There's no delight in owning anything unshared."

- Seneca

⌘⌘⌘⌘⌘

Many years ago, I met a wonderful gentleman named Kevin Sanders. He
has his own marketing firm, and we met many times as he was helping me get my
business started. Over the course of time, we became friends. One day I asked
him about his background, and, to my surprise, he told me he had his Ph.D. in
English Literature. My undergraduate degree was in English Literature.

In that one moment, I had met an old friend. We could sit and talk for
hours about people who had been dead for over 500 years and love talking about
them. We shared lines of poetry, little known tidbits about famous authors, and
our favorite quotes from novels.

There are so many wonderful people in my life, but many of them don't
have the same fondness for Twain, Dickens, and Shakespeare that I do. My new
friend does. He had spent hours pouring over the same text I had, taken the
same tests, and recited the same passages. I had a bond with him that I could
have with no one else in my life.

We have many loves in our life, and what can make these loves even more
wonderful is having someone to share them with. Sharing my love for English
Literature with my friend occasionally brought all the story lines, characters, and
happy endings back to life again.

⌘⌘⌘⌘⌘

"May the God of hope fill you with all joy and peace in believing."

Romans 15:13

AUGUST 26
...TURNING OFF THE RADIO

"A happy life...for it is only in an atmosphere of quiet that true joy can live."
- Bertrand A. Russell

⌘⌘⌘⌘⌘

Have you ever noticed that the commercials on TV and radio appear to be at least 10 times louder than the programs? I have, and it is a major source of irritation to me. As a matter of fact, I have made it a point to refrain from purchasing products or services from a company whose advertisement is loud or obnoxious.

I think we are all victims of noise overload. Ringing phones, beeping pagers, screaming kids, yelling adults, and screeching brakes top off the cacophonous sounds of construction noise, factory noise, office noise, and traffic noise. Enough is enough! I don't know who coined the term "can't hear yourself think," but it certainly is applicable.

With silence comes peace and peace of mind. It is reflective, nourishing, and revitalizing. It allows us to think, to create and to heal. It slows us, calms us, and relaxes us.

Sometimes silence is the most welcomed, wonderful sound in the world.

⌘⌘⌘⌘⌘

"My people will abide in a peaceful habitation...
and in quiet resting places."
Isaiah 32:18

AUGUST 27
...KNOWING THE VALUE OF GOOD POSTURE

"It is the disposition of the thought that altereth the nature of the thing."
-John Lyly

⌘⌘⌘⌘⌘

What do you think of phrases such as "I'm in the dumps," "I have the weight of the world on my shoulders," and "I'm really down today"? Have you ever noticed that these phrases go along with the body posture: slumped shoulders, downcast eyes, dragging feet, a frown. Our posture is usually indicative of our mood.

Opposing phrases, such as "I'm up today," "I'm on cloud nine," and "I really look up to them," also go along with a posture of shoulders back, uplifted face, springy step, and a smile. This posture is also indicative of our mood.

Coming from a family with a strong military background, I learned that emulating the "attention" posture was not only beneficial for my back but also for my mood. I have found out that standing straight, smiling, lifting my head slightly, and walking with a bounce just makes me feel better. And, more than that, it helps me project to the rest of the world that life is fine even on days when it isn't.

With a good posture, I think we indicate that we can meet the world head on, look problems squarely in the eye, and face any challenge nose to nose. We need to be looking up, standing tall, maintaining balance, and displaying composure.

⌘⌘⌘⌘⌘

"And what does the Lord require of you?
To act justly and to love mercy and
to walk humbly with your God."
Micah 6:8

AUGUST 28
...WALKING AND TALKING SOFTLY

"Fair and softly goes far."
- Cervantes

⌘⌘⌘⌘⌘

I have mentioned before that we have created a habitat for the birds. Two of our favorite visitors are Mallards: Granny and Bubba. This year they came with their brood of eight gorgeous little ducklings. I loved to get as close as I could and watch them.

I found out that if I walked very softly and slowly, I could edge my way to the end of the deck, sit down on the steps, and toss them grain and bread. I talked very softly so that they would get used to the sound of my voice. When I would open the patio doors, I would coo to them and let them know that everything was all right. My soft voice and slow approach let them know that they did not need to be afraid or rush off. Day after day, I went through the same routine with them. Now, when I open the patio door and go out on the deck, they walk towards the edge of the deck and wait for me to throw handfuls of corn and cereal.

I think if we approach most situations walking and talking softly, we can accomplish what we want. When we speak softly, others must listen to hear what we are saying. When we walk softly, we eliminate the fear factor of the rush. Another valuable lesson on the power of soft skills.

⌘⌘⌘⌘⌘

"Let your gentleness be evident to all."
Philippians 4:5

AUGUST 29
...EXCELLING IN YOUR OWN ART FORM

"Art is I; science is we."
- Claude Bernard

⌘⌘⌘⌘⌘

Gina is a wonderful artist. Her impressionistic style and use of colors create the kind of beautiful scenes that allow your mind to wander through. One Saturday, one of our play days, she brought over all her art supplies. We were going to create the front of cards. She set out all the chalk, paints, and papers and dug in. I sat and watched. She handed me a piece of paper, and I sat and watched. Finally, she asked if I would be drawing. I said no. I did not have that type of artistic talent. She looked puzzled, so I went on to explain that words were my art.

People speak of art as having passion, of being colorful, or of creating beauty. My words have passion, and, I try to create as many beautiful word pictures as I can. However, at times, they are much more colorful than I would like.

Words have life, history and power. A word can plummet you into an abyss from which you think you may never recover or set you on top of Olympus for days. The pen, and the word, always have been and always will be mightier than the sword. Words cause tears, smiles, bonding, and comfort. Words scorn, cut, and alienate. Words surprise, motivate, and tickle. Words prompt us to action, to remember, and to think.

Words are an art form just as sculpting, painting and composing. All contribute to the enhancement of our lives. We must find out where our expertise lies and establish ourselves as artists in our own right.

⌘⌘⌘⌘⌘

"Each one should use whatever gift he has received to serve others, faithfully administering God's grace in its various forms."
1 Peter 4:10

AUGUST 30
...NOT PUTTING UP WITH PUT DOWNS

"Self-respect is at the bottom of all good manners.
They are the expression of discipline, of good will,
of respect for other people's rights and comforts and feelings."
- Edward S. Martin

⌘⌘⌘⌘⌘

Have you ever gone out on a romantic dinner date with someone and had them tell you that you looked good in dim light? [You have to think about that.] Put-downs are terrible because they are so subtle. Many times, by the time that you have thought about what was said and taken exception to it, the moment and the person have passed you by.

In our personal relationships, we are suppose to be taken as husband or wife, and in our professional relationships, we are to be taken as employee. Unfortunately, some of us are just taken as hostage and continue to put up with put-downs.

Many people like to make statements and never want to be held accountable for what they have said. They don't like having to make an embarrassed explanation or do a lot of back peddling. Our problem with these people arises when we do not speak up when we are put down. We may think that a person will only put us down once and then leave us alone. That is not true. We develop a pecking order, and we put down those that let us put them down. The routine I have developed to stop people from verbally abusing me, being the recipient of my share of put downs, I call "Wide-eyed and Innocent."

A person I once knew was very much a phony and a snob. One day at a meeting, I made several points that he must have considered almost intelligent. After the meeting, he commented that I was intelligent and added that instead of sending me to a local university, you would have thought that my parents would have sent me to some place prestigious like Smith or Vassar. [He didn't stop to consider that we may not have had the money.] To me, this was the equivalent of telling me I looked good in dim light, and I wasn't going to let it pass.

My response was, "My parents knew that I was prestigious. I did not need a university to make me appear so." He never made a comment like that to me again. I walked away from the situation feeling that I, my education, and my mother, who had worked so hard to take care of me and saw to it that I had a college education, were all in tact of our self-esteem.

⌘⌘⌘⌘⌘

"A cheerful heart is a good medicine."
Proverbs 17:22

AUGUST 31

...KNOWING NO ONE DOES THINGS THE WAY YOU DO

"Habit will reconcile us to everything but change."
- Charles Caleb Colton

⌘⌘⌘⌘⌘

I'm an arranger of magazines, flowers, pillows, cupboards, etc. I am also an organizer of meetings, presentations, check books, get-togethers, etc. I am pretty neat and tidy. My mother always told me that my coffee table looked like it should be in a dentist's office; and that when I got married, if my husband got up in the middle of the night to go to the bathroom, when he got back, his side of the bed would probably be made. [Please remember, these remarks come from a woman who got up early every morning to iron one piece of clothing because she thought if she ironed the night before and died before morning, she would have ironed that piece of clothing for nothing.]

Yes, I can tell if a curtain has been moved, a magazine read, or food eaten. That's because no one does things the way I do. We are all in the same boat; no one does things the way we do them.

For quite some time, Stan and I were so busy that we didn't have time to keep up with the house (and the dog hair). We hired someone to come in and clean. The house looked nice and smelled good, and the dogs didn't eat anybody; so we let this person continue helping. She helped us for several months. Finally, my husband's and my schedules slowed down a little, and we told her we did not need her services for a while.

The next week I started my routine cleaning. When I picked up the plants and the bunny collection that sits in the bathroom, I was shocked at the layer of dust that had accumulated behind them. Our helper had spent the last several months just dusting around things. I'm sure it was her way to get many rooms cleaned in the time allowed, but it was not my way.

When others help us, we must always be grateful and praise their help, but we must never think it will be perfect for us. Others do things in the way they are accustomed to, not the way we are accustomed to.

⌘⌘⌘⌘⌘

"You have made known to me the ways of life;"
Acts 2:28

SEPTEMBER 1
...STOPPING UNNECESSARY WORRY

"The crosses we make for ourselves by overanxiety."
- Francois de Fenelon

⌘⌘⌘⌘⌘

I have heard the 80/20 rule to marketing and sales. The other day I heard that there is also an 80/20 rule to worrying, and it makes sense to me. When troubles or unpleasant situations come our way, we should spend 20% of our time worrying about the situation and 80% of our time doing something about the situation. It must relate to being proactive. This 80/20 Rule of Worrying reminded me of a situation a friend of mine went through several years ago. She had a gorgeous pair of pearl earrings. They were a keepsake from her grandmother, and she wore them everyday. One morning, while getting ready for work, she dropped one of the pearl earrings down the drain. She said, "You know, I cussed that earring for 30 minutes, and it was still in that drain." She finally called the plumber and had him undo the pipe and get her earring. The 80/20 Rule of Worrying. Cussing didn't get her the earring; calling the plumber did.

Mother Goose gave us similar information many years ago.

For every ailment under the sun, there is a remedy or there is none.
If there is one, try and find it. If there is none, never mind it.

How much better off we would all be if, every time we began to worry over something, we first decided if there was a remedy for the worry.

I'm not cavalier about life. What I can correct, I want to correct. I'm also not a worrier. If I can't change the situation until Monday morning at 8:00, I simply do not deal with the situation or worry about it until Monday morning at 8:00. One Friday night, my husband and I arrived home to find a package of a dozen promotional video tapes a friend had agreed to do for $500.00. I opened the package and, with the video tapes, there was a bill for $1,000.00. I was shocked. I knew I could not reach the people who had done the video until Monday morning after 8:00. I put the bill and the package on the floor of the study and just enjoyed the weekend with my husband. I called Monday morning and got the situation straightened out after having enjoyed my weekend.

It takes much practice and concentration to live the 80/20 Rule of Worrying, but once mastered, life is much more pleasant.

⌘⌘⌘⌘⌘

"Who of you by worrying can add a single hour to his life?"
Matthew 6:27

SEPTEMBER 2
...MAKING DO

"Nothing has more strength than dire necessity."
- Euripides

⌘⌘⌘⌘⌘

My wonderful friend Carolyn Parrott was married to a man with a military career. For several years of their lives they lived on a military base in Saudi Arabia. Other than talking about the dinners and parties she planned, we never discussed much about her time over there. Carolyn has always been a very private person, and, to be her friend, you must accept that. But, every now and then, a secret part of her slipped out, and you could get a closer look at her.

It was the first time she had come over to the new house. We had cappuccino and waited for the dogs to calm down. Then, I took her on a tour of the house. When we got to the guest bedroom, the look on her face changed. She looked at the spread and drapes covered with yellow and purple Iris, Cornflowers, and Daisies and slowly and sadly said, "This was my bedroom in Saudi Arabia. Over there, it was the only flower garden I could have."

All of us spend a part of our life making do. If flower gardens have to be pictures on spreads and draperies, and aromas have to be from incense, we are still reminded of the real thing. We make dresses by hand when we can't afford originals; we buy generic when we can't afford name brands; and we patch everything from clothing to emotions just to get by.

We are all wonderful mothers of invention arising out of necessity.

⌘⌘⌘⌘⌘

"And God will meet all your needs according
to his glorious riches in Christ Jesus."
Philippians 4:19

SEPTEMBER 3
...NOT ALWAYS TAKING WHAT IS PUT IN FRONT OF YOU

"Too great an eagerness to discharge an obligation is a species of ingratitude."
                                                            - La Rochefoucauld

⌘⌘⌘⌘⌘

CoCo, our little terrier (and I say little as to height not to weight), is a gourmand; she will literally eat anything — dog food, wood chips, dust bunnies, table scraps. If it is on the floor or ground, she will go after it.

My husband and I love fresh asparagus; and for one of our few evening meals together, I was fixing asparagus. I was standing at the sink snapping the tips off of the asparagus. CoCo, as usual, was at my feet waiting for anything that came falling her way, and she was in luck. A piece of asparagus missed the sink and fell on the floor. In less than a New York minute, she snapped it up and ran for the corner of the dining room — her hiding place. I followed her knowing for certain she wouldn't eat a piece of raw asparagus, and I would have to pick it up. I was surprised.

She sat there chewing and chewing with the most pained, disgusting expression a dog can manage. She hated the taste of it; but it was her prize, and she was not about to give it up.

Thinking she could understand a complete English sentence, I said, "CoCo, just because it is on the floor doesn't mean you have to eat it." But my words fell on deaf ears. She continued to chew with her nose in the air, occasionally spitting it out, but always picking it up one more time. I think she was hoping the taste would change with time and chewing. Or, maybe she thought it was like a nut shell, and if you kept working on it long enough, it would reveal a tasty treasure on the inside. She was sadly disappointed in her piece of asparagus and finally abandoned her treasure.

⌘⌘⌘⌘⌘

"Every good gift and every perfect gift is from above."
                                                            James 1:17

SEPTEMBER 4
...RECYCLING IN THE MIND

"What is so tedious as a twice-told tale?"
- Homer

⌘⌘⌘⌘⌘

I spent a large amount of time in psychology classes when I was doing my undergraduate work, and I did learn some extraordinary things about my mind and how it works. Some points that I found very interesting about the subconscious mind, the part that controls most of our reactions, is that it has no sense of humor, doesn't understand magnitude, and doesn't differentiate between what is real and what is imaginary. If our subconscious doesn't differentiate between what is really going on and what we are just imaging, then we could spend a great deal of time recycling bad things through our mind. This type of recycling is not good for us or our environment — the people around us.

Another interesting point about out mind is that we can only hold one thought at a time. Have you ever tried to hum one tune when another is playing on the radio? Your mind flips in and out like the hologram on your credit card.

When I get to the point where I am recycling things in my mind that I shouldn't be, I focus on one of the most amazing things I have ever witnessed. We used to live on a pond with a fountain. The fountain shut off at midnight and came on at 7:00 am. One morning I was standing at the sliding glass door drinking coffee and looking at the pond. Suddenly I realized a flock of geese was sitting on the fountain. I looked at the clock; it was 6:58, and I thought "this ought to be good." I waited, and sure enough, at 7:00 am, the underwater lights came on, the water burst out of the fountain under a huge amount of pressure and blew the geese all over the pond. They were unable to get their wings out and were hitting the water like bags of wet cement. They honked and chased one another thinking it was the other goose's fault, I'm sure. I was hysterical. I called my husband and mother and shared this event with them. This was a great way to start the day.

The next morning, out of curiosity, I walked to the sliding glass doors and found the geese sitting on the fountain again. I'm assuming this was like an amusement park ride to them and got the goose endorphins going early each morning. This incident always makes me smile and laugh. When I remember this, I know I am calming because I am thinking of something positive and stopping the recycling of bad things. I know I certainly look better smiling than frowning.

⌘⌘⌘⌘⌘

"To set the mind on the Spirit is life and peace."

SEPTEMBER 5
...HAVING THE WIND KNOCKED OUT OF YOU

"Wherever life takes us, there are always moments of wonder."
- Jimmy Carter

⌘⌘⌘⌘⌘

My mother and I have a small pony farm. My mother still lives on the farm; we just don't have the stock any longer. Between the barn and the house, we dug a pony track and landscaped it with trees and benches. Hitching up the ponies and driving them around the track was a wonderful way to spend an afternoon whether you were driving the ponies or just watching them run.

Almost weekly, we would scrape the track. Scraping it kept it smooth and free of weeds. We would attach the blade to our old Ford 8N tractor. Mother drove the tractor, and I rode the blade to give it some added weight. When mother was ready to dump the excess dirt in the field, I would jump backwards off the blade. Everything worked very smoothly until we got a new blade that had a level for turning the blade that protruded upward. After years of riding the old blade, I got on the new blade, rode the track; but this time when I jumped off backwards, I got my jeans caught on the lever, jerked severely in mid air, and landed on the track on my back.

I realized I couldn't breathe. The wind had been knocked out of me, and I couldn't breathe. I couldn't yell for help. I was scared. I actually hoped to pass out so that my autonomic system would kick in and start me breathing.

Finally, I got up, bent over, and strained as hard as I could to push air out of my lungs, and I heard myself scream. I knew I was breathing again.

When someone tells me that something someone has said or done has really knocked the wind out of them, I know exactly how they feel: stunned, scared, and panicked. It is a horrible experience, literally and figuratively; and if ever we see that we have done this to someone else, we need to make a strong effort to help them start breathing again. It is the hope they need to know that they will recover.

⌘⌘⌘⌘⌘

"My presence will go with you, and I will give you rest."
Exodus 33:14

SEPTEMBER 6
...ATTENDING

"What you will do matters. All you need is to do it."
- Judy Grahn

⌘⌘⌘⌘⌘

I have been in love with black horses since my mother first read *Black Beauty* to me. I always wanted a black horse, and I made my wishes known.

One Saturday at a horse auction, a groom led in the most beautiful black mare I had ever seen. Her coat shone; her mane and tail moved as she walked and looked like strands of silk. Her forelock was braided with red ribbons. Her name was Jubilee, and I had immediately fallen in love with her. Smitty, the man I trained horses for, didn't have to ask what I thought; he knew. He began bidding on her; and before I knew it, I had the lead in my hand, and we were taking her back to the farm.

What we were not told was that Jubilee had been wild in the fields all her life. For the sale, she was captured, heavily drugged, cleaned up and put in the sale. By the time we pulled up to our barn, the drugs were wearing off, and she was becoming a wild, uncontrollable animal. We finally got her out of the trailer and into a box stall. You could tell she was terrified. It took us months of working with her to get her used to people and being handled. It was dangerous work because she was fully grown. [She weighed about 1,000 pounds and had a wonderful set of teeth and four very active hooves.] In time, she became gentle and manageable.

Jubilee turned out to be a wonderful brood mare and produced some of the prettiest colts we had. We were never sorry we bought her. We just wished our first months with her had been a little easier, and they would have been if people had just attended to her.

⌘⌘⌘⌘⌘

"Let us not be weary in well doing: for in
due season we shall reap, if we faint not."
Galatians 6:9

SEPTEMBER 7
...BEING TICKLED

"Not a gift of the mind, but of the heart."
- Ludwig Boerne

⌘⌘⌘⌘⌘

I like to tickle my husband. He begins this great laugh, his face turns red, and he doubles over. I laugh just to hear and see him laugh, so I figure out ways to make him lose control.

Because we were in our late 40's when we met, we dated for five years to see if we had a long term future. Before getting married, we signed living wills, disclosure statements, pre-nuptials, and a number of other papers. For our life together, we divided the work, the cooking, the errands, and the bathroom sinks — we each had our own side. Now, I must tell you that my husband is a fanatic about bathroom chrome. The rest of the bathroom can look like an abandoned gasoline station, but the chrome will be shining. Basically, I could care less about chrome. It is way down on my list of priorities.

One morning while we were getting ready, my husband commented that my chrome looked very shiny. I thanked him and told him I had a new method for keeping my side clean. He asked, "What?" I replied, "I wait until you leave, and then I use your side." For a minute he just looked at me, and then, in typical fashion, his face turned red, he doubled over, and his laughter began.

I love seeing him get tickled. He is like a kid. We all need these kid or childlike moments of intense joy. It takes getting to adulthood before most of us understand the advantages of childhood: little care, little drudgery – mostly happiness and fantasy.

⌘⌘⌘⌘⌘

"But the cheerful heart has a continual feast."
Proverbs 15:15

SEPTEMBER 8
...MAKING THE MOST OF THINGS

"Second thoughts are even wiser."
- Euripides

⌘⌘⌘⌘⌘

My grandmother worked at a bakery for many years. Almost every day, she would bring home two-day old French Cruller donuts. After two days, crullers are pretty crusty. You could actually bang them on the table, and they would make noise. But we always knew that grandma would find a use for them.

She made use of everything for good reason. My grandmother raised five children through the Depression, and while in her sixties, was raising her three grandchildren. She lived in a world of "making the most of everything" and hand me downs and hand outs. She would stand in lines for hours to get discounted food, clothing, and other things we needed.

Stale donuts were a breeze! She cut them in half, put a pineapple ring on each one, sprinkled them with brown sugar, and put them under the broiler for a couple of minutes. You can not even begin to imagine what a sweet treat this was — not only from the taste but also from her making the most of things one more time.

When we must make do, we can make do.

⌘⌘⌘⌘⌘

"For God did not give us a spirit of timidity, but
a spirit of power, of love and of self-discipline."
2 Timothy 1:7

SEPTEMBER 9
...RELAXING ON THE 19TH HOLE

"Take rest; a field that has rested gives a bountiful crop."
- Ovid

⌘⌘⌘⌘⌘

My older cousin Fran lives in California. She is our family rebel. [None of the rest of us have ever left Indiana.] Some times I go out to visit her and do all those touristy things. We must walk down Fisherman's Wharf, ride the cable cars, drive through the wine country, take the ferry to Sausalito, go into the Boar's Head Inn in Carmel to see if Clint Eastwood is there, have dinner in Chinatown, drive across the Golden Gate Bridge, and go to Seal Rock and just listen to the seals and the ocean. It's great.

On one visit, we drove to Pebble Beach to see the houses and the acclaimed golf course. At the end of the tour, we stopped at the "19th Hole." The "19th Hole" is a little sandwich shop/pub where people stop to relax and enjoy the view. It was one of the nicest parts of the trip.

We hurry so often thinking each moment is always wanting us and has something for us to do. We get so hurried and busy — even on vacations – trying to see and do it all. We take rolls of photographs in front of anything notable, develop the film, and put the pictures into albums seldom to be looked at. Why? Aren't our memories just as good? Isn't relaxing just as beneficial and enjoyable?

I love all the touristy things we do, and I have pictures in front of the Chinatown lions, Monterey Bay, the Golden Gate Bridge, and the Sausalito ferry. I have to dig the albums out to see these pictures, but the picture in my mind of the view from the "19th Hole" is readily attainable any time. When things are too much with us, we all need a relaxing view from our own "19th Hole" to pull away momentarily.

What relaxes us should not be something looked at but something lived in.

⌘⌘⌘⌘⌘

"Come to me, all you who are weary
and burdened, and I will give you rest."
Matthew 11:28

SEPTEMBER 10
...UNDERSTANDING OTHER'S TRIALS

"Sympathy is a supporting atmosphere,
and in it we unfold easily and well."
- Emerson

❀❀❀❀❀

When you teach junior high and high school aged children, the problems you encounter are endless. I figured I had run the gamut of adolescent problems and had helped the students cope as best they and I could.

My classroom was directly across the hall from my yearbook office. There were glass windows by each door, and they gave me the opportunity to view my staff while they were working and I was teaching. One day while teaching, I noticed Shannon, a yearbook staff member, rapidly pacing the floor, wringing her hands and crying. I knew I had to go over and talk to her, so I began to prepare myself for possibilities. Conjuring up my memories of how to deal with students' problems of parental abuse, alcohol, drugs, pregnancies, fights, and running away from home, I took a deep breath, walked across the hall, opened the door and asked what was the matter. Through sobs, she said, "I have an overdue book notice from the library."

An overdue book notice. My initial response was to chuckle, but I knew from the look on her face that would not be the appropriate response. In my very best "we'll take care of it" tone, I said I would go down and see what was wrong.

I did laugh while I walked down the hall. Her problem, compared to some of the other students with problems, was miniscule, but to Shannon it was a big deal, and that was the important point.

Our trials are our trials. It does not matter in what form they come; it matters that they are here.

❀❀❀❀❀

"Praise be to the God and Father of our Lord Jesus Christ, the Father of compassion and the God of all comfort, who comforts us in all our troubles, so that we can comfort those in any trouble with the comfort we ourselves have received from God."
2 Corinthians 1:3-4

SEPTEMBER 11
...USING YOUR TALENTS

"The tools to him that has the ability to handle them."
- French Proverb

⌘⌘⌘⌘⌘

I have always been impressed with the "Parable of the Talents." The parable helps us believe that in giving, we receive: we reap what we sow. When I looked in an etymology dictionary about the word "talents," I found it originally meant "ancient weight and money of account; valuable" and then took on the meaning of "mental endowment or attitude." This latter definition also means something of value.

All of us have talents — money and mental endowment. Just as we invest our monetary talents and reap rewards as in interest; likewise, we need to invest our mental (and spiritual and emotional) talents and reap those rewards as well.

I had reached a point in my life where I was afraid to love. During my childhood I had lost too many people and things that I loved. My heart had reached its breaking capacity, so I shut down emotionally determined not to care anymore. People left, and pets died. I had cared too much and been hurt too deeply. By not caring and "burying my talents," I didn't have to worry about getting hurt. A high level of materialism, shallowness, and callousness ensued, only to be followed by loneliness. I had stopped the hurt, but I wasn't feeling anything at all.

It took me a long time to realize that risk is a condition of life. It is by loving that we are loved. It is by giving to others that we receive from others. It is by being a part of life that we learn to live. We don't always win when we risk, and I get sick to my stomach when I think of losing someone or something that I love. But I do love, and I am loved, and these two talents are of immeasurable worth.

⌘⌘⌘⌘⌘

"For everyone who has will be given
more, and he will have in abundance,"
Matthew 25:29

SEPTEMBER 12
...CARRYING ON

⌘⌘⌘⌘⌘

When I was going through chemotherapy, I felt awful! I was sick to my stomach all the time, my skin was gray, and I had no hair, eyebrows, or eyelashes. And, I worked every day. As a matter of fact, my business was going better than it ever had. I worked; I slept; and I focused on being well.

Occasionally, when I was working with a client, they would find out what I was going through. They never failed to ask, "How do you do it?" I would always respond, "What's my option?" I figured my options were to wallow in self pity, think on how badly I felt, feel incredibly sorry for myself, imagine I was going to die — soon, and dig a hole, jump in and pull the dirt in on top of me. I was not fond of these options. So, I worked, slept and focused on being well.

No matter what type of situation we are in, we have options. These options may only be in the way we view something, but that, in itself, is an option. Isn't that what makes us human beings? We can go or stay, accept or refuse, live or exist, make the most or least of all our situations. The "Serenity Prayer" explains the three options we have: accept the things I cannot change, have the courage to change the things I can, and have the wisdom to know the difference.

Our courage helps us carry on in that it gives us the impetus to go from one thing to the next. To have the courage to carry on helps us grow with life, not succumb to it.

⌘⌘⌘⌘⌘

SEPTEMBER 13
...APPRECIATING UNANSWERED PRAYERS

"I have had prayers answered — most strangely so sometimes — but
I think our heavenly Father's loving-kindness
has been more evident in what He has refused me."

- Lewis Carroll

⌘⌘⌘⌘⌘

I, probably like most of you, have tried to make deals with God. God, I'll
never do (whatever) again if You just let me (whatever). It's never worked for me.
I finally realized the prayer says *Thy will be done.* We ask, but it will be His will.
At one time in my life I was dating a man who was separated from his wife.
He wined and dined me, wrote me poetry, and treated me as if I were very
special. I got very involved – not so much with him but with a life style and the
idea of romance. I knew he was seeing a counselor and was vacillating between
his wife and me. I would sit up for hours praying to let him stay with me. I could
think of all kinds of reasons why I, and our life together, would be better. Finally,
he made a decision. He left me and patched things up with his wife. For several
months I was devastated. I was in the pits and figured I would never recover. I
did.
I got the job of a lifetime in regards to money and travel. I developed a
world of contacts. I trained with prestigious people. I started my own business,
bought my own home and a Mercedes, and started a stock portfolio. I met my
husband; we were married, and our life together is wonderful.
One day at a restaurant where I was meeting a client, I saw my "old friend."
All he could do was whine about his health. His posture and clothing were bad,
indicating to me his state of mind. He had not taken care of himself and kept
talking about this "hangy" turkey neck. Now, he was in the pits. I walked out of
the restaurant thanking God for unanswered prayers. I could have been married
to that man. I cannot even begin to tell you at that moment how glad I was that
my prayers had gone unanswered.
At the time we are praying, we want our prayers answered, all we see is the
result of the "halo effect." Everything about the person or situation is wonderful –
it just couldn't be any better. With time, the halo slips, and we see things
differently — almost in a new light, and in this new light, we are tickled to death
our prayer went unanswered, and God didn't give us what we asked for. As our
Father, He knows best.

⌘⌘⌘⌘⌘

"As for me, I will call upon God; and the Lord shall save me.
Evening, and morning, and at noon, will I pray."

SEPTEMBER 14
...ADDING SEASONING AND SPICE

"Cooking is like love. It should be entered
into with abandon or not at all."
- Harriet Van Horne

⌘⌘⌘⌘⌘

When I was growing up in the age of fast food, preservatives, pre-packaged meals, TV dinners, and canned and frozen everything, the only three seasonings I was aware of were sugar, salt and pepper. I never learned to cook when I was young. My grandmother loved to cook, and she would be offended if you wanted to learn how or tried to help her out. I didn't learn to cook until my mother and I got our own place. I experimented on her with my cooking, and I am proud to say she was strong and survived every meal.

I was almost 35 years old before I began to look at what I put in my body. I attended classes on balancing your diet and eating healthy. I went to Weight Watchers. I actually began cooking food and preparing meals instead of assembling things and eating out of Styrofoam containers.

I met Stan, who is an excellent cook. We went to cooking classes together, learned where to buy all of our fresh vegetables and meats, eliminated anything boxed or pre-packaged, and started our own herb garden.

I cannot believe how good spice and seasonings make things taste. Meat and vegetables marinated and grilled or cooked with fresh herbs taste great. You don't need tons of salt or sugar to make things taste good. Herbs enhance flavors. Just running your hands over fresh rosemary, oregano, thyme, dill and sage makes your hands smell heavenly.

I think our lives are like recipes, and it is up to us to add the spice and seasonings that make it special and ours and heavenly.

⌘⌘⌘⌘⌘

"You are the salt of the earth."
Matthew 5:13

SEPTEMBER 15
...WHEN CLIPPING WINGS IS NECESSARY

"To keep oneself safe does not mean to bury oneself."
- Seneca

⌘⌘⌘⌘⌘

As a child, I always preferred animals to dolls. I love living things. At one time I had two pet ducks, Henny Penny and Ducky Lucky. They were my babies. All the other kids in the neighborhood had dolls in their baby buggies; I had my two ducks.

Grandmother had clipped their wings to keep them from flying off. They were tame ducks and would have been lost in the outside world. I could tie one end of a rope to the handle of my baby buggy and the other to their legs and keep them nice and safe.

There are times in all our lives when we are too tame and too delicate and could not survive in the outside world. We are unprepared for what life is going to deal us. For us to survive, we need maturity, time and wisdom.

We must all meet our destiny, and as Winston Churchill said, "The chain of destiny can only be grasped one link at a time." Handling one link will prepare us for handling the next and the next and so on.

⌘⌘⌘⌘⌘

"The eternal God is thy refuge, and
underneath are the everlasting arms."
Deuteronomy 33:27

SEPTEMBER 16
...PROFITING FROM SMALL BITS OF TIME

"All my possessions for a moment in time."
- Elizabeth I

⌘⌘⌘⌘⌘

I will have to admit that I am time conscious. I feel great when I have checked off all the items from my To Do List, and I have time left over. Left over time is handled very differently from person to person. I don't know how often I have heard people say, "Well, I only have 10 minutes. That's not enough time to do anything now." When I think of all the things I can get done in 10 minutes, I'm amazed to hear that statement.

I use my 10 minutes to throw laundry in the machine, make a bed, grade a paper, clean a counter, take the dogs out to play ball, file miscellaneous papers, etc. I grade papers at stop lights, car washes and traffic jams. I read paperbacks while waiting in lines. I work at my computer while riding in the car with my husband. I practice my presentations while I'm walking the dog. By utilizing these small bits of time and getting things done, I free up larger blocks of time to spend with my family.

What prompted me to write this entry is a song that Marie Fischer, one of our soloists in the church choir, sang on Sunday. The line that had such an impact on me was "If your day is full of daily things, and you have no room to grow." This line haunted me all day long. How true this is for many people. By profiting from small bits of time and quickly ridding myself of daily things, I have room to grow, to relax, and to spend my time the way I choose.

⌘⌘⌘⌘⌘

"Brethren, the time is short."
1 Corinthians 7:29

SEPTEMBER 17
...GREETING THE WORLD EXPECTANTLY

"The best part of our lives we pass in counting on what is to come."
- William Hazlitt

⌘⌘⌘⌘⌘

Several years ago, the previous pastor of our church talked about prayer. One point he made was that we should pray expectantly thanking God in advance for what we had received. We should trust that things will go well. I nearly fell out of the pew. I thought this way of looking at life was just "new age" stuff.

In thinking this through, I realized my family raised me to think and react to life expectantly. My mother, grandmother, aunts, teachers, and friends saw potential in me and constantly told me there was nothing I couldn't do. I believed them.

I learned to train horses, play piano, cook, fold napkins, operate my computer, etc. At fifty years old, I'm still learning — and loving learning.

One of the major things I learned was how to greet each and every day: expecting the best of the day and most people. By starting each day expectantly and saying "Good Morning, God" instead of "Good God, it's morning," I set myself up to receive the best, and I'll be darned if the best isn't usually what I get.

⌘⌘⌘⌘⌘

"Find rest, O my soul, in God alone;
for my expectation is from him."
Psalm 62:5

SEPTEMBER 18
...GETTING BACK TO NATURE ANY WAY YOU CAN

"Man masters nature not by force but by understanding."
- Jacob Bronowski

⌘⌘⌘⌘⌘

I'm a big bread eater. Starch has always been and will always be one of the main stays of my diet. It is sad for me to say that, try as I might, I cannot make good yeast bread. It is never done in the middle. As much as I love natural home made bread, I can never make it. Then someone invented the bread machine. I was excited! I questioned people who had a bread machine to see what they thought. The results were positive. The machine finally went on sale at a local appliance store, and I told my husband I just had to have one. So, we became the proud owners of a bread machine.

I took a great deal of ribbing from my husband when I baked my first loaf. He said it was the only $150.00 loaf of bread he had ever eaten. But even he got hooked. It tastes so fresh, has little fat and no preservatives, and reminds us of the bread our parents used to make.

Going backwards to a simpler time seems to be the rage. How many grocery stores do you frequent that have wooden barrels filled with candy, dog biscuits, and rice? The old fashioned "help your self" general store attitude! Butchers slice our ham while we wait. It doesn't taste as good when it comes pre-sliced and from a cellophane package. Farmer's Markets and specialty stores are the rage. Even the restaurants advertise "down home" cooking.

I certainly agree with this philosophy, and I, for one, am all for getting back to nature any way I can. If getting back to nature, for me, is in using a $150.00 bread machine, then let's hear it for the bread machine.

We have a love and a passion for getting back to nature. It conjures up delights, inspiration, happiness, and remembrance. Christine Pierce wrote, "...'natural' were some sort of metaphysical glue that could hold our claims or values together." We come to trust what is natural.

⌘⌘⌘⌘⌘

"Through these he has given us his very great and precious promises, so that through them you may participate in the divine nature and escape the corruption in the world caused by evil desires."
2 Peter 1:4

SEPTEMBER 19
...WRAPPING PACKAGES

"In choosing presents people should remember that
the whole point of the present is that it is an extra."
- E. V. Lucas

⌘⌘⌘⌘⌘

I had the opportunity and privilege to know a truly "beloved" man. He was
the pillar of his community, a role model, an authority figure, a counselor, a sage,
a humorist and a friend. He was ethical, hard and direct. You may have been in
the minority of those who did not like him, but even as one of the minority, you
respected him.

I was and always will be in awe of this man. I asked his advice on many
occasions and would stop by and talk with him when I just wanted to chat. He
was simply a pleasure to be around.

He and I had only one rough spot: he did not like for women to wear
make-up, and I liked wearing make-up. He always told me I was pretty without
make-up, and that it was what was on the inside that counted, so I tolerated this
interchange. One evening, at a Christmas party and gift exchange, he walked up
to me and rubbed some of my eye shadow off with his thumb. Looking at the
color on his thumb, he again said he just didn't understand why I wore make-up.
Standing there looking at the beautifully wrapped packages, I had an epiphany! I
asked him what present he brought. He pointed to one very nicely wrapped
package in blue and gold with a gold ribbon and gold horn.

I wanted to know why he had wrapped the gift. Wasn't it what was on the
inside that counted? Wasn't the gift pretty enough by itself? Didn't the receiver
know that it was pretty on the inside?

The person matters. The present matters. The packaging is the little extra
that makes the presentation of who or what we are just a bit more special.

⌘⌘⌘⌘⌘

"You are looking only on the surface of things."
2 Corinthians 10:7

SEPTEMBER 20
...UNDERSTANDING ASSOCIATIONS

"A moment's insight is sometimes worth a life's experience."
- Oliver Wendell Holmes

⌘⌘⌘⌘⌘

When we run into anything that reminds us of another person or event, it can be either a shock or a pleasure. Regardless of which it is, it definitely makes the memory work overtime and pulls us in another direction — some of which we don't really want to go.

Although my husband never verbally expressed his concern when I was going through chemotherapy, I knew he was worried. I decided that I would make it seem as insignificant as I possibly could. He sat and watched me intently during the injections. I remember, during the first injection, my vision blurred, I became light headed (and scared), and I had a taste in my mouth and a smell in my head of something that must be similar to embalming fluid. To say the least, I was sick. I was also determined not to let my husband know how sick I was.

Trying to prove to him how un-sick I was, when he suggested lunch, I said sure. We went to one of his favorite Italian restaurants. I sat down and ordered and prayed that I wouldn't throw up and embarrass him and me. The server brought my lunch of a chicken sandwich on focaccia bread, fries and Alfredo sauce. I ate what I could, went to the restroom and just sat there staring straight ahead. I will never forget that meal! To this day, I cannot abide foccacio bread or Alfredo sauce.

I thought that would be the end of it. It was not. Several months after the chemotherapy had ended, we went to the same restaurant. I began to get nervous and upset when we were seated. I couldn't breath. The awful physical feelings were coming back. I stood up from the table, apologized, and told my husband I had to leave — now. Associations.

⌘⌘⌘⌘⌘

"Can a man take fire into his bosom, and his clothes not be burned?"
Proverbs 6:27

SEPTEMBER 21
...OLD HABITS DIE HARD

"It is unpleasant to miss even the most trifling
thing to which we have been accustomed."

- Goethe

⌘⌘⌘⌘⌘

Sometimes, I wonder if we realize how conditioned we are? I wouldn't say
conditioning is bad or wrong; I would just say that we are conditioned. When the
phone rings, we pick it up. When we hear a siren, we pull over. When we see a
red light, we stop; and when we see a green light, we go. When we have the
remote control, we click it. When we have a pencil and paper, we doodle. We
are conditioned. Conditioned responses become habits, and old habits die hard.

When we moved into our new house, we found a place for everything, and
everything, basically, stayed in its place. Our only major difficulty was in regards
to the master bath we shared. I had put all the supplies under my side of the sink
— since I do most of the cleaning. All of our sundries were under his side of the
sink. Most mornings, we get ready at different times, so no problems arose.
Occasionally, such as Sunday mornings, we would use the bathroom at the same
time, and I was always asking him to move over so I could get the things I needed
to get ready. He would sigh and then move aside.

Finally he asked why I didn't keep my things on my side. I asked what
would I do with the stuff under my side of the sink. He said put the waste basket
under his side of the sink. I did.

Now, for three years we had been opening the first set of doors and
throwing the trash in the basket. For nearly six months after I moved the waste
basket behind the second set of doors, we still opened the first set of doors to
throw in the trash. Used tissue and dog hair all over my makeup was pretty
disgusting, but the half full cans of soda were the real problem! YUCK!

It took us almost six months to get used to the waste basket's new location.
I have thought about this silly incident many times when I am trying to introduce a
new routine or eating habit into my life. We want to do it immediately, and we get
frustrated when it doesn't happen immediately. If it takes nearly six months to get
used to a minor change like the new placement of a trash can, how long will it take
to incorporate major changes? Patience is so difficult for us to contend with and
wait for and so necessary for our success with change.

⌘⌘⌘⌘⌘

"Perseverance must finish its work so that you may be
mature and complete, not lacking anything."

James 1:4

SEPTEMBER 22
...SHOWING OTHERS A BETTER WAY TO LIVE

"Example: An eloquent orator."
- Czech Proverb

⌘⌘⌘⌘⌘

I am always seeing articles and hearing leaders talk about the need for mentors and role models. People who will set standards and lead the way for others. People who will give of themselves to others.

During our lifetime, we have the opportunity to give much to others. We give time, advice, talent, knowledge, labor, money. The list goes on and on. All these things are not nearly as important as another gift we have available to give to others.

We know young people are desperate for mentors, role models, and success stories. They want to find people who not only set standards but also live up to them. It isn't necessary to stand on a pedestal and yell, "Look at me." Even without doing this, you can give people a very important gift: the example of your own life working and working well.

Bad news and failures are publicized daily. We don't have to look long or hard to find either. It's the good news and successes people are looking for. And, I do mean "looking" for. Where is the person who not only sets the standard but also lives the standard?

When you live the life you talk about, when you have a good job, healthy relationships, a multi-faceted life, you are giving without going out of your way to give. People see your successes and begin to emulate your philosophy and your lifestyle.

You are the mentor and role model everyone is looking for. Your successes will become other's successes. You are creating a heritage and legacy that can be passed on to the next generation and the next. You are giving while living.

⌘⌘⌘⌘⌘

"Join with others in following my example,
brothers, and take note of those who live
according to the pattern we gave you."
Philippians 3:17

SEPTEMBER 23
...SEEING PERSPECTIVE CHANGE

"It is the eye which makes the horizon."
- Emerson

⌘⌘⌘⌘⌘

One of the great loves of my husband and step son is to go to a Christmas tree farm on Thanksgiving weekend, find the perfect "live" Christmas tree, tag it, pick it up in December, decorate it for the holidays, and then plant it in our yard on New Years Day. It is quite a tradition.

One year they found a beautifully shaped tree and were looking forward to bringing the tree home to decorate for the season and then planting it in the yard to provide shelter, beauty, and memories for the rest of our lives.

Ben, my step son, took his pick-up truck to the Christmas Tree Farm to get the tree. He called us on the way home and told us, when the tree was placed in the back of the pick-up, the front wheels came off the ground. He also told us that the tree took up the entire bed of the pick-up, and he was afraid he might lose it on the way home.

We waited anxiously for him. About an hour after he called, he pulled into the drive. The truck was dwarfed by the tree. With the help of several neighbors, we finally got the tree out of the truck and on the porch. When we pulled the tree through the front door, the hinges on the door broke. We repaired that. We tried to place the tree in the living room, but it took up all the free space, including the walk ways. Finally, we decided to take out all the dining room furniture and let the tree stand there for the holidays.

After the tree was standing firmly in place, and we were standing there in awe of this huge tree inside our home, Ben made a remarkable statement. He said, "It didn't look this big in the forest." I replied, "No, Ben, trees don't look big in the middle of a forest. It's a matter of perspective."

Now before we go for our tree, we measure the area where we want it to stand and take the measuring tape and dimensions with us. This has made our selections more manageable.

Each year, as we decorate the new tree, we talk about the giant fir tree we had in our home and laugh at what we went through. All the fir trees stand in the yard and remind us of many stories of Christmas Past. And the biggest tree always reminds me to keep a good perspective on life.

⌘⌘⌘⌘⌘

"May your eyes see what is right."
Psalm 17:2

SEPTEMBER 24
...WHEN TO GO ALONG FOR THE RIDE

"Every advantage has its tax."
- Emerson

⌘⌘⌘⌘⌘

I laugh when I hear someone ask if anyone wants to go along for a ride. And, I laugh even harder when I hear someone say that they are going along for a ride. I wonder if either knows what they are getting themselves into.

Gina and I had planned a dream vacation. We were going to San Francisco to eat and shop. It's our idea of a really good time. There aren't too many places where you can find the plethora of restaurants, shops and candy stores as you can in San Francisco. It was our idea of heaven on earth.

After we had been there several days, the candy wasn't having the same appeal, and we had shopped so long that our hands had creases from shopping bag handles. Gina decided she wanted to rent a car and drive to Carmel. She asked if I wanted to go along for the ride. I said yes not knowing what I was getting into. In Carmel, we didn't find even one thing to buy. On top of that, we didn't see hide nor hair of Clint Eastwood. So, we headed back to San Francisco.

The trip back to our hotel was less than perfect. Traffic was outrageous, and it began to rain. We came to a place where the road forked. Gina thought she was to go left, but, at the last minute, she decided to go right. I was holding two extra large diet drinks in my lap and putting on lipstick when she veered right. In one swift, brief moment, I looked like a clown and was wet from the waist down. The drive back to San Francisco was much longer under these conditions and to top this off, when we hit the outskirts of town, it was rush hour.

This was what happened to one day of my vacation just because I decided to go along for the ride. I think about that day when I hear someone ask about going along for a ride. I weigh the benefits of what I am doing against what might happen on this ride. It could be an enlightening adventure or material for another entry.

⌘⌘⌘⌘⌘

"I have learned by experience that the Lord hath blessed me."
Genesis 30:27

SEPTEMBER 25
...GOING FIRST CLASS EVERY TIME YOU CAN

"Be content with your lot; one cannot be first in everything."

- Aesop

⌘⌘⌘⌘⌘

The phrase "first class" says a lot. People, computers, cars, restaurants, musicals, almost anything can and has been referred to as first class. In all actuality "first class" simply means being seated first, a few extra inches of leg room, and glass dinner service. What it really is isn't all that impressive; what it implies is! It implies you have arrived. It suggests quality not quantity.

For years I was into quantity. It could be I had fallen for the marketing of so many products and began to believe that more was better. I had many clothes, many shoes, many pieces of costume jewelry, ate many meals out, and went many places. But everything I had or did was inexpensive, just filled up time and space, and wore out or wore off easily. Worth was there; value wasn't.

It was in reading one of my motivational and thought provoking books that I began to look at what my life was saying to others: of worth but not value. At least that was my perception.   I decided to change "many" things. The first thing I decided to change was flying first class as often as I could. I would let my clients purchase my flight ticket, and I would take my accrued mileage and upgrade to first class. I took most of my clothing to the consignment shop. When I received the money from their sale, I bought fewer but better quality clothes. I ate out and vacationed less often, but when I did eat out or vacation, it was in very nice places. I enjoyed how I traveled, what I wore, and where I ate.

I had and did what I wanted — not quite as often — but definitely first class. I did the best I could with what I could afford. I showed myself and the world I had arrived, and I exhibited quality and value not quantity and worth.

⌘⌘⌘⌘⌘

"I have learned, in whatsoever state I am, therewith to be content."

Philippians 4:11

SEPTEMBER 26
...BECOMING MORE EXPRESSIVE

"Good communication is stimulating as black
coffee, and just as hard to sleep after."
- Anne Morrow Lindbergh

⌘⌘⌘⌘⌘

Our church has a large deaf ministry. They have a minister who speaks
and signs at their own services, and they have developed several small groups to fit
the special needs of the deaf members. One of the small groups they have
developed is called "The Singing Hands": a choral group who signs the hymns.
They dress in black and wear white gloves, and when performing any musical
piece, they create quite a sensation.

On several occasions, "The Singing Hands" have performed for the hearing
congregation with one of the choir's soloist . The congregation learns the signs for
the chorus and participates. Their performance of "How Great Thou Art" always
comes to mind. We are associating the signs with the words and, little by little, we
are picking up on signing.

It was Emerson, referring to a handshake, who said, "I hate the giving of the
hand unless the whole man accompanies it." Their signs for the words are so
beautiful and expressive that you know the whole person is involved with the
words of the hymn. Watching "The Singing Hands" perform brings tears to most
people's eyes. I think some of the tears are for the non-hearing people working
hard to function in a hearing world, but I think the majority of the tears are for the
beauty and expression the congregation sees in their movements and faces.

After the first performance "The Singing Hands" did for the congregation,
some members of the congregation began to applaud. They then realized the
deaf couldn't hear the applause. The congregation quickly learned the non-
hearing method of showing appreciation is by waving the hands side to side.

Now, when "The Singing Hands" perform, we all wave our hands side to
side. They have taught all of us how to be a little more expressive.

⌘⌘⌘⌘⌘

"The Lord will fulfill his purpose, for me;
your love, O Lord, endures forever —
do not abandon the words of your hands."
Psalm 138:8

SEPTEMBER 27
...SACRIFICING

> "The first element of religion, and resolves itself
> in theological language into the love of God."
> -James A. Froude

⌘⌘⌘⌘⌘

To give something up or away, expecting nothing or little in return is sacrificing. Some sacrifices are major. We read stories, both fictional and non-fictional, of people who offer up their own life to save someone else. Some sacrifices are minor: giving up a favorite pair of earrings to please another or staying home to watch children so someone else can have a night on the town. One thing that most sacrifices have in common, whether major or minor, is that we feel more noble for having made them. I made a minor sacrifice this summer. Not only did I feel more noble, but I had the opportunity to see something beautiful.

My husband and I grow herbs. Herbs are pretty, for they flower, and they smell wonderful. Each year our herbs do very well with one exception — the dill. For two consecutive years, we could not get the dill to grow. Finally, the third year, the dill grew tall, strong, and healthy. We were excited.

One Saturday, I went out on the deck to snip some dill for a loaf of bread, and I found three caterpillars on the dill plant. My husband came out on the deck to see what was happening. He told me these caterpillars would become Monarch Butterflies. They had attached themselves to the dill plant for nourishment before they cocooned. Now, we had a choice. We could either pull the caterpillars off and save the dill or sacrifice the dill and allow three more beautiful Monarch Butterflies to come into this world. We sacrificed the dill.

Every day I would go out on the deck to monitor the progress. Slowly and surely, the caterpillars stripped the plant bare. The stems turned yellow. The cocoons were spun, and they began their transformation. One day I noticed that the cocoons were empty, and I had missed their coming out. I was so disappointed. Later that afternoon, I went out to exercise the dogs. As I was sitting in the swing watching the dogs, three beautiful Monarch Butterflies flew across the yard. It would be almost impossible for anyone to convince me they were not "our" butterflies for they hovered over the dill plant and the deck as if they were home.

Sacrificing the dill was so trivial next to the beauty these three creatures gave to the world for a short period of time.

⌘⌘⌘⌘⌘

"And do not forget to do good and to share

SEPTEMBER 28
...THE QUIETING OF A VOICE

"An index of character."
- Anonymous

⌘⌘⌘⌘⌘

I have run into some amazing people in my life. These are those special people who have a wonderful, soft, soothing voice that calms and brings peace to a troubled mind. My Aunt June is one of these people. No matter how stressed or distraught I am, all I have to do is pick up the phone, call my Aunt June and listen. It's not what she says; it's the way she says it.

Marie Fischer, one of our choir's outstanding altos, is like that, also. There is such a gentleness and flow with her voice that you find you are mesmerized with the sound of the notes. The words are secondary.

Edmund Burke wrote of "...the healing voice of Christian charity," and that is exactly what these voices are. These voices heal and quiet and calm. When we have run into walls and obstacles, we can get back on a return journey to sanity by listening to the quieting of a special voice.

⌘⌘⌘⌘⌘

"From this time forward I make you hear new things."
Isaiah 48:6

SEPTEMBER 29
...BEING CAREFUL ABOUT WHOM WE UNDERESTIMATE

"What we see first when we look into a region
hitherto unknown, unexplored, unannexed."
- George Macdonald

⌘⌘⌘⌘⌘

When Stan, my husband, and I first started dating, he had decided to go back to school to get his MBA. He wrote well and had a keen understanding of business. However, statistics were not his strong suit.

One evening, while we were together, he was working on some statistics problems. He kept complaining that he did not understand what the problems were asking. He asked me if I had any idea what the terms meant. I told him he was talking to the wrong person; he should call my mother. [I need to point out that my mother did statistical work for Eli Lilly for many, many years.] He kept complaining; so I called my mother and handed the phone to Stan.

He explained the problem to her. She asked him a series of questions to which he responded. When he got off the phone with my mother, he looked at me rather skeptically and said my mother was a nice person, but he didn't think she knew what she was talking about.

The following Thursday, after his Wednesday night class, Stan called and said he owed me and my mother an apology. I asked why, and he said, "You remember all the questions that your mom asked me last week about the statistic problem? The instructor asked the class members the same questions that your mother asked me last week."

Sometimes we underestimate the help, the insight, and the knowledge others can give us.

We must always remember that regardless of whom we are dealing with, or what we are concerned about, there is always some one else out there who can give us the help, insight, and knowledge we need.

⌘⌘⌘⌘⌘

"Though it cost all you have, get wisdom."
Proverbs 4:7

SEPTEMBER 30
...KNOWING YOUR TERRITORY

"I think knowing what you can not do is more important
then knowing what you can do. In fact, that's good taste."
- Lucille Ball

⌘⌘⌘⌘⌘

All the dogs in the neighborhood are very territorial. Most people have the invisible fences, and the dogs run to the safety line, bark, and toss their heads and stomp. [A pretty impressive display to anyone thinking of crossing the line!] The dogs know their territory, their boundaries; they know where the line is drawn.

Animals are not the only creatures who know territory. We all do, and we feel comfortable and safe in our own boundaries. We become so accustomed to our territories that we transfer their boundaries elsewhere without realizing it.

Tag was a big game in our neighborhood. We usually played tag in Mr. and Mrs. Piper's yard because they had the biggest yard with the most trees and the fewest man-made obstacles. We knew the territory of Piper's yard well.

One summer evening one of our friends had a birthday party at their aunt's house. After the cake and ice cream, we decided to go outside and play tag. We did a fair job avoiding the obstacles when it was dusk, but when it became dark, we ran into some difficulty — a clothes line. You would be running pell-mell across the yard and be "clothes lined" across the neck with a real clothes line. You could tell when it happened because you heard that unmistakable gag that someone makes when they are grabbed by the throat. [It was amusing until it happened to you.] We never had enough time to get used to this new territory.

I think when we are interacting with new people — in new territory — that we step on unfamiliar toes, make remarks that are not well accepted by some, and hurt feelings or create animosity that we don't mean to create. It is not a deliberate act; it is an act that occurs because we are on unfamiliar territory

We all have grown up with a "Piper's Yard." We know where each tree is, where the good hiding places are, and where manmade obstacles are placed. But our world must go further than Piper's Yard; and when we are placed in new territory, instead of running through it pell-mell making mistakes, maybe we should slow down and look to see what and who we are facing in our new territory.

⌘⌘⌘⌘⌘

"My purpose is that they may be encouraged in heart and united in love,
so that they may have the full riches of complete understanding, in
order that they may know the mystery of God, namely, Christ,
in whom are hidden all the treasures of wisdom and knowledge."

OCTOBER 1
...ACCEPTING "TRULY" CONSTRUCTIVE CRITICISM

"Speak the truth by all means; be bold and fearless in your
rebuke of error, and in your keener rebuke of wrongdoing;
but be human, and loving, and gentle, and brotherly, the while."
- W. N. Punshon

⌘⌘⌘⌘⌘

I was doing a second series of presentation for a company in Lafayette,
Indiana, on Writing Basics. This was a very early morning presentation. I had
been up since 5:00 am and on the road for 2 hours before I even began the
presentation. My communication powers were functioning in a heavy fog.

I was trying to explain to the attendees that they should not be upset
because they did not know everything about grammar and writing styles. I
explained that no one was "omnipotent." What I actually meant was
"omniscient."

During the first break, a young woman approached me hesitantly. I knew
she wanted to tell me something. I also knew that it was something she was
uncomfortable saying because she was wringing her hands and having difficulty
making eye contact. I assured her that I was "thick skinned," and she could
speak her mind.

She explained what I had said and knew it wasn't what I had meant. She
added, "I hate bringing this up. I know you just didn't realize what you were
saying. Normally, I wouldn't have said anything. It's just that I have so much
respect for you and your skills that I don't want you to look foolish in front of
anyone." I smiled my biggest smile and sincerely thanked her because she was
being so sincere in her criticism. She wasn't being mean or hateful; she had
genuine concern.

There are two types of criticism in this world: constructive and destructive.
Destructive criticism is "you're ugly, and you'll always be ugly." It gives you no
where to go or no way to improve. It's very damaging and ineffective. True
constructive criticism is meant to help us improve and be our best. It's a way
others help us live up to our potential.

When you know that others are genuinely trying to help you, don't get your
nose out of joint and try to rationalize, justify, and explain. Instead, smile and
know that their intent is honorable, comes from the heart and is purposefully to
help you be the best that you can be.

⌘⌘⌘⌘⌘

"As for the person who hears my words but does not keep them, I do
not judge him. For I did not come to judge the world, but to save it."

OCTOBER 2
...LIFE'S "IRONING" PHILOSOPHY

"He who hesitates is sometimes saved."

-James Thurber

⌘⌘⌘⌘⌘

My mother and I are almost clones in some of our physical characteristics and philosophies and at opposite ends of the spectrum on others. On some things she did drove me nuts! [However, I'm sure nothing I did had that effect on her!]

One particular thing she did that drove me crazy was her hanging her clean laundry in her closet unironed, wrinkled, a mess. It looked terrible. I was embarrassed for anyone to see it. You see, I did laundry the correct way. I ironed everything after it came out of the dryer and hung it neatly in the closet ready to go. My mother had to get up 15 minutes early every morning to select what she was going to wear and iron it. I, on the other hand, got to sleep later because my clothing was ready to go.

One day, I told her she was crazy for keeping her clothes in that wrinkled state, and she ought to iron everything so that it was ready to wear. Her response was, "I hate to iron! Suppose I spent an entire day ironing all my clothes and then died the next morning. I would have ironed all that stuff for nothing." I had no response.

We all have things we hate to do (mine is folding underwear), and I suppose there are times when it doesn't hurt to postpone them until they have to be done. By freeing up our time to do the things we really love, i.e. Mother and I going to lunch, shopping, or working with the ponies, the precious few moments that we have together will leave more pleasant memories for each other than standing at an ironing board or whatever else it is we hate to do.

⌘⌘⌘⌘⌘

"Be still before the Lord and wait patiently for him;"

Psalm 37:7

OCTOBER 3
...EASING OTHER'S PAIN

"A man, to be greatly good, must imagine intensely and comprehensively;
he must put himself in the place of another and in many others;
the pains and pleasures of his species must become his own."

- Percy Bysshe Shelley

⌘⌘⌘⌘⌘

When I got my first "high paying" job, I decided to get myself something I had always wanted: a Mercedes. It was a beautiful silver and caused heads to turn. It rode and handled like a dream. It was worth every dime, and I was in heaven when I drove that car.

I was returning to the office after having met with a client. Just as I got off the interstate, it started to rain heavily. I pulled up to a stop light, looked in my rearview mirror and saw a car approaching — too fast for stopping at the traffic light. The car kept coming and slammed into the back of my Mercedes.

I looked at the odometer; I had just turned 2,000 miles. I undid my seat belt, opened the door, and headed to the other car to kill the person who had dented my dream. Out of the other car stepped a 16 year old girl who was sobbing. Through tears she told me she had just passed her driver's test and received her license a week ago, and she didn't understand why the car wouldn't stop. Someone had failed to explain or demonstrate what happened to a car when it hydroplaned. I knew she was scared to death. I took a deep breath, asked her if she were hurt, and told her, "Anything that can be fixed with money is not a problem; it is merely an inconvenience."

She stopped crying, and I calmed down. We called the police, exchanged insurance information, and, in a week, I had my Mercedes back as good as new.

I'm sure it was the Lord who put those words in my mouth and stopped me from wanting to kill her. I realized she was a child who was scared and in an incredible amount of pain. I know I could have screamed at her — believe me I wanted to — but something in my heart couldn't do it. I hope if she is ever in my shoes, and encounters another situation like this, she passes this small kindness along to someone else to help ease their pain.

⌘⌘⌘⌘⌘

"A gentle answer turns away wrath,
but a harsh word stirs up anger."

Proverbs 15:1

OCTOBER 4
...BEING AWARE OF YOUR LIFE FORCE

"It is the acme of life to understand life."
- George Santayana

⌘⌘⌘⌘⌘

Clara, one of my best friends, lives in Colorado. Periodically we visit one another. On one trip to Colorado Springs, I learned how strong a life force can be and how some people are more attuned to their life force.

Clara had many things planned for us to do while I was visiting her. She had only one engagement she couldn't cancel. Two people had flown over from Sweden to do a seminar on Transcendental Kinesiology. I had the option of going with her or staying at her home. I opted to go.

When I walked into the home where the TK seminar was to take place, I stood just inside the front door to get a glimpse of the people attending. At the far end of the room to my left was a tall, handsome blond man, and at the far end of the room to my right was a tall, handsome blond woman. My gaze flipped from left to right as we made eye contact, and without a moment's hesitation, both the man and woman walked straight to me. We didn't say anything to each other for a while. The presence I felt pass through me was overwhelming. I don't actually know what it was. In my uncertainty, I will call it a life force.

I have always had a strong sixth sense; there are some things I just know, and I can't explain. My husband and many others have told me that they see people attracted to my life force. People want to talk to me. People in my seminars tell me they wished they could carry me around in their pocket. Or, if they could listen to me every day, they would never have a problem with self esteem. I am so honored by their compliments.

I am very happy I have a strong life force. It allows me to help other people connect, and I am sure it is what has carried me through trials and tribulations. This combination of strength, charisma, and soul — our life force — helps make our journey smoother, more engaging, and lasting.

⌘⌘⌘⌘⌘

"What no eye has seen, nor ear heard,
nor the human heart conceived, what God
has prepared for those who love him."
1 Corinthians 2:9

OCTOBER 5
...COMMUNION

"Infinite sharing is the law of God's inner life."
- Thomas Merton

⌘⌘⌘⌘⌘

The first Sunday of each month is Communion Sunday. It is always a special Sunday for me. When I hear the words and see the bread and wine, I realize that symbolically we are all sharing the body and blood of Christ.

This particular Sunday, the choir's Offertory Anthem was "My Shepherd Will Supply My Need" by Mack Wilberg/John Carter. The lyrics are lovely and so special that I believe we were all touched by them.

There would I find a settled rest
while others go and come,
no more a stranger, nor a guest,
but like a child at home.

Not only is communion a "religious or spiritual fellowship," but it is also a "a sharing of thoughts or feelings." As I looked at the choir and the members of the congregation, I knew that at that moment there was a shared feeling. The harmony of the chords was created by the voices, organ, harp, oboe, and flute. The harmony of the souls was created by the words.

How lovely it would be to commune with others on many levels enabling us to share this pleasing interaction and appropriate combination as often as possible.

⌘⌘⌘⌘⌘

"Do this often in remembrance of me."
Luke 22:19

OCTOBER 6
...KNOWING THE DIFFERENCE BETWEEN FINE , FINE AND FINE

"For there is good news yet to hear and fine things to be seen."
- Giblet Keith Chesterton

⌘⌘⌘⌘⌘

I have always thought that "fine" was truly one of life's most fantastic four-letter words. For such a simple word, it can say so much to so many. I, personally, have three very favorite uses for "fine".

Use #1: For those "less than perfect" days when I'm trying to convince myself that things are going more smoothly than they really are, I say "fine" through clenched teeth. This particular fine means I'm "Frustrated, Irritated, Nauseated, and Exhausted."

Use #2: For those days – and this is most of the time – when things are going just peachy, I say "fine" with a cheerful heart. This fine means I'm "Fortunate, Idealistic, Nurtured, and Ecstatic."

Use #3: For those days when I haven't gotten up on the good or bad side of the bed and I'm in one of those non-committal types of moods, I say "fine" meaning I'm "Faded, Idle, Neutral, and Emotionless."

My husband tells me that he can always tell what mood I'm in simply by listening to me say "fine." It's the undercurrent that each type of "fine" connotes.

We all have our "fine" words – those words that mean different things to us depending on our state of mind and soul. It's good that we try to cover up a dark mood for the sake of others. It's also good that others know us well enough to recognize and understand which "fine" we mean today: the real meaning from our heart.

⌘⌘⌘⌘⌘

"May the words of my mouth and the meditation
of my heart be pleasing in your sight,"
Psalm 19:14

OCTOBER 7
...REMEMBERING OTHERS

"To be able to enjoy one's past life is to live twice."
                                                    - Martial

⌘⌘⌘⌘⌘

Before my husband and I married, we bought a lot and build a new house. We put both of our own homes up for sale; and while our house was being built, we sorted, packed, and boxed our worldly goods.

Having both been single for some tisme, we had accumulated 5 coffee pots, 3 toasters, 20 sets of sheets, 5 sets of dishes, 2 tea makers, etc. We had multiples of everything, so we decided to have a garage sale to get rid of the excess and use the sale money to buy items for our new house. After several days of organizing and pricing, on the day of the garage sale, I opened the garage door at 8:00 AM, and the customers came.

I was talking with several shoppers while other shoppers arrived. When I turned to greet the new shoppers, I saw a young woman I hadn't seen since she graduated from high school. He name was Jane, and she had been in one of my Senior English Classes.

I looked at her and said, "Hi, Jane." Immediately, she smiled ear to ear. I think her smile was generated because I remembered her. Jane had been one of the very quiet students who always had her homework done, always behaved, and was always pleasant. I'm sure, to most people, she didn't stand out. To me, she did stand out and was memorable because she was a good student and a good person.

Remembering others is very important. It shows them that their existence was significant enough to matter to someone. It shows them they have left a mark on someone. It shows them their life had meaning for someone. Yes, it is very important to remember. How pleased we are when we are remembered by others for it means that we have mattered to someone else.

⌘⌘⌘⌘⌘

"May my tongue cling to the roof of
my mouth if I do not remember you,"
                              Psalm 137:6

OCTOBER 8
...REALIZING THE IMPORTANCE OF TIMING

"Time ripens all things. No man's born wise."
- Cervantes

⌘⌘⌘⌘⌘

Mary, my widowed grandmother, dated Al, a man who owned and ran a dairy farm. Al also drove a school bus. He was a very nice man and one heck of a story teller. One favorite story he told was about his Jersey bull and the school bus.

I had often heard the expression "as mean as a Jersey bull," but I didn't really know what it meant until I heard this story. Al said one of the farm hands must have accidentally left the gate between the barn lot and the bull's pasture open. He had parked the school bus in the barn lot and was making his way to the bus to begin his rounds picking up the kids. He was about 20 yards from the bus when he realized his bull was walking parallel with him in the same barn lot 15 yards to his left. The bull was snorting, stopping to paw occasionally, and definitely picking up speed. Without giving it much thought, Al ran as fast as he could and slid under the bus just ahead of the bull. The bull's head, with horns, was under the bus trying to gore Al. The more the bull tried to reach him and the less successful he was, the angrier the bull got. The bull got down on his knees and stuck his head under the bus. Without understanding the term "leverage," the bull was putting it into practice: he was using his head and shoulders to turn the bus on its side and reach Al. Al crawled to the end of the bus; and when the bull turned the bus on its side, Al jumped out from under the bus, climbed up its side, and jumped through an open window to safety. Al was stuck inside the bus until the farm hands came out of the field, saw what had happened and drove the bull back into the pasture.

Al's timing had to be perfect. He timed how long it would take to make it to the bus, when to jump out from under the bus, and when to climb up the side of the bus and through the window to safety. His perfect timing saved his life.

Timing, the wonderful teacher who prepares and arranges things well, is everything.

⌘⌘⌘⌘⌘

"I tell you, now is the time of God's favor,"
2 Corinthians 6:2

OCTOBER 9
...KNOWING WE ALL FEEL BETTER WHEN THE SUN COMES UP

"A cloudy day, or a little sunshine, have as great an influence
on many constitutions as the most real blessings or misfortunes."
- Joseph Addison

⌘⌘⌘⌘⌘

Several years ago, I had the opportunity to vacation in Hawaii. Naturally, I did all the tourist things — toured the island, visited a pineapple field, shopped for pearls, and bought a flowered shirt. I wanted to do something that was "super" special, and at my hotel I found what I was looking for: a Diamond Head Breakfast Cruise to see the sun come up over Diamond Head. Sounded special to me!

I was at the dock before dawn. There must have been 50 people waiting to board the catamaran. Each passenger was given a tray, escorted to the breakfast buffet, given breakfast and told to find a seat. I was enjoying my breakfast as we left the dock.

The catamaran was undulating on the waves. I love motion, and I was having a great time eating my breakfast while riding on the ocean waves. All of a sudden, I noticed many of the passengers putting down their trays and running for the top deck. Then, I heard sounds from the other passengers that were very unpleasant. Many of the passengers were seasick. They were hanging over the rail losing their breakfast.

As we neared Diamond Head, I went up on the top deck to see the sunrise. As I walked by the other passengers, I saw that many were green and in pain. All of a sudden, the catamaran rounded a curve, and we were facing the sun rising over Diamond Head. This sight will live in my memory as one of the most spectacular things I have ever seen. The colors of the sunrise against the blackness of the rock were a wonderful contrast silhouetting two of God's most marvelous creations.

I looked at the other passengers to see if they were as awed as I was. Not only were they in awe, but they had stopped looking pained, and their green pallor had faded. Their day was going to end much better than it had started. I guess we all feel better when the sun comes up.

⌘⌘⌘⌘⌘

"Do not let the sun go down while you are still angry,"
Ephesians 4:26

OCTOBER 10
...SHARING THE BLAME

"Blame is especially useful in situations in which there is no apparent
villain — those moments that prove, despite our advancement of
learning, how susceptible we are to high winds and wet roads."
- Roger Rosenblatt

⌘⌘⌘⌘⌘

Stan and I were in our study working on the computer, and from the guest
bedroom we hear a crash. We then saw Murphy and CoCo, our dogs, run from
the guest bedroom, down the hall, and into the master bedroom. We looked at
one another curiously. As Sherlock Holmes said, "Something's a foot."

We went into the guest bedroom and found one of the mini blinds on the
floor. As we picked it up, we noticed the cord was wet. The dogs had been using
the cord as some type of pull toy and had succeeded in pulling the blind from its
mounting.

We walked down the hall into the master bedroom to see what the dogs
were up to — now. The dogs were sitting at the end of the bed, side by side,
perfectly calm. Neither dog was making eye contact with us. As a matter of fact,
Murphy was looking to her right, and CoCo was looking to her left. When we
called their names, both dogs looked at us rather indignantly as if to say "What?"
Neither one was going to accept the blame. I think, even in their little dog minds,
they knew by sharing the blame, neither one would be chastised. They had stuck
together in their indiscretion.

There are times when we must share the blame — as an instigator or by-
stander. My Aunt June always told me that "a joy shared is twice a joy, and a
sorrow shared is half a sorrow." Maybe, as we share blame or take on the burden
of another, we can be successful in reducing the blame for one of our
indiscretions.

⌘⌘⌘⌘⌘

"And do not forget to do good and to share with
others, for with such sacrifices God is pleased."
Hebrews 13:16

OCTOBER 11
...KNOWING WHEN YOU HAVE TOO MUCH OF A GOOD THING

"To go beyond is as wrong as to fall short."
- Confucius

⌘⌘⌘⌘⌘

My mother loves violets! She wore violet perfume and had bouquets of artificial violets everywhere. Before we could afford "good" furniture, she would buy inexpensive, unpainted furniture, paint it white and put violet decals on it. In the gourmet shop at Ayres, she found a heart shaped box of candied violet petals to use as decoration, and she was tickled to death with her find. We had cups and saucers with violets on them. Dish towels, bathroom accessories, scarves, and vases were violet covered. Violets were as much a part of my mother's life as one of her four basic food groups: ice cream.

She loved real violets, and each spring we would travel the country roads in search of violets. One particular road in Martinsville had an abundance of roadside violets, and one Sunday afternoon, we found ourselves on that road picking them.

Mother saw a new, large clump of violets just on the other side of the ditch. She was making her way towards them when I told her I thought we had picked enough. Just as she stretched her arm out to get to this fresh clump of violets, a very large black snake made a grab for her arm. She jerked her arm back, screamed, and nearly fell into the ditch.

She turned around, looked at me with "silver dollar" eyes, and through gasping breaths said, "I think you are right. We have enough violets, and we don't want too much of a good thing." And, if my memory serves me correctly, I don't think we ever went back to that particular spot on that particular Martinsville road again.

⌘⌘⌘⌘⌘

"Watch out! Be on your guard against all kinds of greed; a man's life does not consist in the abundance of his possessions."
Luke 12:15

OCTOBER 12
...BEING PREPARED FOR CIRCUMSTANCES THAT ARE CERTAIN

"Everything is funny as long as it is happening to somebody else."
- Will Rogers

⌘⌘⌘⌘⌘

For several years, three single friends and I were the best of friends. We went to each other's homes, out for dinners, and on vacations. We also played absolutely hideous practical jokes on each other. If you were wise, you were always on guard. We decided to go to King's Island for the weekend. We were excited and on our guard.

The first practical joke strategy was developed watching the White Water River Raft ride. We stood on a bridge watching the rafts go by to determine which passenger got drenched with the most water. When we were being loaded into the raft for the ride, I was the last one in; consequently, I was given the selected seat and soaked by the time we ended the ride. After we left King's Island, we went to the mall. To compound my "almost drowning" incident, as we passed a hair salon, one of the stylists ran out and gave me a 20% off coupon on a hair set. My friends thought this was hysterical!!! I smiled and reminded them of paybacks.

After a dinner where everyone in the restaurant stared at me because I looked like a drowned rat, we went back to the hotel room. I was determined to be the first one in the shower, and while in the shower, I heard the bathroom door creak. I stared at the top of the shower rod and saw a hand with an ice bucket inch over the top. I jumped aside just as the ice fell into the tub. That was the last straw.

After my shower, I dried, applied my body lotion, dressed in my pajamas, and filled the tub with water. Once the tub was full of water, I put all of *their* dry washrags, hand towels, bath towels, and bath mat into the tub. What a surprise it was for them, and what a joy it was for me.

It's very wise to be prepared for things that we know, for certain, will happen.

⌘⌘⌘⌘⌘

"For we are God's workmanship, created in Christ Jesus
to do good works, which God prepared in advance for us to do."
- Ephesians 2:10

OCTOBER 13
...GETTING OTHERS ON YOUR BAND WAGON

> "Lofty words cannot construct an alliance or
> maintain it; only concrete deeds can do that."
> - John F. Kennedy

⌘⌘⌘⌘⌘

The term "networking" had become trite. It took people a while to realize that walking into a room with an armload of resumes, handing them out, and expecting strangers to network them into an immediate position or on-the-spot business usually didn't happen.

It isn't networking that helps you get ahead; it's building alliances. Even the analogy points out the differences. A net can be weak, and it is certainly full of holes. Building alliances creates an image of something that is constructed or planned and made of very firm material.

It isn't important who you know; it's more important who knows you. People get to know you by building alliances, and building alliances comes from good deeds.

I write a column at no charge on Corporate Etiquette for a paper. I'm always on time, have my correct word count, and answer the questions asked by the readers. I do presentations for some non-for-profit organizations at no charge. I serve on boards and committees and hold offices in a few organizations. All of these activities take time and do not net me an immediate financial gain. What it does net me is getting people on my band wagon.

The "old fashioned" band wagons paraded through town. They were so colorful, and the music was so enticing that people followed them through the town, wanted to climb on board, and told other people about them. The word spread.

Building alliances and getting other people on your band wagon have a lot in common. It takes time to construct both. It is something others want to be a part of, and the word spreads.

⌘⌘⌘⌘⌘

> "By wisdom a house is built, and through
> understanding it is established;"
> Proverbs 24:3

OCTOBER 14
...EXPECTING THE UNEXPECTED

"Unless you expect the unexpected you will never find
[truth], for it is hard to discover and hard to attain."
- Heraclitus

⌘⌘⌘⌘⌘

My husband knows many intelligent, dedicated, amazing people in his industry. Although I could mention many individuals, one man in particular comes to mind when I think of expecting the unexpected. My husband has learned to expect the unexpected on most Monday mornings.

This "unexpected" gentlemen is, most likely, a self-made millionaire. A mover and a shaker who exudes corporate power. He is loyal to his staff, respected by upper management and has a great sense of humor. This man is also accident prone. Almost every Monday morning he tells my husband a story of what happened to him on the weekend.

One weekend, he fell out of a tree while operating a chain saw. Another weekend, while at the lake and walking around barefoot, he ripped his toenail off on a nail in the dock. This was rather ironic because he had just told his grandson, who also wanted to go barefoot, that as a young boy he must always wear his shoes on the dock to avoid hurting his feet. One weekend he dropped a set of pull-down stairs on the head of his son-in-law who was helping him. He screwed a screw into his thumb, dropped a drill down his leg, hit himself with a mallet on more than one occasion and operated his table saw without a guard.

My husband admires this man and has often said he is looking forward to their retirement because then they can be more than colleagues — they can be friends. I told my husband I wasn't sure that would be a good idea as I would like him to stay as injury-free as he could.

I always look forward to Monday evenings because I'm eager to hear about the weekend's happening. It's nice to know that regardless of how high we have climbed up the corporate ladder or how much money we have or how highly we are regarded, we are all human, and we all must be ready for the unexpected things that we and others do.

⌘⌘⌘⌘⌘

"So you also must be ready, because the Son of Man
will come at an hour when you do not expect him."
Matthew 24:44

OCTOBER 15
...MAKING MOUNTAINS OUT OF MOLE HILLS

"We do what we can, and then make a
theory to prove our performance the best."
- Emerson

⌘⌘⌘⌘⌘

Stan and I have two sets of neighbors we really like. We help one another with projects and spend quite a bit of time chatting about the other neighbors. All of us decided it would be fun to have a supper together. Since Stan and I have a large deck, we volunteered for the first dinner party.

This dinner was a comedy of errors. First, what we had planned to serve for dinner was not turning out well. Second, the rain began to pour down in buckets just as our neighbors arrived, so we had to move everything indoors. Third, and most important, Murphy, our retriever, was coming off of steroids and was quite literally a lunatic dog. Murphy had started pulling out the hair on her legs. She was quite a sight with long black silky fur and bald legs. We had taken her to the vet, and he put her on steroids. After two days on the medication, she began to change drastically. She would sit in the corner and growl or run through the house wildly and throw herself on the floor. Her behavior was so bizarre she scared me. I called the vet. He said a few dogs react badly to steroids and you have to stop the medication immediately. We stopped her pills, and she began to go through some type of "roid rage" withdrawal.

Our neighbors arrived, and we sat down to dinner. Murphy began to pace the table and stare at us with a wild-eyed look. She began to pant, drool and growl. I couldn't put her outside because it was raining. I put her in the garage, and she frantically dug at the door and would not stop. It was one of the longest evenings of our lives. After the neighbors left, Stan and I decided our neighbors would probably never have anything to do with us again.

I apologized a hundred times over. Our neighbors assured me they knew that Murphy must really be suffering because that was not her nature. They told me to relax and to stop feeling bad. Things happen. For them it was their children running through the house naked or throwing up in the middle of the room.

We are all still friends, and we still have dinners together. I guess I was truly making a mountain out of a mole hill.

⌘⌘⌘⌘⌘

"Then you will know the truth, and the truth will set you free."
John 8:32

OCTOBER 16
...BEING PERSISTENT AND POSITIVE

"The person who makes a success of living is the one who sees
his goal steadily and aims for it unswervingly. That is dedication."
- Cecil B. De Mille

⌘⌘⌘⌘⌘

When I was four years old, our family moved into a neighborhood called University Heights. I loved living there because our neighbor four houses down had this gorgeous Newfoundland named Zeke. Zeke had gone to obedience school, and there was nothing — in the dog world — that he couldn't do. Zeke and I bonded instantly. I guess he wanted a little girl as badly as I wanted a big dog. Zeke and I were pals, and we played together all day long. At night, when his owners came home, Zeke would go home for dinner, but after his dinner, he would come back to play with me until dark.

Since my Mother had to work during the day, she and I would try to do something special together in the evening. During the summer our special treat was going to the Dairy Queen for an ice cream cone. As we got in our old car and headed to the DQ, we had to pass by Zeke's house. The dog would see us and begin to run behind the car. We would look back and see Zeke running at top speed with his tongue flapping in the breeze and his ears standing straight out on each side of his head; he was trying to catch the car. Mother said he would get tired, stop chasing the car, and go home, but that didn't happen. He just kept running.

We finally stopped the car and let him in. Zeke would sit in the middle of the back seat as happy as if he were a movie star being chauffeured around town. Then he learned about ice cream, and his happiness changed to ecstasy.

Zeke was always a perfect gentleman, and he would sit politely with me at one of the picnic tables waiting patiently while Mother went to the window for three vanilla ice cream cones. Everyone in the neighborhood loved to watch Zeke lick his ice cream cone. He was quite the spectacle, and I'm sure he was good for DQ's business. Zeke loved being loved and petted, and, by being persistent in his pursuit of the car, when we arrived at DQ, he certainly got his share of attention.

One of my fondest memories is seeing Zeke run behind the car. That big old dog was not only persistent and positive, but he was also so uninhibited in his need to be loved and included. We can all learn a lot from Zeke.

⌘⌘⌘⌘⌘

"Behold, we consider blessed those who have
perservered. You have heard of the patience of Job."
James 5:11

OCTOBER 17
...GOING DORMANT

"Inside myself is a place where I live all alone and
that's where you renew your springs that never dry up."
- Pearl Buck

⌘⌘⌘⌘⌘

This summer, we went through a time when its was very hot with little rain.
Unless people watered their lawns, they simply died. My husband and I were
going into choir practice at the church by the back door. I mentioned to him that
the grass really looked terrible. He replied, "I guess it (the grass going dormant) is
the way it is suppose to be. We are the ones who force it to do unnatural things."
I was impressed by this wisdom. It caused me to realize that grass isn't the only
thing that needs to go dormant periodically; humans do, also. We need
tranquility: time to rest and relax. We need to listen to our inner self.

When people try to force us out of our dormancy, we don't get the
opportunity to rest. Only by withdrawing can we protect ourselves from further
damage. At times forcing is just as unnatural a thing for us as it is for the grass.

I'm reminded of a wonderful quote by Indra Devi: "Like water which can
clearly mirror the sky and the trees only so long as its surface is undisturbed, the
mind can only reflect the true image of the Self when it is tranquil and wholly
relaxed."

⌘⌘⌘⌘⌘

"...a time to be silent and a time to speak,"
Ecclesiastes 3:7

OCTOBER 18
...SHARING IN UNEXPECTED JOY

> "Grief can take care of itself, but to get the full value
> of joy you must have somebody to divide it with."
> — Mark Twain

⌘⌘⌘⌘⌘

Sharon and I were having lunch one day at a local restaurant and solving all the world's problems. Our waiter, who was especially entertaining, made the meal even more enjoyable with his wonderful sense of humor and zest for life. As my grandmother would have said, "He was a hoot!"

At the next table was a middle aged man and woman who, apparently, were treating one of their mothers to a birthday lunch. She was one of those lovely, happy, little old ladies who loved living. She made eye contact with people and smiled at them. She had a zest for life that was easily seen.

Sharon and I and the people at the next table had finished our lunches and were preparing to leave. When our waiter brought both tables the checks, the birthday lady asked if she could have a "to go" cup for her drink. The waiter said he would be right back with one. When he returned to the table, his arm was down to his side. As he reached the birthday lady, he gave the lady a child's cup, the kind with the sealed top and the drinking spout. The lady put her head down and began to laugh. Her shoulders shook, and her face got red. All of us, including the waiter, laughed and laughed. It was a great way to end the meal.

It was not only incredibly delightful to share in this unexpected joy, but it was also incredibly delightful to share in people's zest for life.

⌘⌘⌘⌘⌘

> "He that is of a merry heart hath a continual feast."
> Proverbs 15:15

OCTOBER 19
...KNOWING WHO AND WHOSE WE ARE

"The cornerstone of our culture and our civilization."
-Joseph Proskauer

⌘⌘⌘⌘⌘

A few Sundays ago, Terry Coe was giving the prayer. One of the statements she made in this prayer was "help us to know who and whose we are." That statement made quite an impact on me.

Murphy, our retriever, knows she is a retriever. She watches birds and automatically points when she sees a bird in the trees or bushes. She has never been trained to do this. It's her instinct; she knows who she is. CoCo, our terrier, knows she is a terrier. Any place she goes, her nose is always on the ground. If she finds a hole in the ground, she will sit by it motionless for hours waiting for something to pop up. She has never been trained either. It is her instinct; she also knows who she is.

During our evenings at home together, when Stan and I sit down to relax and watch TV, Murphy will immediately go and sit by Stan, and CoCo will immediately come and sit on my lap. Not only do these dogs know **who** they are, but they also know **whose** they are. Dogs are not nearly as advanced as we humans are, yet they certainly have a handle on their identity.

No one or thing has the ability to know us as well as we know ourselves; we must come up with those answers. We must determine by our own instinct who we are, not who others say we are or think we should be. We cannot discover ourselves by letting others tell us who we should be.

Just as Murphy and CoCo have a personal strength, confidence, and sense of purpose by knowing who and whose they are, so should we by discovering our identity and our belonging. To make our contribution in life, we must know what we have to offer. We must know who and whose we are.

⌘⌘⌘⌘⌘

"If you have any encouragement from being united with Christ,
if any comfort from his love, if any fellowship with the Spirit,
if any tenderness and compassion, then make my joy complete
by being like-minded, having the same love,
being one in spirit and purpose."
Philippians 2:1-2

OCTOBER 20
...BEARING FRUIT

"A plant is like a self-willed man, out of whom we can obtain
all which we desire, if we will only treat him his own way."
- Goethe

⌘⌘⌘⌘⌘

My husband and I love fresh food. Almost everything we cook has been
cooked from scratch. We buy ground round and make hamburger; we make
home-made bread and pasta;
and we always use fresh herbs for cooking. We also love fresh vegetables and
fruits.

Our yard isn't very large, so when we wanted to have our fruit trees, we had
to be creative. We bought three apple trees that could be grown in pots and two
dwarf nectarine and two dwarf peach trees. Because all these trees were planted in
pots, they had to have special care. They needed extra fertilizer and water. They
could only survive in temperatures that were 20 degrees above zero; so, when it
got too cold, we had to bring them inside. We had to create a special place for
them in the garage during the winter. We sprayed, pruned, and nurtured these
trees. And, finally, they all bore fruit.

These apples, peaches and nectarines were, without a doubt, the sweetest,
most delicious pieces of fruit we had ever tasted. They were soft and juicy and
had an intense fruit taste. All the extra effort we had gone through was worth it.
We will certainly go to this extra effort again.

When I eat the fruit or work on the trees, I relate this to people. I wonder
what people would be like if we went to all this extra effort for them — sweet,
tender and the best they could be.

⌘⌘⌘⌘⌘

"By their fruits ye shall know them."
Matthew 7:20

OCTOBER 21
...LAUGHING AT YOURSELF

"He is not laughed at that laughs at himself first."
- Thomas Fuller, M.D.

⌘⌘⌘⌘⌘

For 10 of the 14 years I taught, I was the advisor for our high school's yearbook. Each March, during Spring Break, I would take next year's yearbook staff to a week long Journalism Workshop at Columbia University in New York City to update everyone on the latest publishing trends and to get next year's yearbook completely outlined.

One year, the staff and I designed a very attractive cover with the crown — we were the Royals — imprinted on the cover. The following year, I was asked to give a brief talk on making a brass mold. I was honored.

I wanted to dress really sharp so my students would be proud of me. I had on a beautiful royal blue sweater with multi-colored stripes on the left sleeve and down the left front panel and royal blue slacks. I thought I looked pretty cool. This particular sweater had been made with a plastic zipper. Many of you will remember plastic zippers. For a while they were quite popular; however, their popularity declined because they had a nasty habit of popping open in the center. They usually popped open at inconvenient times.

As a speaker, it is my habit to take a very deep breath before I begin speaking. I stood up and walked to the podium to do my presentation. As I was accustomed to doing, I took a deep breath, and the plastic zipper of my royal blue sweater popped open. A most inconvenient time! There I stood, in front of these high school students, in the glory of my bra and sweater. I grabbed the sides of the sweater to pull it together and looked up to see the many high school faces staring at me in my underwear. The look of shock on the student's faces was so intense, I just burst out laughing. Everyone else laughed, also.

I turned around, got my zipper back on track, and then proceeded to do the presentation on the cover. I know my presentation was memorable — maybe not for the information I imparted but certainly for the situation I conquered by laughing at myself.

⌘⌘⌘⌘⌘

"The Lord has done great things for us, and we are filled with joy."
Psalm 126:3

OCTOBER 22
...HAVING A GUIDE

"One who breaks new paths into unfamiliar territory."
- Gerald White Johnson

⌘⌘⌘⌘⌘

I had the opportunity to take a trip to Falun, Sweden, with a group of people. Because none of us had been to Sweden before, we hired a guide to show us around.

The guide took us to castles and museums. We saw the Wasa, a resurrected Viking Burial Ship from the year 1628. We spent a day at a "living" museum being told the stories of Swedish customs and being shown the way the houses were built and the land was farmed. We took a luncheon cruise to see all the summer homes and, later that same day, toured the site where the Nobel Prizes were awarded. We saw beautiful countryside's peppered with flowering Lilac Bushes. We toured many wonderful places, but, of all the places we toured, my favorite was the Copper Mine.

Our guide had us suit up in rain coats and hard hats before we went underground. As we walked the tunnels, she told us of the great cave in that happened on a Christmas Day and of the man who was lost and buried in the tunnel for over 50 years and was so well preserved that his fiancée recognized him when he was exhumed. The guide also told how the miners mined the copper. We kept following her lead as she told us one exciting tale after another and ended our journey in the Room of Gold. Each Swedish monarch had been there and etched his/her name in a wall of gold. A fir tree was cut once a year and placed in the Room of Gold. Because of the cool, damp atmosphere, the trees survive there. It was awesome! Without our guide knowing the stories and the locations, we would have — quite literally — passed right over the top of the mine and missed these wonderful tales of history.

How wonderful it is for each of us to have a guide that not only knows the way, but also makes the trip so enjoyable.

⌘⌘⌘⌘⌘

"Since you are my rock and my fortress,
for the sake of your name lead and guide me."
Psalm 31:3

OCTOBER 23

...HAVING CONCERN FOR OTHERS OVER YOUR OWN

"Understanding human needs is half the job of meeting them."
- Adlai Stevenson

⌘⌘⌘⌘⌘

Gina, my friend, and I have many things in common. One of our most obvious likenesses is being impatient. Gina and her family had just moved from their home in Lebanon into a home in Indianapolis. The home in Indianapolis fit their room requirements but not their aesthetic requirements. Drapes needed to be hung; wallpaper needed to be applied; furniture needed to be set in place. Both Gina and I are very strong, and under normal circumstances, she could have done this by herself; however, when the move was made, Gina was seven months pregnant with her daughter, and my name sake, Anna.

I called her to ask how the move had gone. She said the move had gone well, and she intended to take the week off to unpack and decorate. I wasn't sure what "decorate" included, so I decided to drive over and take a look for myself. When I walked up the stairs to the master bedroom, I saw Gina sitting on the floor, with her back up against the bed, trying to push the bed into place. Now, I pointed out — very politely — that she really shouldn't be doing this. I stayed the rest of the day and helped with the furniture and the wallpaper and the drapes. I knew if I left her alone she would not stop. She is too much like me, and I know I would not have stopped.

I had things scheduled to do that week, but I also knew that this was a time when I needed to put her needs before of mine. We, as women, have a need to get our nest in perfect order so that we can relax and enjoy our home.

Anna, a perfectly beautiful baby girl, was born several months later. I'm so very glad for Gina, Anna, and me. Gina is a very special person, and she has put my needs before her own on more than one occasion. The most recent time was the day she sat with my husband while I had surgery for breast cancer.

At times, I do wonder how things would have gone if I hadn't put Gina's needs before my own. I also wonder how things would have gone for Stan if Gina hadn't put our needs before her own.

⌘⌘⌘⌘⌘

"So in everything, do to others what you would have them do to you,"
Matthew 7:12

OCTOBER 24
...GIVING BACK THE "HOT POTATOES"

"Guilt is ever at a loss, and confusion waits upon it; when
innocence and bold truth are always ready for expression."
- William Congreve

⌘⌘⌘⌘⌘

My mother and I love one another very much. The love we have for one
another does not mean we always like what one another does. There have been
times when one of us has gotten into a bad cycle; and when the other attempts to
help, the one who is down desperately tries to pull the other one into the bad
cycle with her. It's as if we are drowning; and when someone throws us a life
preserver, we try to pull both the preserver and our rescuer in at the same time.

My mother was going through some bad times; and when one trouble
follows another trouble, it doesn't simply add to the situation — it compounds the
situation. Mother was getting into the "always and never" cycle that we all go
through. On some of her really bad days, she would tell me that I really didn't
love her. I, like most daughters, began to enumerate all the things I had done for
her, and I also mentally thought of all the things I hadn't done for her and felt
guilty. This scenario happened several times. Each time the guilt would eat at me,
and I realized she was pulling me into her bad mood.

I tried to think the situation through logically and finally realized I was
accepting her "hot potato," and I didn't want it! I thought of how to handle the
situation and prepared myself. Several days later, Mother made the comment
again. She said I didn't love her. I responded, "Mother, those words came out of
your mouth, not mine. I know I do love you. This is your problem, not mine.
You are going to have to figure out a way to deal with it."

These were very difficult words to say, but these words made both of us
realize that taking someone else's "hot potato" was not pleasant. Now, when
either one of us is in a bad mood or going through bad times, we stop giving "hot
potatoes," and we certainly stop trying to pull the other one under.

If someone is around who can throw us a life preserver and try to help pull
us out of bad situations, the worse thing we can do is try to drag them under with
us. We need to learn to accept someone's help without jeopardizing them and
without causing them to feel guilty.

⌘⌘⌘⌘⌘

"The way of the guilty is devious, but
the conduct of the innocent is upright."
Proverbs 19:8

OCTOBER 25
...NOT GOING TOO FAR OUT

"It is the eye that makes the horizon."
- Emerson

⌘⌘⌘⌘⌘

Our honeymoon was postponed for several years. When we finally got around to taking a honeymoon, we went to Tahoe for five days. We had a splendid time. We went to the casinos, and we went shopping. We drove through the mountains and picnicked. We took pictures and hiked. And, because my husband loves to bike, we biked and biked.

Now, I like to bike, but I don't love it. It is not something I do often, so I'm rather out of shape. One morning, we rented bikes and started down the Truckee Trail. It was a cool morning, and the trail out was all downhill. Instead of realizing it was an easy morning, I thought I was getting into better shape, so I kept going and going. We rested for a short while before we started back to town.

Our trip back was a little different. First of all, I was fatigued. Second, the sun was out in full force, and it was getting hot. Third, and most important, the ride home was uphill!!! I had gone too far out on too easy a ride and had not calculated the price I would have to pay.

We overextend ourselves too many times. We overextend in relationships, finances, and commitments. We go out on a limb and jeopardize our mental and emotional stability.

When we begin a project of any type, it's important for us to take into consideration how many other projects we have going, how centered we are, and what kind of support we have. If we don't take these things into consideration, we will go too far out just as if we were biking downhill in the early morning at Tahoe.

⌘⌘⌘⌘⌘

"For I am already being poured out like a drink offering, and the time has come for my departure."
2 Timothy 4:6

OCTOBER 26
...KNOWING WHAT TO AVOID

"The man does better who runs from
disaster than he who is caught by it."
- Homer

⌘⌘⌘⌘⌘

When I was the Executive Director of the Indianapolis Entrepreneurship Academy, I had many opportunities to hear some of our city's most outstanding entrepreneurs tell their stories. These business people told their background, why and how they started their own business, and answered questions of aspiring entrepreneurs. All of the attendees learned a great deal and had a good time.

Some of the speakers added humorous touches to their stories. One gentleman quickly comes to mind. He was in his late 50's and swore, at his age, that the more money he made, the more handsome he became. During the question and answer session, a member of the audience asked him what he would suggest avoiding in a business career. His response was "Modern Hotels." This seemed a rather odd statement. He explained.

He had just returned from a trip to Hawaii where he had stayed at one of the new hotels that was done in glass, brass, and marble. He said his bathroom had floor to ceiling mirrors, and being in his late 50's, there were just some parts of his body that he didn't want to see anymore. From this point on, he was going to avoid the modern hotels and stay in the older hotels that had solid walls instead of mirrors. Everyone in the audience was very amused.

I guess our perspective isn't all that changes with age.

⌘⌘⌘⌘⌘

"Oh that I had the wings like a dove!
for then would I fly away, and be at rest."
Psalm 55:6

OCTOBER 27
...KEEPING YOUR PERSONAL AND PROFESSIONAL LIFE SEPARATE

"No one tests the depth of a river with both feet."
- Ashanti Proverb

⌘⌘⌘⌘⌘

I have mentioned before that, when I was going through chemotherapy, I was busier doing seminars for clients than I had ever been before. I had contracted with one of the fire departments to do 16 presentations on "Understanding Gender Differences." For 16 days, I would get dressed, put on my wig, and go do one of the presentations.

Two years later, I was asked by the same fire department to do follow-up programs to remind the attendees of the subject matter and to focus on our work relationships. One of the statements I made was "try to keep your personal and professional life separate." One of the attendees said that was impossible. I told him it wasn't, and I had proof.

I asked him if he thought my hair looked different. He looked at me for a while and then replied that it looked lighter and was a different cut. I told him the reason it looked different was when I did the presentation two years ago, I was wearing a wig because I had lost all my hair while going through chemotherapy. He asked me why I didn't say something. I told him I had said nothing because I was hired to get the job done, not to tell people my personal problems. He looked down and became very silent.

We want people to like us. We want people to have sympathy for what we are going through. We want friends, fun, and interaction. However, most of us do not earn a living for admiration, sympathy, or friendship. We are paid for our skills and ability, and part of our ability is keeping our personal and professional lives as separate as we possibly can.

⌘⌘⌘⌘⌘

"Commit your work to the Lord,
and your plans will be established."
Proverbs 16:3

OCTOBER 28
...MATCHING THE MOMENT

"Timeliness is best in all matters."
- Hesiod

⌘⌘⌘⌘⌘

Stan, my husband, loves to watch the Olympics. I love to watch certain events and moments, but an 18 day span of sports is a little too much for me.

Normally, I do presentations at dinner meetings, so I am not home every evening of the week. However, this week's evening presentations were limited to one, and for the three or four other nights, we watched the gymnastic competitions.

I really needed to talk to Stan about some difficulty I was having with a computer software program. As I was cleaning up the kitchen, I was trying to talk to him about the problem. I finished what I was saying with a question and got no response. I looked around the corner of the family room. He was standing in front of the TV watching the gymnasts and was oblivious to what I was saying.

I decided I had to get his attention, and I thought it would be good if I could match the moment to keep in the spirit of the games. I called to him and ask him to turn around. When he did, I took two of three skips across the room, did a cartwheel as best I could, and landed in the gymnastic dismount pose with my back arched and my arms in the air. He looked at me deadpan and said "What?" Then we both laughed.

Corita Kent said that we must "Love the moment, and the energy of that moment will spread beyond all boundaries." Now, when we see the gymnasts perform, not only do we enjoy the competition, but we also laugh at my feeble athletic ability and the humor of matching the moment.

⌘⌘⌘⌘⌘

"A word spoken in due season, how good it is!"
Proverbs 15:23

OCTOBER 29
...BEING A MASTER OF CAMOUFLAGE

"Self-deception is sometimes as necessary a tool as a crowbar."
- Moss Hart

⌘⌘⌘⌘⌘

CoCo loves to be outside. Each morning, she spends about 30 minutes in the back yard with her nose pressed to the ground picking up smells from all the night creatures that have visited the feeders.

You can tell by the intensity and dedication in her mission that she wants to track something and kill it. She does all she can to camouflage herself and make her appear non-dog. She rolls in whatever she can find that will take away from her dog smells. This is also the reason she gets a bath on a regular basis. When she sees something that might be game, she sits motionless waiting for the game to relax its guard and run across her path.

The other morning I let her out and went about my daily chores. About 30 minutes later, I went out in the back yard to get her. I called and called, but no CoCo came. I began to walk the yard looking for her. I looked in all her hiding spots under the fir trees and still no CoCo. I sat down on the steps of the deck and tried to figure where she might have gone. I felt something staring at me. I looked to my right, and there, hidden under the long leaves of the day lilies, sat CoCo.

To see these two brown eyes and grey moustached muzzle among leaves and flowers was amusing. Since rolling in the other smells or sitting motionless didn't net her any prey, she tried desperately to camouflage herself to look like a day lily. She must have thought she was a master at camouflage because you really have to stretch to image a little grey chunky dog looking like a day lily. But, in her mind, I'm sure they were one and the same.

⌘⌘⌘⌘⌘

"You are my hiding place and my shield;
I have put my hope in your word."
Psalm 119:114

OCTOBER 30
...BEING CONNECTED

"Two lives bound fast in one."
- Alfred Lord Tennyson

⌘⌘⌘⌘⌘

Stan, my husband, had done part of a project for Duke University. For being involved in the project, he was flown to the university to hear the results of the entire project.

I took him to the airport on a Friday afternoon. I let him off at the terminal, kissed him good bye, and began my drive back home. As I neared home, my stomach began to hurt. I had eaten very bland food that day, so I was having difficulty figuring out what had made me feel so awful. I felt worse with each passing minute. My stomach hurt so badly that I finally went upstairs, got in bed and curled up in the fetal position to try and get some relief. I lay there for about and hour, and the pain started going away. I was relieved.

Later that evening, my husband called to tell me he had arrived safely. He told me he was very happy to be on the ground. The flight encountered rough weather, and the plane bounced from take-off to landing. He said he was sick to his stomach the entire trip.

When we got off the phone, I checked his itinerary. His flight had taken off just about the same time I started to get an upset stomach, and his flight landed just about the same time my upset stomach started to feel better. For me, it was another example of how strongly I am connected to the people I care for. There are times when I know I must call my mother, aunt, cousin, or friend.

I can't prove it, but I will always think that I was connected to him while he was on the flight. I don't know if he was so unnerved that he thought the plane might go down, so he was thinking strongly of me. I do know that the timing of the flight and my discomfort was a very strong coincidence.

⌘⌘⌘⌘⌘

"And they too shall be one flesh."
Ephesians 5:31

OCTOBER 31
...TUNING IN ON YOUR OWN SELF AWARENESS

"The test of a civilized person is first self-awareness, and
then depth after depth of sincerity of self-confrontation."
- Clarence Day

⌘⌘⌘⌘⌘

Mission Statements are a big thing. Not only do companies have Mission
Statements, but teams, groups, and individuals are also supposed to have Mission
Statements. I spent time trying to define my Mission Statement — just in case I
was asked — and came up with a statement that I try to live daily: "I want to make
a difference with my life." It may not be very profound, but it certainly is very
sincere.

I have had many opportunities to share my Mission Statement with others.
One person in particular was a student in one of the Adult Education Classes I
taught; her name is Careen. We became "woodwork" friends and got together
occasionally to solve the problems of the world.

When Careen found out through the grapevine that I had breast cancer,
she called to
find out how I was feeling. It was the evening of the second surgery, and I was still
groggy and unhappy. She told me that everyone in class was praying for my
speedy recovery and a good prognosis. I thanked her for her kindness in calling.

She added one other comment that brought tears to my eye: "You always
told the class you wanted to make a difference with your life. Your verb tense was
wrong; you have made a difference with your life."

I guess I had been so busy trying to make a difference that I hadn't realized
that I had. Some type of enlightenment always comes out of tragedy.

⌘⌘⌘⌘⌘

"I pray also that the eyes of your heart may be enlightened in
order that you may know the hope to which he has called you,"
Ephesians 2:18

NOVEMBER 1
...BEING CREATIVE

"It is not the finding of a thing, but the making
something out of it after it is found."
- James Russell Lowell

⌘⌘⌘⌘⌘

I love cookies. In fact, that's the nickname I was given by my family because "cookie" was the first two-syllable word I said as a child. Each Christmas, I am the "official" cookie maker. I make a dozen different kinds of cookies and take great pleasure in putting them in tins to give to family and friends.

Each type of cookie makes a particular statement. Chocolate Chips are decadent, and Oatmeal Raisins are "down home." Shortbreads are elegant, Peanut Butters are casual and fun, and Butter Cookies are rich.

Even though I love all types of cookies, I have a favorite cookie: a Fig Newton. Fig Newtons were a special treat I received as a child. Fig Newtons helped make tears go away and made Chicken Pox and Measles heal faster. Stubbed toes weren't quite so painful and unkind remarks from playmates were more easily forgotten with a Fig Newton in your hand.

When you come to my house, you are more than welcome to eat anything in the pantry, cabinets, or refrigerator — anything except my Fig Newtons. My husband is particularly forbidden to eat my Fig Newtons. I will eat one Fig Newton at a time, but he will eat one package at a time. Then I have to go to the store for more.

One day his desire for my Fig Newtons overpowered him. After he had eaten at least half the package, he looked at the clock. He knew I would be home soon, and he would have to face my Fig Newton Wrath. To avoid my wrath, he pulled the plastic divider out of the wrapper and turned the empty section to the back of the bag so I would believe I still had the entire package of Newtons. Several days later, I pulled the plastic divider out of the wrapper and found the back half of the package empty. When my husband came home, I asked him what had happened to my Fig Newtons. He said it was one of three things: they evaporated, the dogs ate them, or aliens had visited the kitchen.

If nothing else, my husband is creative.

⌘⌘⌘⌘⌘

"I will give you a new heart and put a new spirit in you;"
Ezekiel 36:26

NOVEMBER 2
...COMPENSATING FOR A LOSS

"Every sweet hath its sour; every evil its good."

- Emerson

⌘⌘⌘⌘⌘

When my husband and I decided to have dogs in our lives, instead of buying pedigreed animals, we decided to rescue animals already in this world with no one to take care for them. We picked Murphy out of a litter of 12 puppies and brought her home when she was 6 weeks old. We acquired CoCo differently. She was 6 years old the first time I saw her. Her owner had boarded her at the vet for over 30 days. For over 30 days this little dog had been in a cage just a little bigger than she. She had lost much of her zest for life — including eating. She was one of the boniest little dogs I had ever seen.

When I first brought her home to live with us, she was timid and trying desperately to find a place in our house and our lives. After a brief time, CoCo and Murphy became buddies, and CoCo was a happy little dog. She regained her zest for life — including her appetite. She ate so much that she is now about 15 pounds overweight.

I told the vet I walked her a mile each day and measured her food. Short of starving her, I didn't know how to get her weight off. The vet told me that many times when an animal has been starved or stops eating; when they begin to eat again, they make up for lost time. They gorge themselves so, if they have to go without food again, they will have a bigger reserve. They compensate for the loss of food.

I think we all compensate for what we have lost. Whether our starvation is for food or attention, we find a way to make it up to ourselves. Being an introvert, I compensated by being a public speaker in the spotlight. Having no children, I compensated by raising animals. Being an overweight, unpopular teenager, I compensated by having many friends as an adult.

Have you ever stopped to think what you have today that is your compensation for a loss? Like food filling a dog's belly, the vacuum goes away, and we don't have to deal with fear, sadness, or pain that the emptiness helped to create and brought to the forefront of our lives.

⌘⌘⌘⌘⌘

"For where your treasure is, there your heart will be also."

Matthew 6:21

NOVEMBER 3
...WANTING TO TAKE A TURN BEING THE SAN DIEGO CHICKEN

"There is nothing that gives more assurance than a mask."
- Colette

⌘⌘⌘⌘⌘

One Saturday, my husband and I were visiting carpet stores. As we passed a car, I looked over and discovered the driver of the car was dressed in a clown costume. I giggled and told my husband to look to his right. When he saw the clown, he laughed, too. The clown looked at us, smiled a little bigger smile expanding the painted smile he had on his face and waved. We waved back.

My husband and I decided it would be fun to be a clown. All that make-up would give you concealment. You could do crazy things and never worry what others would think because they wouldn't know it was you.

We remembered a time we had been at Disney World waiting in line to go on the Pirates of the Caribbean ride. Two people dressed as Chip and Dale were playing with the kids. Chip or Dale had been tickling this little boy who had an infectious laugh. Everyone standing in line was laughing at the chipmunk's actions and the laugh of the little boy. At that moment, I think all of us wanted to be able to dress up as the chipmunk, or the wolf, or the San Diego Chicken.

I would love to be the San Diego Chicken. Disguised, I would do things in front of thousands of people that I wouldn't even think of doing unless I was home, alone, in front of my own mirror. I would do silly dances, fall down on the ground, wave at strangers, put my arms around strangers, and anything else I could think of. And, the really funny part of this scenario is, dressed up as the Chicken, other people would not only tolerate this behavior, but they would also enjoy and encourage it.

Guise means manner, and when we are dis-guised so our regular manner is not recognized, we don't worry about what people will think. Our outlandish behavior can camouflage our true self right under other peoples' noses.

⌘⌘⌘⌘⌘

"The kingdom of heaven is like treasure hidden in a field."
Matthew 13:44

NOVEMBER 4
...TAKING A BREAK

"Take rest; a field that has rested gives a bountiful crop."
- Ovid

⌘⌘⌘⌘⌘

As you already may be aware, my husband and I sing in our church's choir. From September to June we practice every Thursday night and sing in at least two services each Sunday.

We do get a break. In July, we do not practice on Thursday nights. For the month of July we sing anthems that we have practiced during the year and are congregational favorites. We arrive 15 minutes earlier than usual to warm up our voices and brush up a few notes. In August, we do not practice, nor do we sing on Sundays.

The choir members are thankful for the break. Many go on vacations, and some use the opportunity to sit in the congregation with their families. Toward May and June, it takes extra effort to get to choir practice, and, once there, it seems to last a little longer. I feel like my car phone when the battery is low: I'm not as loud, as clear, or as accurate as I am when the batteries are fully charged.

With a two month break to rest, I come back to choir refreshed, enthusiastic, and ready for another 10 months of practices and services. My spirit is fresh, my voice is strong, and my heart is happy to be there. It is amazing what a short rest will do.

⌘⌘⌘⌘⌘

"For six days, work is to be done, but the
seventh day is a Sabbath of rest, holy to the Lord."
Exodus 31:15

NOVEMBER 5
...MAKING DECISIONS

"Take time to deliberate, but when the time for
action has arrived, stop thinking and go in."

- Napoleon Bonaparte

⌘⌘⌘⌘⌘

I have mentioned that Murphy's favorite toy is her Frisbee. Her second
favorite toy is a yellow gum ball. When my husband or I take her outside to play,
she brings one of her toys with her. Most of the time, Murphy will just grab the
one nearest the door; however, if both toys are within sight of one another, she has
a difficult time making a decision.

To avoid making a decision, Murphy will try to get both the ball and the
Frisbee in her mouth. This doesn't work well, so her next routine is picking up
one and dropping the other and dropping one and picking up the other. It can be
a long drawn out process. To get her out the door, my husband or I will grab
either the Frisbee or the ball and throw it out the front door knowing she will
immediately follow.

The decisions we make are not always easy either. At times, we try to book
two events on the same day and then enjoy neither one. We try to do two things
at once, not doing either one well. And, we continue to vacillate between two
alternatives, driving other people, who are involved with the scenario, crazy.

It would be a great relief for us to have someone make a decision when our
decisive powers are less than perfect. My husband and I realize this; so when we
have days where we have made too many decisions and are decision-impaired,
the other one takes the initiative and decides for both of us.

⌘⌘⌘⌘⌘

"The lot is cast into the lap, but
its every decision is from the Lord."

Proverbs 16:33

NOVEMBER 6
...TEMPERING "OFF THE CUFF" REMARKS

"First learn the meaning of what you say, and then speak."
- Epictetus

⌘⌘⌘⌘⌘

When I was in my late teens and early twenties, I was very critical. I was overly concerned with image, impressions, and implications. My teen and twenty years were spent during the "hippie" era. This was a time when saying and standing up for what you believed was more important then the accepted norm. It was the age of sit-ins and protests. Boys grew long hair, and girls abandoned traditional undergarments.

Coming from a very conservative family (to the point of not going out unless you coordinated your accessories), this new era was not a comfortable time for me, and I was overly critical of the hippie behavior and attitudes.

During my college years, I became good friends with one of my Psychology Professors who was one of the few people I knew who majored and minored in the same areas I did: English and Psychology. Some days, I would go over to the building where the Psych Classes were held a little early just to talk with him. On one such day, I passed a segment of the campus female "hippie" population. A group of girls were standing there smoking pipes. I was appalled!!!

I walked into my prof's office fuming and told him what I had just seen was an abomination. He looked at me and said, "Suzanne, I think the world of you, but I have often wondered if you would have made fun of Jesus." Now I was even more appalled!

It took me several days to think about that statement. As with most things, I needed distance. Jesus walked about saying and standing up for unpopular things — things He believed that others did not. He protested many issues and sat-in where He was not always wanted. I truly may have been one of the people standing on the side lines wondering what he was all about. I wasn't comfortable with that thought.

I don't think I ever really liked the hippies, but I did learn to temper "off the cuff remarks." It was another "real-life" example of not speaking before you think. I learned it was better not to give your two-cents worth until you had two-cents worth of accurate information to give.

⌘⌘⌘⌘⌘

"If the snake bites before it is charmed,
there is not profit for the charmer."
Ecclesiastes 10:11

NOVEMBER 7
...BEING VIGILANT

"It is our less conscious thoughts and our less conscious actions which
mainly mould our lives and the lives of those who spring from us."
- Samuel Butler

⌘⌘⌘⌘⌘

One evening I returned home at 10:00 PM after doing a dinner
presentation. I was tired and looked forward to going to bed. I walked into the
family room, and there stood my husband, looking anxious, holding CoCo, our
little terrier. His shirt was covered with a mixture of blood and — for lack of a
better word — goo. He told me he had been holding her on his lap when
something erupted.

We have a nearby emergency center for animals, so we got in the Blazer
and took CoCo there. After an examination, the vet told us CoCo had ruptured
an impacted anal gland. I had never heard of this, so I did not know how serious
this was. He told us that many dogs have died from this problem.

The vet asked if we had noticed CoCo dragging her butt on the carpet or
grass. Yes, we had, but we knew she didn't have worms, so we didn't pay much
attention to her actions. The vet also asked if our other dog had been sniffing at
her. Yes, we had noticed that also, but dogs sniff so many things, we didn't pay
much attention to this either.

CoCo had given us the signs that something was wrong the only way she
knew how. Because we had not paid attention, or been vigilant, we almost lost
her. Now, any time we see the signs the vet asked us about, we take CoCo back to
the vet for an examination.

If being vigilant saved the life a little dog, what wonderful results would
occur by being vigilant about people?

⌘⌘⌘⌘⌘

"Be sober, be vigilant;"
1 Peter 5:8

NOVEMBER 8
...MATURING

"To mature is to go on creating oneself endlessly."
- Henri Bergson

⌘⌘⌘⌘⌘

I was asked to give a presentation to the youth group at church. It was the first time I had been around that many young people since I stopped teaching high school 14 years ago. I noticed in that 14 years that young people have changed. Critiquing the crowd, I realized I was looking at the people of this younger generation with a more critical eye than I would the people of my generation. Why not? We are mature, and they are immature.

There was one young woman in the crowd who I thought looked a lot like me when I was in high school. Looking at her reminded me that I, too, spent days in immaturity.

I can't answer for others, but I can answer for myself. When I was immature, I was the center of my universe. I had more days than I care to remember and did more things than I care to relate that proved I was cold, heartless, and hateful. With maturity and life's lessons, I know I have become more compassionate, more understanding, and more tolerant. Learning to be "more" is the wonderful thing about maturity.

I think the Prayer of St. Francis is a very accurate comparison of immaturity and maturity. Hopefully, as we age, we replace hatred with love, injury with pardon, doubt with faith, and despair with hope. Life's lessons, although difficult and at times seemingly insurmountable, help us learn to console, understand, and give when once all we wanted was to be consoled, understood, and take.

No, maturity does not come easy nor at the same time for everyone. Some of us need to experience harder lessons and more lessons. These lessons help us learn to laugh at ourselves, deal with realities, keep secrets, and look at life with a less critical and more compassionate eye.

⌘⌘⌘⌘⌘

"...become mature, attaining to the whole measure of the fullness of Christ."
Ephesians 4:13

NOVEMBER 9
...BEING A SILENT HERO

"Our deeds determine us, as much as we determine our deeds."
- George Eliot

⌘⌘⌘⌘⌘

When I was teaching high school, I sponsored the yearly Blood Drive. Each student that donated a pint of blood was given a sticker that read "Silent Hero." As I watched the students walk around wearing their stickers, I thought how they had saved someone's life: a person they would never know. Silent Heroes.

I have had the opportunity to be a Silent Hero from time to time. At Christmas time, one of the other churches I attended had beautiful pieces of children's clothing placed all over the sanctuary. If you wanted, you chose a piece of clothing, and your gift was to complete the outfit from underwear to overcoat. I chose a Size 4 child's sweater. It was Royal Blue with a strawberry design on the front. I had such a great time buying the matching pieces and wrapping them. I could only imagine how this little girl would squeal with delight when she opened her present from Santa. Now, at St. Luke's, my husband and I buy two cart loads of toys so that children less fortunate will have a toy from Santa. I always get misty-eyed when I drop the toys off at the church.

When I was in junior high, my grandmother went to the store and happened upon two little boys digging broken watermelons out of the dumpster behind the grocery. She asked them what they were doing. They told her that they, and their sisters, lived down by the river with their mother. The father had left the family, and they had to fend for themselves. We took the little boys to their home. Their home and possessions had suffered water damage. They had little. For almost a year we helped them until they could get back on their feet. Finding toys and "stuff" for the little girls in the family was exciting and rewarding for me. Being a Silent Hero won't net you accolades, but that isn't the point. The point is to do something for another human being without being asked, thanked or rewarded. It is to ease hard times and hurts and make the trip on rough roads quicker and more bearable. The benefit from being a Silent Hero is in learning to like yourself for whom you have become and what you will do to help others.

⌘⌘⌘⌘⌘

"By this shall all men know that ye are my disciples, if ye have love one to another."

NOVEMBER 10
...MAKING LIGHT OF SOME SITUATIONS

"Some degree of affection is as necessary to the
mind as dress is to the body; we must overact our part
in some measure, in order to produce any effect at all."
- William Hazlitt

⌘⌘⌘⌘⌘

On most Sunday evenings, our dinner is home-made soup and home-made bread. There is something special about winding down the weekend by spending the last few hours together breaking bread with the people you love.

Some Sundays, however, we get tied up with errands or special projects, and we don't have time for our Sunday Evening Ritual. One such Sunday, Ben, Jill, Stan and I had been running errands all day. About 6:00 that evening, we decided we were hungry. Jill remembered a coupon in the Sunday paper for a complete dinner for four at Boston Chicken. This dinner came with all the "fixins" including a whole apple pie.

Acting as hostess for our dinner party, I served the dinner and then served the dessert. Not realizing that the pie was frozen, all I had to cut the pie with was a plastic knife. As I applied pressure to the frozen pie with the knife, the knife broke in two. The blade part of the knife flew up and hit me in the forehead. Not only my family, but everyone in the restaurant laughed.

Making the most of the situation I asked, "Am I bleeding? Will I be scarred for life? Is the pie ruined? Are we going to be charged for breaking the dinnerware?" Each question, and response, got sillier and sillier. Everyone in the restaurant had fun making light of the situation.

So many times we must take situations seriously, and then there are other times when we take situations way too seriously. When we can all share in a funny situation and laugh together, we create good memories. We call it "making light" of a situation. Maybe this light isn't "magnitude" but rather "insightfulness." It could be that we are opening our lives up to be visited by another human being. This "light" is the kind that we share — one human being to another.

⌘⌘⌘⌘⌘

"For with you in the fountain of life;
in your light we see light."
Psalm 36:9

NOVEMBER 11
...ACCEPTING THE OCCASIONAL BIZARRE AS BIZARRE

"Curiosity is one of the permanent and certain
characteristics of a vigorous intellect."
- Samuel Johnson

⌘⌘⌘⌘⌘

In a recent church bulletin, one of the entries read "Bizarre Men Needed."
I'm sure the meaning really was "Men Needed To Help With Bizarre."
However, by the way it was stated in the bulletin, it not only caused people to
laugh, but it also got their attention.

Occasionally, the bizarre is just that — bizarre. *The bizarre is curious.* It
causes us to look at things in more than one way thus helping us expand our mind
and our outlook on life. *The bizarre is thought provoking.* It charges our mental
energy giving that extra boost of insight. *The bizarre is humorous.* Some of the
strange things we run into cause us to laugh out loud at its ridiculousness. *The
bizarre is rare.* Thank heavens, it does not come along every day. Every day
would be more than we could bear. *The bizarre is natural and humbling.* It helps
us realize we can not know it all. *The bizarre is flexible.* It helps us learn to roll
with situations. *The bizarre is subjective.* It causes us to question.

And, occasionally, the bizarre is to be accepted. It has a definite purpose:
to help us realize our world is full of endless possibilities.

⌘⌘⌘⌘⌘

"Everything is possible for him who believes."
Mark 9:23

NOVEMBER 12
...SAVING SOME THINGS FOR TOMORROW

"Never let the future disturb you. You will meet it, if you have to, with
the same weapons of reason which today arm you against the present."
- Marcus Aurelius

⌘⌘⌘⌘⌘

The first time I saw "Gone With The Wind" I was impressed. As a
teenager seeing the movie for the first time, I was in love with the costumes, the
scenery, the characters and the romance. I think I comprehended most of the
story line; I felt as if I were right on target up until the end. When Scarlet O'Hara
said "I can't think about that today; I'll think about that tomorrow," I remember
thinking that was just about the dumbest thing I had ever heard. My philosophy
was my grandmother's "Bull Frog Philosophy": If you have to eat a bull frog, do it
first thing in the morning, and the rest of the day is downhill. I always tried to get
unpleasant things dealt with immediately. If something needed said or done, I
said or did it. That way I didn't have to worry about it all day. I found I have
changed in many ways as I have aged, and one of the ways I have changed is by
occasionally adopting the Scarlet O'Hara Philosophy.

As an adult, there are more days than we care to think of when one
problem seems to come after another problem. Commitments, job requirements,
relationships, duties, schedules, and matters of personal choice can certainly fill up
a day. Then, if you add those little unexpected situations like a car breaking
down, a loss of a friend, or having to deal with something from your past that you
thought was dead and buried, you realize that the word "overwhelmed" won't
quite cover the circumstances. This came to light when a friend asked me
something personal about my childhood. Unpleasant memories I thought I had
buried rose to the surface, and I started to become extremely melancholy. I knew
I couldn't deal with the issue this day. I smiled and replied, "I can't think about
that today; I'll think about that tomorrow."

I finally understood Scarlet. I finally understood that, as adults with
commitments, job requirements, relationships, duties, schedules, and matters of
personal choice, there are days when we need the Scarlet O'Hara Philosophy just
as badly as the Bull Frog Philosophy. Philosophy. The Love of Learning. The
Love of Learning the right course for us each moment of our lives.

⌘⌘⌘⌘⌘

"Therefore do not worry about tomorrow, for tomorrow
will worry about itself. Each day has enough trouble on its own."
Matthew 6:34

NOVEMBER 13
...KNOWING THE PURPOSE OF HOPE AND FAITH

"Hope is a waking dream."
- Aristotle

⌘⌘⌘⌘⌘

It took me nearly a year to write this book. It was my hope that I had something of value to share with others that made me start the book, but it was my faith that kept me going on 365 entries.

I looked up the definition of hope. Hope is "to entertain a wish for something with some expectation, to look forward to with confidence." That is why hope started my journey. Even on days when the stories didn't sound right, the quotes didn't come easily, or there wasn't enough time to write, I did not put the book to rest. I looked forward, with confidence, to finishing what I had started.

I also looked up the definition of faith. Faith is "a confident belief in the truth, value, or trustworthiness of a person, idea, or thing." When the stories and the quotes came easily and I worked and enjoyed each writing hour, it was because I believed in the value of what I was doing.

Hope is life's spark plug. Faith is life's fuel. Only by having both can we run the course of our lives and continue on our journey.

⌘⌘⌘⌘⌘

"You will be secure, because there is hope;"
Job 11:18

"...if you have faith as small as a mustard seed,
you can say to the mountain, 'Move from here to there'
and it will move. Nothing will be impossible for you."
Matthew 17:20-21

NOVEMBER 14
...PUTTING OUR LIFE BACK TOGETHER

"The growth of understanding follows an
ascending spiral rather than a straight line."

- Joanna Field

⌘⌘⌘⌘⌘

I needed to pick up Stan, my husband, at the hospital where he is
employed. I went to his office to get him. He wasn't there, so I decided to sit
down and wait for him. His computer was on, and the screen-saver had kicked in.
I was fascinated with what I saw.

On the screen was a spinning orb. It would spin briefly on a small section
of the screen and then break into many little pieces. The pieces would also spin
in the air; and while they were spinning, they would change colors and gradually
pull back into a new place on the screen as a different orb of a different color.
The process was repeated again and again. I finally realized that what I was seeing
was symbolic of our lives.

Every time we go through a major upheaval in our routine existence that
causes us to fall apart, we change just like the pieces of the exploding orb. After
we put our lives together, we also are different just as the pieces of the orb which
had changed in color and location.

Instead of being angry because our life does not follow "the" straight line or
we can't handle everything "straight on," I think we should be glad we have the
ability to pull ourselves back together, to profit from what has taken place and to
become that new person as a result of what has happened.

⌘⌘⌘⌘⌘

"The meditation of my heart shall be understanding."

Psalm 49:3

NOVEMBER 15
...ELIMINATING INTIMIDATING

"No passion so effectual robs the mind of all
its powers of acting and reasoning as fear."
- Edmund Burke

⌘⌘⌘⌘⌘

Ben was a pretty impressive sight when he was playing Big 10 Football. At his prime, he was 6'4", 273 pounds, and only 13% body fat. Pretty impressive!

One Saturday after a very tough game, Stan and I took Ben to dinner. Ben was hurting, and he hadn't eaten all day. There was a very long wait for dinner, and we weren't seated until 7:00 pm. Because he was so tired, he wasn't saying much. He honestly looked as if he were in slow motion.

After our barbecued rib dinner, a young high school boy came around to clear the table. This high school boy was as tall standing as Ben was sitting, and you saw this young man's eyes widen as he approached Ben. He kept looking at Ben's face as he picked up the plate. The plate became unbalanced, and a knife, loaded with barbecue sauce, fell into Ben's lap.

With an unsmiling, grim face, and in slow motion style, Ben looked down at his lap and then at this young high school boy. This young man looked stunned, shocked and scared, and as Ben's eyes met his, and this young man said, "Oh, s__t." We waited until the young man had cleared the rest of the table and was gone before we burst into laughter.

Ben's size alone was intimidating, and with the grim look on his face, we all agreed there were times when Ben needed to smile more.

⌘⌘⌘⌘⌘

"A gentle answer turns away wrath,"
Proverbs 15:1

NOVEMBER 16
...LISTENING TO INSTINCT

"The difference between the reason of man and the instinct of the beast
is this, that the beast does but know, but the man knows that he knows."
- John Donne

⌘⌘⌘⌘⌘

Jim and Alex each have a dog. They are both Huskies. Jim's dog is a
beautiful little red Husky named CoCo. Alex's dog is a dramatic, large grey
Husky named Sheena.

As puppies, these dogs got along wonderfully well; however, as they
matured, they each thought the position of the dominant or "alpha" female should
go to them for appropriate reasons: CoCo was the oldest, and Sheena was the
biggest. The contest was on!

Even though CoCo is the smaller, she certainly is a scrapper and went into
each battle with determination; however, CoCo is missing her canine teeth.
Needless to say, she lost every fight and finally was badly injured.

If Jim and Alex were to keep their dogs, some changes had to take place.
The yard was divided down the center. Each dog had designated rooms in the
house. Only one dog at a time was allowed to be in the main part of the house.
Jim and Alex have the system down pat.

One Saturday afternoon, Alex and I were out in the yard playing with
Sheena. Jim and Stan were inside the house with CoCo. Both Sheena and CoCo
walked past the bay window at the same time, and snarling, bared fangs, clawing,
and growling ensued. Jim pulled CoCo away from the window, and Alex pulled
Sheena away. As we led Sheena back to her side of the yard, Alex said, "I can
tolerate the aggression in animals because I know it's instinct. It's the aggression
in people that I have trouble with."

We humans have much less instinct than animals. We also have more
reasoning power or intellect. Keeping these two things in mind, we should be
capable of tempering our emotions. We should be able to reason and talk things
out. We should be kinder to other human beings. We should be more
Christian. I guess the operative word is "should."

⌘⌘⌘⌘⌘

"If you are so pleased with me, teach me your ways
so I may know you and continue to find favor with you."
Exodus 33:13

NOVEMBER 17
...UNDERSTANDING WHO WE CAN MAKE HAPPY

"Nothing is more difficult, and therefore
more precious, than to be able to decide."
- Napoleon I

⌘⌘⌘⌘⌘

I have had the pleasure of attending many football games. For 14 years, while teaching high school, I attended the Friday night football games. For four years while Ben was playing for Purdue, I attended the Saturday afternoon football games. And, for three years, a friend and I had season tickets to the Colts games. Having personally watched this much football, in addition to the games I have seen on TV, the one occupation I would not want to have is the job of referee.

When the referee makes a call, one half of the stadium cheers and the other half boo's. If, for some reason, a mis-call is made and a reverse decision is handed down, the cheering half of the stadium begins to boo, and the booing half of the stadium begins to cheer. There is no way you are going to leave that stadium making everyone happy.

I thought this predicament was only for referees. However, when I am teaching classes, making a decision for the family, or relating to a client what I can and can't do, I'm not making everybody happy, either.

Decisions divide. Decisions are, many times, unpopular, but decisions must be made. To quote David Lloyd George, "Don't be afraid to take a big step when one is indicated. You can't cross a chasm in two small jumps."

⌘⌘⌘⌘⌘

"What you decide on will be done,
and light will shine on your ways."
Job 22:28

NOVEMBER 18
...SAVING MEMENTOS

"How we remember, what we remember, and why we
remember form the most personal map of our individuality."
- Christina Baldwin

⌘⌘⌘⌘⌘

I have never been a collector or a keeper of things. I hate to dust, boxes
drive me crazy, and display cases are expensive. Instead of keeping a ton of things
from people, I keep one special memento from each person that I love. Each of
these mementos remind me of the person. They actually bring the person back to
life for me.

I have my grandmother's candy jar. Every time I look at the candy jar, I
think of our trips to the Old Country Store in Brown County for watermelon
slices and marzipan. I remember watching her hands arrange the candy in the jar
so that you could see each piece plainly. I remember how my Aunt June and I
would try to sneak some of the candy when we thought she wasn't looking, but she
always was. We would turn around and see her blond hair disappearing around
the corner.

From my Aunt Annabelle I have a handkerchief embroidered with pansies.
I remember seeing her putting on her Sunday best and tucking her handkerchief
into her purse. She would wash it out by hand and iron it face down into a towel
so the embroidered flowers would not look flat.

From my Aunt June I have a book of Bible School Lessons. When I was
young, she used to let me sit on her couch and look at the pictures. She would tell
me about going to Sunday School and coloring the pictures while hearing the story
of the person from the Bible. I see her walking around dusting and feel the big
green, scratchy couch on the back of my legs.

From my Mother I have a white cap-sleeved jacket she made for me. I
remember the touch of her hands as she fitted the jacket to me. I remember
walking by the sewing room watching her sew, and I remember seeing her sitting
in her red recliner sewing on buttons. Pins would be protruding from the arm of
the chair and spools of thread would by sitting on the floor.

The things I kept from these people I love are not objects to be honored or
handed down. They are mementos that have value for no one but me, and that
value is they will always keep these people I love alive — if only in my mind.

⌘⌘⌘⌘⌘

"These things I remember
as I pour out my soul:"
Psalm 42:4

NOVEMBER 19
...LIVING WITH SENTIMENT

"It is as healthy to enjoy sentiment as to enjoy jam."
- G. K. Chesterton

⌘⌘⌘⌘⌘

Many years ago I met Susan. This 5'10" (mostly legs) strawberry blond was the Director of Sales of a medical equipment company. Susan was not only beautiful, but she was also an astute businesswoman and incredibly funny. For many years we traveled together on business; and after we both left the same firm, we maintained our friendship. She moved to Texas, and even though we don't see each other as often as we used to, we still send cards and talk on the phone.

For Susan, this year was filled with sadness. Her mother was diagnosed with breast cancer, she had a scare with breast cancer herself, and Calvin died.

Calvin (Klein) was Susan's 150 pound Golden Retriever. He was huge. He was also lovable and cute. He'd curl his lip if you told him to give you his mean look. He'd do the Conga with you, and he would sit with a dog biscuit on his nose until you told him to eat it. He had a big old beach towel he drug with him from place to place, and each night when Susan went to bed, Calvin would get his beach towel and crawl under her bed to rest for the night. He was a sweetie.

When Susan called to tell me about Calvin, her voice quivered. She said he had a stroke and his front paws were almost paralyzed. She told me she had to make the decision to put him down. After a pause to regain her composure, she said, "You know how Calvin always slept under the my bed? Well, he still does. I had him cremated, put his ashes in an urn, and put the urn under my bed. He's still sleeps in his spot."

It was a quite a while before I could say anything. She truly was living with sentiment. Calvin wasn't just her dog; he was her companion. Calvin, like all things we care for, wasn't a disposable.

Sentiment: "The sediment of emotion." Anonymous.

⌘⌘⌘⌘⌘

"The Lord is good to all; he has
compassion on all he has made."
Psalm 145:9

NOVEMBER 20
...KNOWING STILL WATERS RUN DEEP

"When we are unable to find tranquility within
ourselves, it is useless to seek it elsewhere."
- La Rochefoucauld

⌘⌘⌘⌘⌘

Autumn, my younger cousin, is an amazing person. From the day she was
born, she was different than the rest of us. As an infant, she never cried. Autumn
would just lay in her bassinet and look around. For a while, we thought she might
not be able to speak. We found out she always could speak; she just chose not to.

Her high school years were spent under some rather brutal, dark clouds.
After high school, she worked very hard to obtain her license for a career at the
hospital. She loved working in the nursery because of her love of children. To
date, she has been unable to have a child of her own. She also possessed the
strength and courage to work in the hospice and oncology wards: something I will
always be in awe of. After enjoying her career for several years, she suffered a
disability and is now unable to work at the hospital. As our Grandmother would
say, "She had more than her load of sticks." I think her ability to help others and
find humor in almost any situation is the result of the life she lead as a child and
young adult. I also think her life as a young adult caused her to turn more inward.
She is introspective with herself and with others.

It seems to me that Autumn has spent her life watching people. As a result
of watching, she has developed uncanny understanding and compassion. When
people in our family discuss a person, it is Autumn, who very succinctly, hits the
nail on the head relating what they have gone through and how it has affected their
outlook on life. Because she is the youngest in our family, we usually turn and
look in her direction trying to determine where these "words of wisdom" came
from.

She is truly the living example of "still waters run deep." Sometimes when
you look at her, you don't think she is connected with you or what you are saying.
Then, when you least expect it, she opens up with insight that is amazing for a
person her age. Autumn's awareness of all the details of the situation and the
people involved make her a unique and interesting person and a person I'm
proud to be related to!

⌘⌘⌘⌘⌘

"I will help you speak and teach you what to say."
Exodus 4:12

NOVEMBER 21

...EXPLAINING WHEN THERE IS A NEED TO EXPLAIN

"To question a wise man is the beginning of wisdom."
- German Proverb

⌘⌘⌘⌘⌘

I was born looking like Charles Laughton. I had a double chin. It made no difference if I weighed 6 pounds or 160 pounds; the double chin was always there! When I turned 40 years old, I decided I was tired of looking at this pocket of unwanted fat on my neck. I went to see a plastic surgeon; and after talking with him, I decided to have it removed.

The surgeon gave me a long list of instructions. I had to avoid whiplash, so I couldn't travel by car. My face would be bandaged, swollen and bruised for two weeks, so he wanted me to plan my schedule so that I could stay home. While at home, I had to be careful of what I did; consequently, I would have to hire someone to do my yardwork.

In a local paper, a person who did part time yard work had placed an advertisement. I called him and asked to meet him. He came over, and through conversation, I learned he was a police officer and enjoyed doing yardwork.

He had been doing the yardwork for about a month before I had my plastic surgery. On Monday, I had the surgery; two days later, the gentleman came to do the yardwork. Without realizing I had not told him I was going to have this type of surgery, I opened the door and let him in. My entire head was wrapped in bandages. My face and neck were bruised and swollen. I suppose I looked like someone had hit me. He looked at me and asked, "Who did this to you?" Suddenly, I remembered he was a police officer. I told him I had plastic surgery done.

We think because we know what we are doing, the rest of the world knows, too. Most of the time, we don't fail to explain, we just forget to explain. In this situation, it was just a mild misunderstanding, but in other situations, we unthinkingly create agony, hostility, and fear. Hurt feelings can harden hearts, and sometimes those hearts never soften. How much better off we would be if we just remembered to explain what and why we do what we do.

⌘⌘⌘⌘⌘

"And now I will show you the most excellent way."
1 Corinthians 12:31

NOVEMBER 22
...VALUING, NOT TAKING FOR GRANTED, THE EVERYDAY

"Good friends, good books and a sleepy conscience:
this is the ideal life."

- Mark Twain

⌘⌘⌘⌘⌘

I have always taken for granted the fact that I am a native Hoosier. For 50 years, even though I have moved around town several times, I have always lived in central Indiana. I can't go anywhere without bumping into someone I know. This was very much taken for granted until Stan and I became friends with Harry and Denise.

Harry and Denise moved across the street from us several years ago. One day, they were just there. I never saw a moving van, boxes, or big trash heaps. What I saw were delivery trucks bringing in new furniture and appliances. The reason was Harry and Denise had just moved back to the United States after living overseas for many years.

Since Harry and Denise were first married, they have lived in South Africa, Mexico, New Zealand, etc. Harry works for Firestone; consequently, his work takes them from place to place. They moved here for a brief time when Harry was assigned to the Firestone in Noblesville.

The four of us did many things together. We went out to dinner, took cooking classes, dined on each other's decks, and went to local events. One such event was the "Symphony on the Prairie" at Conner Prairie. At Symphony on the Prairie, people take picnic baskets and lawn chairs and dine under the stars while listening to the beautiful music played by our symphony orchestra.

On one such visit, I kept running into people I knew. I would introduce each person to Stan, Harry and Denise, and we would chat for a few minutes. We finally found a place on the prairie to set our chairs, and, just as we began to eat, someone sitting next to us called out my name. She was a student I had had in class years ago. All through the evening we talked and laughed about old times.

Denise and I were sitting in the back seat on the way home. During our conversation she said, "You are so fortunate." I asked her why she would say that. She said, "Because I've never lived any place long enough to have that many friends." Denise helped me realize how fortunate I really am.

⌘⌘⌘⌘⌘

"Greater love has no one than this,
that he lay down his life for his friends."
John 15:13

NOVEMBER 23

...APPRECIATING OLD WAYS

"What would the future of man be if it were devoid of memory?"
                                                    - Elie Wiesel

⌘⌘⌘⌘⌘

Stan and I have been very fortunate in knowing two wonderful people, Jim and Alex, with whom we enjoy spending time and with whom we have much in common. Jim is in construction, and Stan loves wood working. When they get together, it is as if they were two kindred spirits who have known one another forever.

Alex and I have much in common. We love Charles Dickens, Chopin, shopping and playing Solitaire on our computers. We are never at a loss for words, thoughts or ideas.

The four of us share common origins, a modicum of success, and the love of simple lives. Our loves in our simple lives include reading, sitting in front of the fire talking, petting the dogs and sharing wonderful "home-cooked" meals. These old ways and old pleasures are high on our lists.

Stan and Alex try to out-do each other in cooking — old world cooking. Alex has shared with us some incredible old world recipes her mother taught her to make: Pierogis (pa-ro-ges) and Golumpkis (ga-lump-kes).

When freeze-dried, pre-packaged, and concentrated anything first came out, they were the rage. To some extent they still are; however, when going through the store, I can't help but notice home-cookin' soups, orange juice with pulp, and fabric softeners that make clothes smell as if they had been dried outdoors.

I appreciate old ways. Spending extra time to cook from scratch helps carry on and hand down a legacy from generation to generation. Sharing the plots of novels we have read helps open our minds to new worlds. Reviving the art of conversation simply by spending an evening talking instead of being glued to the TV set helps us learn more about our fellow human beings. Sharing simple times relaxes, enlightens, and refreshes.

⌘⌘⌘⌘⌘

"He will teach us his ways, so
that we may walk in his paths."
                                    Isaiah 2:3

NOVEMBER 24
...PAYING ATTENTION

"All that we do is done with an eye to something else."
- Aristotle

⌘⌘⌘⌘⌘

Because my Grandmother had a baby grand piano, she was determined that someone, besides herself, would know how to play the piano. I was selected.

Once a week my Mother took me to the home of my piano teacher. While we lived in a suburb, my piano teacher lived out in the country, and she had horses. I was always anxious to take my piano lesson. My Mother assumed it was because I loved playing the piano. It was several months into the lessons before Mother commented that I didn't seem to be learning very much. My progress was painfully slow. What Mother didn't realize was that when she dropped me off for my lesson, my piano teacher and I spent a good deal of our time together petting and talking about the horses.

Mother finally told me that she thought I was not paying attention. I was. I was just paying attention to what I wanted to pay attention to. I was learning a great deal — not about the piano but about the horses.

One day, after dropping me off for my lesson, Mother drove back past the house of my teacher and saw us out in the field petting the horses. She mentioned it that evening when she picked me up. My Mother was always very patient and understanding. She knew how much I loved horses, so she suggested we compromise. I would take my piano lesson during the appointed time and then my teacher and I could play with the horses for 15 or 30 minutes after the lesson.

This helped me focus my attention on one thing at a time. I learned to play a little piano and read music, and I learned much about horses. Piano lesson day was my favorite day of the week.

⌘⌘⌘⌘⌘

"Listen, my sons to a father's instruction:
pay attention and gain understanding."
Proverbs 4:1

NOVEMBER 25
...STRIKING UP A CONVERSATION

"To listen closely and reply well is the highest
perfection we are able to attain in the art of conversation."

- La Rochefoucauld

⌘⌘⌘⌘⌘

With all the things that each of us try to do daily, sometimes our lives get complicated, and we feel overwhelmed. In our occasional overwhelmed state, we tend to focus more on us and less on the people around us. Facial expressions or tones of voices from others, indicating that someone wants to tell us something special, are overlook.

My husband and I notice that we go through these stages. Each of us has developed a different way to get the other person to focus on what we are saying.

My husband tends to be more direct — and he adds "less sarcastic" — when trying to get my attention. When I get into my overwhelmed, self-absorbed state, he either follows directly behind me from place to place or stands directly in front of me with a big smile on his face until I say "What?"

My way is more subtle — not sarcastic. Years ago, my mother bought me the "Little Women" dolls. When I am dying for him to ask me if any thing special has happened that day, and he is in his overwhelmed, self-absorbed state, I get one of my "Little Women" dolls, set her in front of me (and him) and say, "So, tell me, Meg, how did your day go? Fine, Suzanne. And yours?" By this time, my husband has received the message, and he looks at me and says "What?"

Each of us have our own ways of starting conversation. It really doesn't matter that others may think it is too direct or sarcastic. I suppose it is just our way: the way we are comfortable with. The point is we are trying to "start" a conversation with another being. We are trying to bond, to share, and to relate. Whether we comment on the weather, something someone is wearing, or the event we are attending, we are relating the only way we know how: our conversation.

⌘⌘⌘⌘⌘

"A word aptly spoken is like apples of gold in settings of silver."

Proverbs 25:11

NOVEMBER 26
...SEEING EPIPHANIES IN ACTION

"Where there is an open mind, there will always be a frontier."
- Charles F. Kettering

⌘⌘⌘⌘⌘

My husband and I were asked to attend a "couples" dinner party. We were rather surprised to be asked, but we won't be surprised if we are not asked again — at least I won't.

By now, the affection I have for animals is rather apparent. During the evening at the home of our hosts, a large black dog came wondering out. For a brief while, I turned my attention to the dog. I've never understood how you can avoid a friendly dog. They stick their nose in your face, nudge your hand and arm with their nose to be petted, and wag their tail when you do pet them. Dogs are truly unabashed in their need and demand for attention.

As we were putting on our coats to leave, the dog again came to me. As I stooped down to pet him good bye, one of the attendees said it was just a "dumb animal." Remembering Anne Sewell's wonderful philosophy from Black Beauty, I reminded everyone that "we call them dumb animals because they can't speak, not because they don't think or feel."

As I looked into the faces of some of the guests, I saw "epiphanies in action." How wonderful it is to see people take something they have heard or learned and view it in a new light. To see the same old things with fresh eyes always brings a smile to my face. How truly remarkable the mind is.

⌘⌘⌘⌘⌘

"The Advocate, the Holy Spirit...will teach you everything, and remind you of all that I have said to you."
John 14:26

NOVEMBER 27
...LOVING UNUSUAL GIFTS

"The spirit in which a thing is given determines that in
which the debt is acknowledge; it's the intention,
not the face-value of the gift that is weighed."
- Seneca

⌘⌘⌘⌘⌘

Every now and then you have a friend that is very difficult to buy gifts for.
They are the type of person who has almost everything, and if they want
something, they just go out and buy it. I have one such friend.

This particular friend of mine received a wonderful gift one year for
Christmas: a star named after her. As part of the gift, she was given a map
showing her particular constellation, and the star named after her was highlighted.

She was tickled to death. She has the constellation framed and proudly tells
anyone and everyone who would listen about "her" star.

Unusual gifts don't have to be expensive or elaborate. The richness and the
beauty of the gift comes from its uniqueness. It's not another toaster, pen or pair
of gloves that you run to the store and buy in less than 15 minutes; it's the gift that
takes thought, time and the desire to please in a special way.

I believe my favorite, most unusual gift was "One Square Inch of Ireland"
that my aunt gave me. I have always believed that owning "One Square Inch of
Ireland" makes me "Landed Gentry."

⌘⌘⌘⌘⌘

"But eagerly desire the greater gifts."
1 Corinthians 12:31

NOVEMBER 28
...APPRECIATING SEMANTICS

"Words are used to express meaning; when you understand
the meaning, you can forget the words."

- Chuang-tse

⌘⌘⌘⌘⌘

Ben, my step-son, and his wife Jill just bought a beautiful bright red sports car. They drove the car over the same evening they purchased it, and we went out to dinner to celebrate.

Ben kept referring to the salesperson as "she." I have a friend, Thelma Wilson, who sells sports cars at a local dealership. I thought the "she" might be Thelma, so I asked Ben who sold him the car. He said, "Some little old lady." I asked if her name was Thelma Wilson, and he said yes and questioned how I knew her. I smiled, looked right at him and told him that Thelma and I went to school together. I could tell by the look on Ben's face he remembered he had called her a "little old lady." He immediately began to back-track. He told me I looked much younger than she and so on. I kept laughing. I wasn't angry; I just thought it was funny.

Jill mentioned that she was very nice and personable, but she kept calling them "kids," and, being in their mid-twenties, they didn't think of themselves as kids. They think of themselves as "young adults."

Semantics, the relationship between signs and symbols and what they represent, is a wonderful thing. I never realized, until this incident, that I, too, may be a sign of a "little old lady" to somebody, and I'm sure Ben and Jill never realized they could be the sign of "kids" to somebody else.

We learn many things by viewing them through someone else's eyes.

⌘⌘⌘⌘⌘

"Have you never read, 'Out of the mouths of
babes and infants thou hast perfected praise?'"
Matthew 21:16

NOVEMBER 29
... UNDERSTANDING THE PREFIXES AND SUFFIXES OF OUR LIVES

"Great is the art of beginning, but greater the art is of ending."
- Longfellow

⌘⌘⌘⌘⌘

One evening while teaching class, during the break I went out to the soda machine for some refreshment. There was a study group sitting at one of the tables working on a project. As I waited for the machine to deliver the goods, I eavesdropped on their conversation. It seemed they were having an in-depth discussion on which prefix was the correct one to use.

As I walked back to the classroom, I began to think about prefixes and suffixes and how they change the meaning of the root word. If you take the word *establish,* it means "to make firm; to secure." However, if you add dis- to establish, it means "to alter the status of or deprive." An establisher is one who establishes. An establishment is a place of business. Established is past tense and means the action is finished. Establishing is the act of making firm or secure, and reestablish is to establish again. Just by adding prefixes and suffixes, we alter the words original meaning.

I believe events that happen to us are like prefixes and suffixes. Our real-life events alter us just as the prefixes and suffixes alter the meaning of the root words. We are the root word, and whether we are dis-, anti-, un-, or non-something alters our perception or viewpoint about issues. If we are -ed, -ing, -ment, or -ish, we have already been affected by what has gone on.

If it is as easy to change a meaning of a word by adding a few letters to its base, it is just as easy for an event to change the base of a person's life.

⌘⌘⌘⌘⌘

"Better is the end of a thing than the beginning thereof."
Ecclesiastes 7:8

NOVEMBER 30
...BEING THE CANDLE THAT BURNS

"It is better to light a candle than to curse the darkness."
- Chinese Proverb

⌘⌘⌘⌘⌘

I am very fond of the candles that are very large: these candles are six inches in diameter and have three wicks. I put them on the coffee table and kitchen island. I light them when guests come over because I was taught that a lighted candle demonstrated the warmth you feel for your guests. They also smell good, look good, and create a relaxing atmosphere for chatting with friends.

Last year, I asked for one of the large candles for Christmas and received two of them. They were identical except for one thing: one of the candles did not burn well. I would light this candle, turn my back to do something; and when I turned around, it would be out. If I pulled at the wick, it broke off. If I melted the wax around the wicks, the wax overwhelmed the wicks, and they again went out. Finally, I became so frustrated that I decided to figure out a way to make this candle burn just as well as the other one.

I took the candle out in the garage, turned it upside down, and propped it up on three pieces of wood. I lit the wicks and let the candle burn — upside down — for about 30 minutes. The excess wax dripped off, making the wicks finally long enough to provide a warm, lovely light for my guests and for me.

⌘⌘⌘⌘⌘

"If the ax is dull and its edges unsharpened,
more strength is needed but skill will bring success."
Ecclesiastes 10:10

DECEMBER 1
...LETTING OTHERS SHINE

"The applause of a single human being is of great consequence."
- Samuel Johnson

⌘⌘⌘⌘⌘

I recently traveled to San Antonio to do a training session on "Generations." This particular presentation is designed to give people a better understanding of the Silent Generation, Boomers, and Generation X, thus helping each generation have a better working relationship with the others.

The attendees and I were discussing the Boomer's philosophy. It was amazing to most of the attendees in tracing the evolution from Hippies to Yuppies to Dinks to Dinkods. One of the gentlemen remarked how strange it was to look at a man in a three-piece suit and know at one time he wore tie-died clothing and sandals. I agreed and added he might possibly be a RUB.

I could tell from the looks I received that RUB was an unfamiliar term. I was just on the verge of "telling" the attendees what RUB stands for, when I stopped, remembering that it is more important to let those attending training sessions show their peers what they know. I asked if anyone knew what a RUB was. A gentleman in the back of the room raised his hand. He then smiled and said, "Rich Urban Biker." Every one in the room laughed and applauded, and he beamed. During break he came up and talked to me about an article he had written on RUB's. We also talked about the beauty of Harleys and our personal experience with RUB's.

I could have told everyone what a RUB was. Most would have remembered, and the training session would have ended well. However, letting him shine and have a moment of glory among his peers assured me that everyone in the room would always remember what a RUB was and how great this training session had been.

It was such a little thing, but you could tell how much it meant to him. Letting someone else shine gives them their moment in the sun. The VP of this organization later told me he was a cancer survivor in remission. This made the event even more special.

⌘⌘⌘⌘⌘

"So in everything, do unto others what
you would have them do to you,"
Matthew 7:12

DECEMBER 2
...APPRECIATING "THE" EFFORT

"When you drink the water, remember the spring."
- Chinese Proverb

⌘⌘⌘⌘⌘

It was the time when all the special events seemed to coincide. First, it was my birthday. Second, Stan and I had just gotten engaged. Third, Sarah, his daughter, had just learned to drive.

Sarah, being excited at having a license and feeling new-found freedom, drove over to Stan's house with one of her friends. Upon learning it was my birthday, Sarah and and her friend decided to bake me a cake. Of course, they had to "drive" to the store to get a mix. Having accomplished this task, they set to work baking the cake. Neither of them had ever cooked before in their life. To say the least, this cake was quite a sight to be seen.

They hadn't greased the pan well, so part of the cake stuck to the bottom. They turned the cake before it had cooled, so the cake split into sections. They wanted to ice the cake to hide its brokeness, but the cake was too hot and the icing ran. It was a mess of pink and yellow on a plate. However, Sarah and her friend were so proud of their first cooking masterpiece. You could see them beaming as they placed it on the table.

Stan and I smiled that special smile to each other agreeing to say nothing that would spoil their feeling of accomplishment. We ate the cake pieces out of a bowl with a spoon and enjoyed each and every bite.

The enjoyment did not come from the taste of the cake; the enjoyment came from the effort these two young women had put forth to show another person that she was cared for.

It doesn't get much better than that!

⌘⌘⌘⌘⌘

"So in everything, do to others what you would have them do to you,"
Matthew 7:12

DECEMBER 3
...SEEING "IGNORANCE IS BLISS" IN ACTION

"The condition necessary...for existence itself. If
we knew it all, we could not endure life for an hour."
- Anatole France

⌘⌘⌘⌘⌘

I was making a trip to Orlando to do a site check of a hotel where we were planning to hold a conference. Our lead time was drawing to a close; consequently, the trip "had" to be made.   It was springtime, and the area was being bombarded with unusually high winds. I called the airport before I left home to determine if the planes were flying. They were, so I headed for the airport.

The passengers boarded the plane. My seat was next to a window. Sitting next to me in the middle seat was a little girl, and her father sat on the aisle.

Everyone on board could feel the plane sway as it rolled down the runway. Just as we were about to take off, the tower shut the airport down until some exceptionally strong winds passed by. We sat on the tarmac and waited.

Finally, we did take off; and after a short climb, we hit what must have been an air pocket because the plane dropped many feet in a very short time. It was the kind of drop you feel when you are going over a bridge a bit too fast, and the wheels leave the pavement. The kind of drop that gives you that funny tickling sensation in your stomach.

The little girl, who was sitting between her father and me, began to giggle loudly. This was the kind of fun feeling you get from an amusement park ride. I must tell you she was the only one laughing. The rest of the passengers gasped and gripped the arms of their seats. I looked at her father out of the corner of my eye, and he said, "Ignorance is bliss." We smiled. I knew it would be many years before this little girl understood the seriousness of what had happened. I was glad.

When we are young or fragile, there is much in this life that we don't need to know. We don't need to know that Santa Claus and the Easter Bunny are really our parents in disguise. We don't need to know of major tragedies when we are emotionally weak or ailing. Sometimes, we are better off not knowing what people truly think.

It is true that we cannot know everything. We are not omniscient. Maybe we should be a little more selective as to what we choose to know and the times we choose to know it.

⌘⌘⌘⌘⌘

"Many will go here and there to increase knowledge."
Daniel 12:4

DECEMBER 4
...CELEBRATING EACH YEAR WE AGE

"Only a number, a cipher for the records.
A man can't retire his experience."
- Bernard Baruch

⌘⌘⌘⌘⌘

Today is my birthday, and I am fifty years old. I have no difficulty telling people I'm fifty years old. I'm not proud of it; I'm not ashamed of it. There simply is no getting around the fact that I am fifty years old.

When I tell people that I am fifty, I get several different reactions. Some are in disbelief and want to see my driver's license. Some can't believe that I tell people my age. And, more often than not, some people complain and bemoan the fact that they are aging, also. When I am confronted by this latter group, I enjoy asking them what is the alternative to aging. You can actually see them thinking, and it suddenly dawns on them that the alternative to aging is death. I usually respond, "Thank you, I'll age."

I have never understood why people get upset about aging. I look back at the things I have done or said when I was younger, and I am not proud of many of them. I have probably been every "un-, dis-, il- and non-" you can think of. As I have aged, I have become wiser, more compassionate, more involved, and more concerned about my world and the people in it. With each passing year I have become a better person, and I am thankful for that. With each passing year I have become more aware of the beauty of small things like butterflies and bunnies. I have become more concerned with people's needs. I have become more compassionate about the physical and emotional pain that people go through and how I might possibly help. My desire for material goods has waned, and my desire for precious moments has grown. And, with each passing year, I have grown closer to God and have realized the importance He has in each minute of my life.

I am fifty years old. The lines in my face show more years than they used to. They show more years of smiling than frowning, of caring than apathy, of wisdom than stupidity, and of spirituality than secularism. Thank God for aging, for maturity, for wisdom, and for compassion.

⌘⌘⌘⌘⌘

"Even in your old age and gray hairs I
am he, I am he who will sustain you."
Isaiah 46:4

DECEMBER 5
...DUPLICATING — THE SINCEREST FORM OF FLATTERY

"We are, in truth, more than half what we are by imitation."
- Lord Chesterfield

⌘⌘⌘⌘⌘

My family's favorite vacation spot is Gatlinburg, Tennessee. We love the mountains, the streams, the ski lift, the lodge, and the little town. We would browse through the little specialty shops and spend hours at the outlet malls. There are few "chain" restaurants in the town, so just about any place you choose to have a meal offered a wonderful view and wonderful menu items.

Our favorite restaurant is the "Pancake Pantry." They serve a light lunch, but their real claim to fame is their breakfasts — especially their pancakes. As an example, their Caribbean Pancakes are served with pineapple, coconut, and bananas. You can get "silver dollar" pancakes, pigs in a blanket, and pancakes made with apples, blueberries, and strawberries. Of all the pancakes they serve, our uncontested favorite is the "Cherries Jubilee Pancakes." They are the light Swedish style pancakes topped with Bing Cherries in a rich, sugary sauce and whipped cream. Breakfast just doesn't get much better than this! When we return home from our trips to Gatlinburg, our talk usually turns to breakfast at the Pancake Pantry and how long it will be before we have the pancakes again.

One Sunday morning my mother made a special surprise. We came down to breakfast to find orange juice, coffee, ham and Cherries Jubilee Pancakes. She had been working all week to duplicate the recipe and had hit the nail on the head. They were just as delicious as what we had on vacation.

Working on the technique to duplicate something that someone is fond of and holds special memories of is a labor of love. The song we learn to play or sing to remind someone of a special time or the chicken we learn to fry just the way that mom did to conjure up memories of our childhood is the labor. The love comes from trying to pull fond memories from the past and our subconscious and create a smile, a warm heart, and a moist eye. I guess that is why duplication or imitation is called the "sincerest" form of flattery.

⌘⌘⌘⌘⌘

"Go, and do thou likewise."
Luke 10:37

DECEMBER 6
...KEEPING ON KEEPING ON

"Every new adjustment is a crisis in self-esteem."
- Eric Hoffer

⌘⌘⌘⌘⌘

Many of the clients that I have are the wonderful "repeat type" of client. They ask me back year after year to speak to their employees. They find ways to make the presentations I do fit their needs, or they ask me to construct and present a special presentation that their staff has requested. Even though the requested seminar may not be my special area of expertise — communication — the company likes my style, and from past experience, they know I will do a good job meeting their needs.

Topics of interest in communication change from year to year, and new studies and concerns emerge. To keep meeting my clients' needs, each year I develop new presentations or update my current presentations.

I have to admit that I am not always overjoyed when I begin a new study. I think of all the books I have to read, the seminars I must attend, and the hours I must spend at the computer. After a while, I notice a change of attitude. The books interest me. I pick up new and valuable information at the seminars (and meet some new friends), and organizing the material is challenging. Once the new presentation is completed, I'm excited, interested, committed, and anxious to present the material. I have become refreshed by the new material and the new presentation, and this attitude carries over to the seminars I present.

My willingness and determination have led me to a new level of success. If I had not followed through or kept on going, I would have missed this exhilaration. If I had let the thought of beginning something new overwhelm me, I would have missed the growth of mind and spirit that resulted from my endeavor. My new found wisdom was the result of a "golden opportunity" to accept the challenge, the work, and the possibility of success that our lives so often offer us. Keeping on keeping on is most definitely a blessing.

⌘⌘⌘⌘⌘

"Teach us to number our days aright,
that we may gain a heart of wisdom."
Psalm 90:12

DECEMBER 7
...DOUBLE-CHECKING DIRECTIONS

"The trodden path."
- Legal Maxim

⌘⌘⌘⌘⌘

Business people have certain restaurant hang-outs. Usually it is a place close to their office that offers good food at good prices and a certain ambiance that allows people to discuss business deals. On the Northeast of town, three restaurants come to mind: Houlihans, The Sunrise Cafe and Le Peep. At one time there was only one of each, but, along with the growth of business, comes the addition of restaurants. There are now two Houlihans, two Sunrise Cafes and two Le Peeps, and each restaurant is within five miles of its twin. I have been waiting to have breakfast with a client at the Sunrise Cafe at Keystone at the Crossing while my client has been waiting for me at the Sunrise Cafe on Meridian Street. I have waited for my lunch partner at the Houlihan's at Keystone while my lunch partner waited for me at the Houlihans at Glendale. More than one of anything can be very confusing.

I was reminded of this when I was searching the Bible for quotes. I could find the very same idea expressed four different ways. One way in Matthew, one way in Mark, one way in Luke, and one way in John. These gospels tell the same story four times. They are four different points of view of different individuals. If you ask people which gospel they prefer, they will tell you which is their favorite and tell you why they like this particular gospel the best. Maybe one appeals more to the heart, or one is more grounded in fact.

Just as we are allowed to choose one of identical restaurants because we like the staff or the view or the location over the twin, we are allowed to choose which gospel we enjoy the most.

Being thinking beings, isn't it nice that the Lord allows us to choose?

⌘⌘⌘⌘⌘

"Ask and it will be given to you; seek and you will
find; knock and the door will be opened to you."
Matthew 7:7

DECEMBER 8
...KNOWING THERE ARE ALWAYS EXCEPTIONS

"There is no useful rule without an exception."
- Thomas Fuller

⌘⌘⌘⌘⌘

For 14 years I taught grammar to high school students. It was not an easy task. High school students are usually more interested in what they will be wearing to the prom and with whom they will be going out on Saturday night than grammar. When I had persevered long enough to get the students to understand grammar basics, then I had to get them to remember all the exceptions.

For some reason, I only equated exceptions to grammar rules. That changed one summer day when I was watching the birds at one of our feeders. A dove was sitting on top on the feeder looking at the seeds in the tray. This was rather unusual because doves are supposed to be ground feeders, and all of the other doves were on the ground feeding. The dove keep walking closer and closer to the edge of the roof, and when he reached the edge, he leaned forward trying to get a better look at the seeds. Finally, the dove lost his balance. He swung under the feeder roof, did a 360, and landed upright in the feeder tray. You could tell he didn't know exactly how he got there, but he was certainly happy that he was there. This "ground feeding" dove sat in the tray and ate every last seed. Watching the dove made me realize that there are exceptions to almost everything.

We set rules and then make exceptions to them. We make blanket statements and then add that there are always exceptions to the statements. And, many times, when we pray, we ask God for certain things, and then we add all these exceptions. We may want one thing to happen except if something else happens, and so on.

Things will happen in His way with His exceptions. He will clear up the confusion, help us learn what is needed, and lead us in the way we should go.

⌘⌘⌘⌘⌘

"He will teach us his ways,
so that we may walk in his paths."
Isaiah 2:3

DECEMBER 9
...BEING UP FRONT

"An honest man's the noblest work of God."
- Alexander Pope

⌘⌘⌘⌘⌘

I have never thought I was a very good cook. I can cook, but I must follow a recipe step by step with no variation. My husband and I take cooking classes, and we have made a point to eat healthier and cook almost everything from scratch: even pasta and ice cream. This can be a challenge for someone who is "cooking impaired."

My husband loves Lemon Meringue Pie, and I try to make this pie for him at least once a month. It is not an easy pie to make. When the pie starts to cook, all the ingredients must be ready to add immediately, or the pie will be overcooked.

While at the store, I noticed the lemons. They were big and bright yellow. They looked perfect, so I decided it was time to make another pie. I spent the better part of an afternoon making this pie, and it looked like it came out of a magazine. I was very pleased.

We had had a nice dinner together and a pleasant relaxing evening. I made coffee and brought out the dessert. When I tasted the pie, I was disappointed. The lemons may have looked good, but they were tasteless. I had spent all afternoon making a pie that didn't taste like lemon. My husband kept telling me how pleased he was and what a special treat the Lemon Meringue Pie was, so I just clammed up. All evening long he kept following me around asking me what was wrong. I kept saying nothing was wrong.

We went to bed, and he said he hoped tomorrow evening was better than this evening. I asked why. He said I had been a grouch all night long. He then said he didn't know what he had done to upset me, but he certainly wished I would tell him what was wrong. I finally said, "Okay. My pie didn't taste like lemon." He sat up and looked at me in disbelief. He told me he had been worrying all night about what he might have done or said to upset me, and my "mood" was all because the pie didn't taste like lemon. He was incredulous.

I now realize it is much easier to be honest and up front with all my emotions. It not only helps me get things off my chest, but it also stops others from worrying about what they have done. And, when they have done nothing to create a "mood," it is truly unfair to put them in that position.

⌘⌘⌘⌘⌘

"Always be prepared to give an answer to everyone who asks you to give the reason for the hope that you have."
1 Peter 3:15

DECEMBER 10
...APPRECIATING SERENDIPITY

"Wherever life takes us, there are always moments of wonder."
- Jimmy Carter

⌘⌘⌘⌘⌘

I once heard a speaker refer to a home-cooked dinner with her husband as their "annual hot meal." Because I spend many nights out speaking and my husband attends several meetings each month, this humorous statement has begun to ring more true. One evening we were both going to be home. It was time for our "semi-annual" home-cooked hot meal. I asked my husband what he would like for dinner. He responded, "Lasagna!"

I checked the pantry for the ingredients. I needed more lasagna noodles, so I rushed to the nearest grocery. I was walking through the store looking up at the directories for "pasta" when I heard someone call my name. I turned to my left and saw Susanne McAlister, a long time friend whom I hadn't seen in several years. We exchanged information on what each of us had been doing. I was writing a book, and she had become an agent for publishers. Coincidence? I don't think so!

So often we speak of accidental meetings: someone stopping by or just running into someone. When we tell others of the event, we usually precede it with "you'll never believe this." Isn't it odd how the unplanned interaction leads to renewed friendships, making the right connections with a third party, or one person being in a new business that will complement what the other is doing?

I guess now I know what is meant when I hear that "someone has called out of the blue" and what particular "blue" they are talking about.

⌘⌘⌘⌘⌘

"And we know that in all things God works for the good of those who love him, who have been called according to his purpose."
Romans 8:28

DECEMBER 11
...REALIZING ONLY "THINGS" ARE DISPOSABLE

"Those things are dearest to us that have cost us most."
- Montaigne

⌘⌘⌘⌘⌘

Over the course of our lifetime, we have the opportunity to observe and to learn from what is going on around us. We may watch related events taking place, and for years we don't understand their relationship to each other. Then, one day, someone says something that makes the years of observation fall into place — an epiphany.

One such epiphany happened to me recently. I was teaching a class on Professional Communication. The students and I were discussing typical workplace troubles: span of control, visionary leadership, lack of company loyalty, high turnover, etc. The discussion turned to the attitude that many companies have about their employees. Early retirement, downsizing, moving companies to new locations, and buy-outs are areas of concern. One woman made the statement that "companies are treating people as if they were disposables," and she didn't understand why.

For me, the light bulb finally went on. I said, "For years we have treated our environment as if were disposable. We bulldoze, excavate, cement, and build whatever and wherever we want. Thought to animals' habitats or the need for a balanced ecosystem is way down on the list of priorities. How long have we treated animals as if they were disposables? How many species have we wiped out or come close to wiping out? How many of us see a cute puppy or kitten, take it home; and when it doesn't behave the way we expect, we dump it on the side of the road never concerned about its survival? What amazes me is that people thought it would stop there! We are simply proceeding up the chain."

I was truly amazed at this epiphany. It only took me 50 years to figure this out. Hopefully, with a new perception of life and its value, it won't take me another 50 years to do what I can do to share with others that our environment, our creatures, and ourselves are not disposables.

⌘⌘⌘⌘⌘

"God saw all that he had made, and it was very good."
Genesis 1:31

DECEMBER 12
...LISTENING TO WHAT'S IN A PERSON'S HEART

"Where the heart lies, let the brain lie also."
- Robert Browning

⌘⌘⌘⌘⌘

Several of my careers have allowed me the opportunity to travel. Being wedged between two strangers, when travelling by air, usually forces you to become more of a conversationalist. Putting in thousands of air miles has helped me strike a conversation with almost anyone.

On one particular flight, I was seated by the window, the middle seat was vacant, and a business woman was seated on the aisle. Waiting for a longer take-off than planned, I decided to engage this woman in conversation to make the time go faster.

I asked her if she was from Indianapolis (my home town). She replied, "No, I'm here on business. I live in Boston." She kept looking around, and finally noticed that I had noticed her looking around. She smiled and said, "I'm very interested in watching these two mothers with their babies." She nodded in their direction and continued, "Next week I'm taking vacation, and I am flying for the first time with my one-year old daughter. We are going out to see her grandmother. I'm very interested in seeing how these mothers handle their babies. Maybe I can learn some tips to make travelling with a one-year old easier." Now, you don't have to have a Ph.D. to know what this woman wanted to talk about. She wanted to talk about her one-year old daughter.

If we would just spend a little more time listening to people, we would hear not only what is in their minds but also what is in their hearts. From our hearts come our true desires. What comes from our hearts is what makes us tick in more ways than one. When we speak from our hearts, we are sincere. When we listen with our hearts, we are compassionate. And, when we understand with our hearts, we have empathy for other souls who are also going through this life's journey.

⌘⌘⌘⌘⌘

"My mouth shall speak wisdom; the
meditation of my heart shall be understanding."
Psalm 49:3

DECEMBER 13
...TURNING OFF THE ALARM

"Throw out an alarming alarm clock. If the ring is loud and
strident, you're waking up to instant stress. You shouldn't be
bullied out of bed, just reminded that it's time to start your day."
- Sharon Gold

⌘⌘⌘⌘⌘

I love Friday mornings for several reasons. It is the start of the weekend,
and my husband's and my date night. It's putting the suits away and getting out
the jeans and sweatshirts. It's cooking nice dinners, going to see a movie, and
playing with the dogs. But my favorite reason for loving Fridays is I can turn off
the alarm.

I, half-jokingly and half-seriously, tell people I became an entrepreneur
because I didn't want to get up early every morning. Then I married Stan, who
gets up every weekday morning at 5:20 AM. The dogs, creatures of habit, also
wake up when the alarm goes off. At 5:20 each weekday morning, I let the dogs
out, let them back in, feed them, and go back to bed to talk with my husband
while he dresses for work. Being wide awake, seldom do I go back to bed for a
cat nap. My day has begun. Ugh!

On Friday morning's, I do the same routine with one exception: before I
get back into bed, I turn off the alarm! This simple action brings a wonderful
sense of relief. This simple action denotes unstructured time, enjoyment,
relaxation, and fun. This simple action removes the senses of dread, drudgery,
and panic. This simple action means no schedules, no meetings, or no
unwelcome interaction with people we prefer not to interact with. This flick of the
wrist makes my spirits soar, my heart sing, and my entire face smile. I love turning
off the alarm.

⌘⌘⌘⌘⌘

"My people will live in peaceful dwelling places, in
secure homes, and in undisturbed places of rest."
Isaiah 32:18

DECEMBER 14
...COORDINATING OUR ENDINGS

"What is there more of in the world than anything else? Ends."
- Carl Sandburg

⌘⌘⌘⌘⌘

Our choir director and choir members do not like to hear sloppy endings. In singing, sloppy endings occur when 100 different voices pronounce the last letter of a word at different times. As an example, if the last word of a measure is God, and you hear the letter "d" four or five different times, that is a sloppy ending.

When singing our T's, P's, D's and N's, it is our goal for each choir member to end at exactly the same time. We accomplish this by either writing "look up" or drawing a pair of eye glasses just before the ending of the letter and note. When the director sees 100 pair of eyes, he touches his index finger and thumb together, and we have a beautiful ending of 100 voices blended together as one. The choir members are always pleased to accomplish this uniform ending. Speaking for myself, I think it makes us sound more professional.

Having someone coordinate our endings is a blessing. There is a sense of comfort and relief knowing when an end has come. For me, a sense of closure makes things bearable. I could deal better with the chemotherapy and radiation treatments when I knew how many there were because I knew when they would end. I could handle working with a group of people I am not particularly fond of when I know the class will only last for six weeks.

We speak of ending points, the end of the road, the end of an era and even being at the end of our rope. When it comes to endings, there is only one thing better than an individual coming to an end: a group of people reaching an end together. Rather than just producing closure, a group produces closure with unity.

⌘⌘⌘⌘⌘

"...then make my joy complete by being like-minded,
have the same love, being one in spirit and purpose."
Philippians 2:2

DECEMBER 15
...VALUING THOSE WHO DOUBLE CHECK

"Only in growth, reform, and change, paradoxically
enough, is true security to be found.
- Anne Morrow Lindbergh

⌘⌘⌘⌘⌘

When I began doing presentations, I used handouts and overheads. Technology and I progressed, and I began using PowerPoint Slides on a projector with my overheads. Then technology and I took another leap, and I progressed to PowerPoint Slides shown directly from my computer. The slides shown on the projector were nice, but they were awkward to carry and very set in their order. It was very difficult for me to add just one new slide or customize a title slide. My computer changed all that. Now I can add one new slide or one hundred new slides, and I change the title slide with each presentation to each new company. I can also put in people's names, scan in company logos and mission statements, and add company humor or pictures. What I can do with my laptop is amazing.

Each time I do a presentation for a company, I send the company a letter of agreement, and, in this letter, the place, amount, time, etc. of the presentation are explained. The last line states what type of computer I will be using and what type of hook-up I need for the computer. What I have found, to my dismay, is that people say they understand the type of hook-up you need; but when I get to the company or hotel, the equipment I need is not there or the hook-up does not accommodate my software. This is very frustrating especially when I have worked for many hours customizing my presentation that is visually appealing with colors, pictures, and artwork. I have learned always to bring hard copies.

I had been contracted to do a presentation in San Antonio, Texas. I had sent the letter requesting the hook-up. A week before I flew to Texas, I received a call from the Audio/Visual person at the hotel. She asked all the particulars about my computer and the software I was using. She told me the hook-up I would have and in what room I would be speaking. She learned from the people at the front desk when I would be arriving; consequently, she told me when she and the room would be available for me to do a run through. It was a detailed and thorough interaction regarding my presentation and set up. I wished everyone, including myself, would be as meticulous and thorough on follow through.

⌘⌘⌘⌘⌘

"Because God wanted to make the unchanging nature of his purpose very
clear to the heirs of what was promised, he confirmed it with an oath."
Hebrews 6:17

DECEMBER 16
...DOING "ONLY" PLANNED THINGS ON BUSY DAYS

"It is best to do things systematically, since we are
only human, and disorder is our worst enemy."
- Hersiod

⌘⌘⌘⌘⌘

Errands. Those time consuming, much needed, immediate, necessities of
life. I would venture to say that most of us do not find running errands a pleasure.
When it's 90°, going in short bursts from one place to another never allows the
car to cool off, and we are hot, miserable and sweaty. When it's pouring down
rain, and we usually run in and out without an umbrella, and, we, and our
purchases, are dampen and soggy. Or when it is 20°, we either bundle up to
survive the cold or run around poorly clad for the weather, never getting warm or
ending up with a cold. Errands!!!
I plan when I need to do errands. I do as many as I can at one time to save
myself from going out again and again. To top this off, I usually do errands when
I am on my way to a speaking engagement just to save time. On one such errand
day, even though it was not on my list of "things to do," I decided to make a quick
stop at Cracker Barrel to exchange my audio book. This would allow me to listen
to a new novel while I did the rest of my errands and drove to my destination. In
an excited state, I ran in and focused all my attention on the audio carousel racks.
I had my selection. I turned to go to the checkout and saw a line of 50 people. I
was dumb-founded as to this mass of people. I was unaware it was "Beanie Baby
Day": the first day the new selections of Beanie Babies hit the stores. People were
packed about 10 deep at the counter calling out "moose, duck, zebra, etc."
Now, I think the Beanie Babies are cute. I have a the moose. I want the
children (or adults) to get their babies, but not on this particular day and time. I
broke out in a sweat and had difficulty breathing because what I had planned was
not going to be carried out.
The manager stepped behind the counter and, over the commotion, asked
if anyone was there for any other reason than getting Beanie Babies. I yelled,
"YES." He motioned me to the side, exchanged my book, and I was on my way.
This was a wonderful lesson for me to seriously consider not doing
unplanned things on busy days. When we are hurried, the last things we need are
added stress and irritation.

⌘⌘⌘⌘⌘

"Let all things be done decently and in order."
Corinthians 14:40

DECEMBER 17
...BEING USED TO HEARING THE NOTES OF OTHERS

"If we were all determined to play the first violin we should never have a full ensemble. Therefore respect every musician in his proper place."
- Robert Schumann

⌘⌘⌘⌘⌘

I may have mentioned before that our church is doing a $7.5 million expansion. We are expanding because every room in the church is filled to capacity. This includes our sanctuary and our choir loft. The choir loft will no longer hold the entire choir, so, last year, all the altos sat in the pews with the congregation directly beneath the loft.

I have to admit it was not a bad arrangement for one reason: it was much easier to sing the alto part when you had no other voices near you. After a year on the floor, our director decided it was unfair to single the altos out; consequently, now all the voices are taking their turn on the floor. Because we keep moving our positions, sometimes we have the tenors behind us and other times we have the sopranos behind us. It can be very distracting. Once you are used to hearing a certain set of notes behind you, a change is made, and you hear a completely different set of notes.

At first I was very frustrated. It took much more focus to sing the alto part when the sounds around you kept changing. Then I realized how pretty the other voices sounded. The descant of the sopranos sent a chill down my spine. The tenors high range was such a beautiful contrast to the low notes of the basses and baritones.

It takes each voice to create the beautiful sound, and we can only appreciate this beautiful sound by mixing our notes and the notes of others. It's the sum of the parts that make up the whole.

⌘⌘⌘⌘⌘

"How beautiful on the mountains are the feet of those who bring good news, who proclaim peace, who bring good tidings,....."
Isaiah 52:7

DECEMBER 18
...KEEPING TRACK OF OUR OWN MILEAGE

"The great and glorious masterpiece of man
is to know how to live to purpose."

- Montaigne

⌘⌘⌘⌘⌘

I keep a mileage log of the business related miles I drive; and at the end of each month I total up the miles and write myself a mileage check. Then, the mileage log goes back into the car to start afresh keeping track of next month's mileage. I am very meticulous when it comes to my company's records. I have to be for tax purposes. Knowing that someone is figuratively "standing over your shoulder" makes you more careful.

It occurred to me that I should be just as meticulous in keeping track of my own mileage. When we are recording too many miles without a break or a chance to become refreshed, we wear thin like tires, we lose spark like our plugs, and we become exhausted by running out of gas. We need a tune up.

When we take our cars into the shop to be tuned up after 25,000 or 50,000 miles, how much better the car runs. We, as human beings, are no different. When we give ourselves a brief break for a personal tune up, we can be ready to go again at top speed and performance level. We can only do this by keeping track of our mileage. It helps if we know how many consecutive meetings we have attended, how much sleep we have had the night before, how many problems we have dealt with, and how many variables have arisen to sap our spirit and life force.

Not keeping track of mileage and never getting a tune up usually results in a car that is unsafe to drive. By not keeping track of our mileage, we become unsafe to be around. Tempers flare, arguments ensue, and confrontation occurs. The result is ill-will to whomever we interact with. Taking time to tune up provides us with safety of spirit, mind and body, refreshed emotions, and the ability to express good will.

⌘⌘⌘⌘⌘

"You will be secure, because there is hope; you
will look about you and take your rest in safety."

Job 11:18

DECEMBER 19
...KNOWING WHEN IT IS THE "RIGHT" TIME

"Persons who are born too soon, or born too late, seldom
achieve the eminence of those who are born at the right time."
- Katharine Anthony

⌘⌘⌘⌘⌘

I think most of us go through life unaware of how intuitive we are in
knowing the "right" time. As strange as it sounds, time is a constant in our lives.
For many of us time provides order, purpose, and meaning to what we are doing.
On certain days or during certain events, we are obsessed with the ticking of the
clock and focus all of our attention on the passing of each minute overlooking our
internal clock which knows the right time.

On night I was having difficulty getting to sleep. I hate to toss and turn and
sigh because I'm always concerned that I will keep my husband awake. He has to
get up at 5:20 AM, so early to bed and a good night's sleep are especially
important to him. I went to the guest room to sleep, and after a restful night,
woke up early. What woke me was the sound of a car starting and stopping. I
realized it was the person who delivers the paper. I thought to myself that it must
be 5:30 AM, and then, just like "clockwork," our two dogs pushed the door open
to wake me up to feed them. I looked at the clock, and, sure enough, it was 5:30
AM.

How silly a thing this was: a sound had told me it was 5:30 AM. During the
day, I became more aware of time and its significance to me. My stomach told me
when I was hungry; I didn't need to look at the clock. My eyes told me when I
had spent too much time at the computer. I even watched the dogs go to look out
the front windows at 4:30 PM because that is the time Stan usually comes home.

If we listen, we will know the "right" time for things. Things such as
laughter, tears, friendship, learning, and even regrouping and waiting for a better
time. Knowing when it is the "right" time for us helps make whatever we need to
do go smoother, faster, and more pleasurable. I think some struggles we go
through are a subtle way of telling us that this time may not be right for this
particular endeavor.

⌘⌘⌘⌘⌘

"A word spoken in due season, how good it is!"
Proverbs 15:23

DECEMBER 20
...APPRECIATING RAIN

"Rain! whose soft architectural hands have power to cut stones,
and chisel to shapes of grandeur the very mountains."
- Henry Ward Beecher

⌘⌘⌘⌘⌘

I love rain storms. Rain makes the air smell clean, washes the dirt off the streets, makes the grass and trees green, makes the flowers grow, and gives a momentary break from the rush of the day. Rain cools the hot temperatures of the summer months.

I have such wonderful memories of rain storms. My grandmother had a big, old front porch with white metal rockers. As I child I remember curling up on those cold chairs after a sweltering summer day and rocking rhythmically to the sound of the rain. We used to catch the rain in a rain barrel to wash our hair because, back then, rain water was purer than tap water.

We usually stay in when it rains. We stand at the window and watch the rain come down. We open the door and take a breathe of fresh air. We relax, read books, bake cookies, and occasionally engage someone is conversation.

We sleep better when it rains. The sound is hypnotic, and I think most of us are listening to the sound of our troubles being washed away for a time.

Without rain there would be no rainbows and, consequently, no way to find the pot of gold. *"I have set my rainbow in the clouds, and it will be the sign of the covenant between me and the earth." Genesis 9:13.* Without rainbows we will be missing more than just the connection between on moment of sunshine and the next.

The water of the rain cleanses us and the world, produces life and beauty, and provides rest and a momentary pause from our fast pace. We speak of showers of blessings, washing away our sins, and drenching cake with icing. We know that "April showers bring May flowers" and sometimes it even rains "cats and dogs," but for one who loves dogs, that's okay.

Rain dilutes some of our troubles and purifies part of our world by literally and figuratively washing the unwanted down the drain.

⌘⌘⌘⌘⌘

"I will send down the showers of their
season; they shall be showers of blessing."
Ezekiel 34:26

DECEMBER 21
...UNDERSTANDING MANY THINGS RISE TO THE TOP

"Even as the holy and righteous cannot rise beyond the
highest which is in each one of you, so the wicked and the
weak cannot fall lower than the lowest which is in you also."

- Kahlil Gibran

⌘⌘⌘⌘⌘

My mother and grandmother were always fond of the expression "It's the
cream that rises to the top." I guess we were more aware of the meaning of that
expression because we lived in the days of the "neighborhood milkman" who
delivered milk every morning in glass bottles. Through the glass bottles you saw a
heavy layer of cream that had risen to the top of the milk. Seeing that milk bottle
pulled from the "ice box" every morning was always a reminder that only good
things rose to the top.

In a small suburb of town there is an infamous card shop. You will not find
clouds, babies, flowers and heart-warming sentiments on these cards. These are
the type of cards you buy when you want to send a more direct, unflattering
message. A friend was looking for a special card for a person who had just
dumped her, so we went to this special card shop. While she was looking for her
specific card, I browsed. I ran across a congratulatory card that stated
"Congratulations on your promotion. Scum always rises to the top."

Now, I never believed that scum was a good thing, but it rose to the top just
as cream did.

This was another one of my "life experiences" that caused my perception to
change. I realized that a position did not actually indicate goodness or badness. A
position indicates a position. The goodness or badness is applied by us and how
we are relating to the position at that time.

We think of success as the climb to the top and high visibility, but there are
many successful people who work in the background, and there are untold
treasures buried from view. Each of these things can change in a moment.

⌘⌘⌘⌘⌘

"Every valley shall be raised up, every mountain and hill made low;
the rough ground shall become level, the rugged places a plain."

Isaiah 40:4

DECEMBER 22
...COORDINATING OUR EFFORTS

"No one knows what he can do till he tries."
- Publilius Syrus

⌘⌘⌘⌘⌘

Gina and I have spent much time travelling together. Most of our travelling was done on company business, and we were on planes, in hotels and in rental cars. However, some times we would go off on a weekend shopping spree to Chicago or Cincinnati, and we would drive Gina's little black, un-air-conditioned Escort with a stick shift. This mode of transportation wasn't bad during the cool months, but it was pretty awful during the summers. To help keep cool, we made frequent trips through the drive-thrus for iced teas.

When we would get our iced teas, Gina would hand them to me to put in the sweetener. Unfortunately, she would accelerate while I was doing this. I would have one iced tea between my knees, the lid off the other iced tea — which was filled to the brim — and a torn packet of sweetener in my teeth. I would begin to pour the sweetener in the tea, and she would begin shifting gears and driving away. I would try to keep the packet of sweetener low, directly over the tea, and move both the tea and sweetener back and forth at the same speed as she shifted into another gear.

By being accustomed to the speed of the car, the pause while shifting gears, and the amount of sweetener in the packets and the length of time it took to pour it into the tea, I actually became quite good. It is amazing what you can do when you coordinate all your efforts. Now, I can even rub my stomach and pat my head at the same time.

⌘⌘⌘⌘⌘

"The race is not to the swift or the battle to the strong,
nor does food come to the wise or wealth to the brilliant
or favor to the learned; but time and chance happen to them all."
Ecclesiastes 9:11

DECEMBER 23
...SNEAKING IN THOSE SPECIAL TIMES

"To know that one has a secret is to know half the secret itself."
- Henry Ward Beecher

⌘⌘⌘⌘⌘

In the early days of television, there weren't hundreds of channels. We were very fortunate to have four channels. The four channels weren't on 24 hours a day. These channels went off well before midnight — with one exception: Channel 4 on Friday nights. This late show was always the same — Sammy Terry.

Sammy Terry was a local television personality. At the beginning of the show, he rose out of a coffin, and during the movie breaks he talked with his pet "rubber" spider. Obviously, Sammy Terry showed monster movies. I loved these old monster movies of Frankenstein, Dracula, and the Werewolf, but they gave me nightmares. Mother got tired of my waking her up with these nightmares, so she banned me from watching Sammy Terry.

As the saying goes "if there's a will, there's a way," and my way was my Aunt Annabelle. She would ask my mother if I could come over on Friday nights and stay with her because she was lonely. Mother agreed, and Annabelle and I would cuddle under warm blankets while eating popcorn and drinking hot cocoa and watching Sammy Terry.

Even though we never breathed a word about this to my mother, I was sure she knew. It was one of those times she let you think you were getting away with something. That was the best part. The secret!

Most of us love secrets. It makes us feel as if we are the only ones in the know. It makes us feel special and connected to the person we are sharing the secret with. Secrets bring about the "knowing" smiles and moments of glee.

Secrets: I know something you don't know!

⌘⌘⌘⌘⌘

"The secret things belong to the Lord our God,"
Deuteronomy 29:29

DECEMBER 24
...MAKING HOLIDAYS SPECIAL

"It's a rare thing, graciousness. The shape of it can
be acquired, but not, I think, the substance."
- Gertrude Schweitzer

⌘⌘⌘⌘⌘

For a company which I previously worked, one of my jobs was doing site checks of hotels as possible seminars locations. Flying into cities for a few days sounds glamorous, but it gets old after a while. You are by yourself hauling luggage, rushing to make connections, eating alone, trying to carry on conversations with strangers, and spending a great deal of time in hotel rooms with room service and movies. This type of work is tiresome, grueling and lonesome.

It was a few days before Christmas. One of the hotels we had contracted with was unable to provide all they had promised. Our brochure was ready to go to press, but we couldn't send it to press until we had *all* the locations of the seminars listed. On December 23rd, a day when you spend special time with family and friends, attend parties and have fun, do last minute shopping, listen to carols, and go to church, I flew to Texas to do a site check of a hotel. I was not happy.

On the day of the 23rd I met the hotel sales person and did my tour of the hotel looking at the ballrooms and breakout rooms, talking with catering, and planning side trips with the event coordinator. After our lunch together, the sales person asked me if I had plans for the evening, and I told her that I did not. She told me that she had been invited to a party at a friend's house, and she wanted me to accompany her as her guest. I was so stunned that I almost didn't know what to say. However, I agreed. She picked me up at 6:00 PM, and we drove to a little suburb outside Dallas. It was a strange Christmas Party for someone being from the midwest. People were in shorts and shirt sleeves. Doors were open, and wagons, instead of sleighs, were being pulled by horses.

That was a very special evening for me. Every December 23rd I think of the Christmas Party in Texas. It was so gracious. Not just the food, but also the people. I never once felt like an outsider. It was as if I only lived a few houses away instead of quite a few states away. I was greeted "cordially" which means "warm hearted," and the warmth I felt from them, their smiles, and their touch shone down upon me and was gracious to me.

⌘⌘⌘⌘⌘

"the Lord make his face shine upon you and be gracious to you;"
Numbers 6:25

DECEMBER 25

...APPRECIATING THE GIFT OF THE MAGI

> "The great art of giving consists in this: the gift
> should cost very little and yet be greatly coveted,
> so that it may be the more highly appreciated."
>
> — Baltasar Gracian

⌘⌘⌘⌘⌘

I remember reading the story "The Gift of the Magi" in high school. It was a wonderful story, and I was moved by it.

It is a story about a young couple — very much in love and very poor – at Christmas time. They each had a prized possession: she had long, gorgeous hair, and he had a pocket watch that had been handed down from his father. Wanting to make Christmas special for each other, she sold her hair and bought him a chain for his watch, and he sold his watch to buy her combs for her hair.

I have been fortunate to have a life experience similar to this. One Sunday, while browsing through the paper, I noticed a furniture store had platform rockers on sale, and I mentioned to my husband that I had always wanted one. He replied that we didn't have the money; but if we got any extra money, we'd get one. On Tuesday of that same week, he called and said we would go look for a platform rocker. I asked where we would get the money. He said that, to his surprise, his employer had given a year end bonus of $500.00. He originally had thought to invest it but remembered how much I had wanted a platform rocker, so that was what the money would go for.

I was speechless for I realized, again, how much my husband loved me. I also realized that I was receiving a modern day Gift of the Magi. How much more precious is a gift when you know it comes from the heart.

⌘⌘⌘⌘⌘

> "There are different kinds of
> gifts, but the same Spirit."
> 1 Corinthians 12:4

DECEMBER 26
...TRYING NOT TO SCARE YOURSELF

"A good scare is worth more to a man than good advice."
-Edgar Watson Howe

⌘⌘⌘⌘⌘

When I was graduated from college and began my first career — teaching — I didn't have much disposable income. Instead of a huge color television, I had a little black and white 12" television. It sat on a stool in my bedroom so I could pull it next to my bed because the screen was too small to be seen from across the room.

I learned to go to sleep to the sound of the television. For me, it is a great tranquilizer. Sometimes I would wake up in the middle of the night to static or some B-movie. I wouldn't want to move too much; so, instead of turning the television off with the knob, I would reach for the nearby cord and jerk it out of the outlet. Consequently, it didn't take long for the cord to wear thin. Sometimes the television would just go off by itself, and I would have to jiggle the cord to get the set back on.

It was the first time "The Exorcist" was broadcast on local television. Having not seen it at the theater, I was anxious to watch it snuggled in my bed. I was wrapped in my blankets watching the set with wide eyes. Just as Linda Blair began to spit up green slime and her head spun around, the screen on my television went blank. I was terrified! In my soul I knew the devil had possessed my television and was going to rise out of the screen any minute. I couldn't even move. Then I remembered the cord. I cautiously stuck one hand out from under the covers and jiggled the cord. The screen showed white, and Linda Blair's head finished its 360°.

Even though I knew in my mind that the cord was weak from being jerked from the outlet, I was having trouble buying it. I had truly scared myself. The next day I had the cord repaired. It's one thing when others scare us; it's quite another when we scare ourselves.

Postscript: Now all my television have timers I set when I go to bed. I never have to worry about the cord. At least I have stopped scaring myself on this level.

⌘⌘⌘⌘⌘

"I will fear no evil, for you are with me;"
Psalm 23:4

DECEMBER 27
...KEEPING THINGS LEVEL

"Better one safe way than a hundred on which you cannot reckon."
- Aesop

⌘⌘⌘⌘⌘

Level means "a natural or proper position; without abrupt variations, uniform, consistent." It took building fence for me to truly realize the importance of this statement.

I had to build a new fence around our pasture for our horses. A friend offered to help. I knew having someone help would make the work go faster, and the time spent would be more fun. I was more than happy to accept her help.

One of the easiest ways to carry a roll of barbed wire is to put a pole in the center of the roll, hoist it up to should level, and carry it on the shoulders between two people; one person in front and one person in back. Most of the time this arrangement works well; however, I am 5'9", and my friend is 5'4". Unless she raised the pole up five inches, a heavy roll of barbed wire was continually sliding into her. Being in the lead of this duo, I didn't realize what was happening. My friend was trying to tell me about the situation; however, her asthma made it difficult for her to speak. So, to show me what was happening to her and to get my attention, she raised her end of the pole over her head so the roll of barbed wire slid down into the center of my back. I immediately understood the problem. To keep things "level," we rolled up a saddle blanket and placed it on her shoulder under the pole.

It was a safe and easy solution to the problem. I can't help thinking how nice life would be if all difficulties could be solved the same way. As the definition indicates, level is a "natural" position, and a natural position is the "expected order of things."

⌘⌘⌘⌘⌘

"And now I will show you the most excellent way."
1 Corinthians 12:31

DECEMBER 28
...APPRECIATING VOLUNTEERS

"Throw your heart over the fence and the rest will follow."
- Norman Vincent Peale

⌘⌘⌘⌘⌘

Many people think that horses are rather stupid. I'm here to tell you that is not true. Having trained and worked with horses for many, many years, I have watched horses roll under electric fence, stick their head under a gate and lift the gate off its hinges, walk a fence down, and work with a latch until they figure out how to unlock the gate when they choose. Horses are patient; they study how things work. Keeping a horse corralled can be a challenge.

As careful as we were, our horses managed to escape several times. We would look out the front window to see them eating flowers out of our flower beds or look out the back door to see them standing on the patio looking in at us. Most of the time when the horses did get out, they stayed close to home. However, one morning we got a call from a neighbor, a sweet little lady about 70 years old, who lived three houses away. She told me our horses were in her backyard. I asked her to keep an eye on them while I got dressed and drove down to get them. Bless her heart, she volunteered to help catch them and asked if there were some way she cold keep them from wandering off. I told her that horses love sugar; and if they get a whiff of sugar, you couldn't drive them away.

I got dressed, put a bucket full of oats in the car, draped four lead straps around my neck, and drove to her house. I walked into the back yard of my dear neighbor lady. There she stood in her robe and fuzzy slippers with a sugar bowl filled with loose sugar. She had a tablespoon; and when she approached one of the horses, she would offer them a tablespoon of loose sugar. The horses recognized the smell but not the form; horses only know how to eat sugar "cubes." They would stick their nose next to the spoon, snort, and blow the loose sugar on the ground. It was everything I could do not to fall down laughing at this sight. I shook the oat bucket, then dumped the oats on the ground. One by one the horses came for the oats, and I hooked the lead straps to their halters.

What a sweet lady to volunteer to help me catch my horses. She did keep them in her yard; and if I had been more explicit in my explanation of the type of sugar horses eat, she probably would have caught them.

⌘⌘⌘⌘⌘

"You, my brothers, were called upon to be free. But do not use your freedom to indulge the sinful nature; rather, serve one another in love."
Galatians 5:13

DECEMBER 29
...WATCHING OUT FOR SHARP EDGES

"However well organized the foundations of life
may be, life must always be full of risks."
- Havelock Ellis

⌘⌘⌘⌘⌘

One slow day I was watching TV, and an info-mercial came on advertising a "state of the art" slicer and dicer. The man demonstrating the machine shredded cheese, cut thin onion slices, made lovely lemon garnish slices, and on and on. Well, I had to have one! I called the 1-800 number, and my new miraculous slicer was on the way.

The slicer arrived in a holder for easy storage. The holder had another purpose as well: to keep your fingers away from the blades. Unfortunately, I didn't understand the holder's second purpose until it was too late. I reached into the holder to pull out the slicer, touched the blades with my fingers, and cut the tips of all four fingers. My new slicer certainly did what it said it would do! Had I read the directions or guide to usage, I could have avoided this.

I realized I had purchased the slicer without giving any thought to the holder. How happy I was that the creator of the slicer had seen the need for the holder as well. This particular creator definitely understood the saying "watch out for sharp edges" and "don't get too close" and had done his or her best to guard us from possible injury.

Guides and guards always serve a purpose: to lead us in the right direction and to protect us from possible harm. We have guides and guards in almost all areas of our lives. How nice it would be if we would immediately recognize them for the help they can provide.

⌘⌘⌘⌘⌘

"And the peace of God, which transcends all understanding,
will guard your hearts and minds in Christ Jesus."
Philippians 4:7

DECEMBER 30
...KEEPING A SAFE, MODERATE PACE

"Desire to have things done quickly prevents
them being done thoroughly."

- Confucius

⌘⌘⌘⌘⌘

Walking two dogs is more of a challenge than just walking one dog. You have ten feet to coordinate, two leashes to keep straight, two different temperaments to deal with, and usually one to scold and one to praise. Add to this that the dogs differ in size: one dog is four feet tall, and the other dog is two feet tall. This means that the four-foot tall dog walks twice as fast as the two-foot tall dog.

Murphy, the larger dog, usually walks in front at a rapid pace. CoCo, the smaller dog, usually trails behind with what is, for her, a fast trot. It seems to be my job to coordinate and keep a moderate pace.

I experience a little difficulty keeping this moderate pace. There are times I almost fall over Murphy because she has stopped to sniff at something. There are also times when I am pulled off balance because CoCo is lagging behind to sniff something. The leashes get tangled. I have to watch CoCo around other dogs and Murphy around people.

The dogs also look to me for protection. When we are going through a strange or new neighborhood, and an aggressive dog runs to the curb, both dogs glue themselves to my legs for protection. What is truly funny about this particular situation is that as long as they are next to me, they bark and snarl and act very aggressive because I am there to protect them. The dogs enjoy their walk.

How nice it is to have someone keep a moderate pace for us. Someone who is not too far ahead so we can never reach them, and someone who is not too far behind so they slow us down. Someone who helps coordinate our lives and deals with our temperamental moods. Someone to scold us and show us the correct behavior, and someone to praise us when we have done well. Someone we can lean on when we are uncertain or afraid. Someone who keeps a safe, moderate pace for us.

⌘⌘⌘⌘⌘

"Even though I walk through the valley of the shadow
of death, I will fear no evil, for you are with me;"

Psalm 23:4

DECEMBER 31
...KNOWING THE LORD HAS ALWAYS HAD A WEBSITE

"What is conceived well is expressed clearly,
And the words to say it with arrive at ease."
- Nicolas Boileau

⌘⌘⌘⌘⌘

For the past year I have been working on *Learning Through Living....Some Assembly Required.* I have been blessed again and again by the Lord jogging my memory and helping me understand the far reaching applications each "seemingly" insignificant event has had on my life — and, hopefully, other's.

I had outlined most of the December stories, but I couldn't figure out what story to use for December 31st. I wanted something very special.

One Sunday, during the silent prayer time, I was praying fervently for the Lord to let some spectacular story come to the forefront of my mind. As we ended the Lord's Prayer, I felt disappointed because my mind was blank. I opened my eyes and realized I was staring down at the weekly bulletin. My eyes had focused on the bottom of the front page that read "www.stlukesumc.com." I knew this was my answer, for I suddenly realized the Lord has always had a website.

You have 24 hour access on a website. You can reach almost anyone or anything on a website. You gain new information, some of it not always wanted, on a website. You have to be the one to take the initiative to operate the website, and you have the ability to shut it down anytime you want. The website is accessible from many different locations. It has taken someone a great deal of time to load the website with the information. There are times when the information you receive is not always correct because it has been supplied by the website's "false prophets." What an incredible connection!

If the Lord had an actual website address, I wondered what it would be. Even though I am not certain what His address would be, I do have one that I think would be appropriate: "**www.iamwithyoualways.calm.**" What a wonderful comfort and calm this readily accessible companionship can bring.

⌘⌘⌘⌘⌘

"And God is able to provide you with every blessing
in abundance, so that by always having enough of
everything, you may share abundantly in every good work."
2 Corinthians 9:8

About the Author

Dr. Suzanne Metzger holds Masters' Degrees in both Education and Management and a Doctorate in Business Administration. She is the President of Corporate Masters, a company providing keynotes and breakout sessions at conventions, workshops and seminars. Over the past 15 years, she's developed over 25 customized presentations in the areas of communication, motivation and leadership for businesses, corporations, and professional organizations. Also, as a 9 year breast cancer survivor, she speaks to medical professionals and survivors' groups on behalf of breast cancer patients and survivors.

Suzanne's passion for "soft" skills goes far beyond the edge of the stage and each story that she tells. She knows that communication is the only way we have to relate to any other person, and it is meant to bond, not repel.

Her humor, ranging from sophisticated to down-home, is her trademark. From her speaking experience, she has found that audiences are more focused and are more open to change if you incorporate humor into the content of the material presented. That is why all of her presentations use humor as an attention-getter. Each presentation and entry in this book are designed not only to enlighten but also to entertain.

Her attendees certainly agree that "she will change the way you look at leadership, communication, and life".

****

For more information about Dr. Suzanne Metzger's keynotes,
you may contact her at
Corporate Masters, Inc.
suzannecmi@earthlink.net
www.corporatemasters.com
317-718-1855